JUDAISM AND ISLAM IN PRACTICE

Judaism and Islam compare because they concur that God cares deeply not only about attitudes but actions, not only about what one says to God but how one conducts affairs at home and in the village.

In this sourcebook, the authors have selected key passages from the laws of Judaism and Islam which allow a close examination of their mode of expression and medium of thought as well as the substance of the laws themselves. The selected passages concentrate on areas critical to the life of piety and faith as actually practised within the two faith-communities – the relationship between the believer and God, between and among believers, at home in marriage, outside the home in the community and between the faithful and the infidels (for Islam) or idolaters (for Judaism).

Judaism and Islam in Practice presents an invaluable collection of sources of Jewish and Islamic law and provides a unique analysis of the similarities and contrasts between the two faiths.

JUDAISM AND ISLAM IN PRACTICE

A Sourcebook

Jacob Neusner,
Tamara Sonn
and
Jonathan E. Brockopp

London and New York

First published 2000
by Routledge
11 New Fetter Lane, London EC4P 4EE

Simultaneously published in the USA and Canada
by Routledge
29 West 35th Street, New York, NY 10001

Routledge is an imprint of the Taylor & Francis Group

Typeset in Adobe Garamond by Bookcraft Ltd, Stroud
Printed and bound in Great Britain

British Library Cataloguing in Publication Data
A catalogue record for this book is available from the British Library

Library of Congress Cataloging in Publication Data

Judaism and Islam in Practice : a sourcebook / [edited by]
Jacob Neusner, Tamara Sonn and Jonathan E. Brockopp.
252pp – 23.4 x 15.6 cm.
Includes bibliographical references and index.
ISBN 0-415-21673-7 9 (hc.). — ISBN 0-415-21674-5 (pbk)
1. Judaism—Relations—Islam—Sources.
2. Islam—Relations—Judaism—Sources.
3. Jewish law—Sources. 4. Islamic law—Sources.
5. Comparative law—Sources.
I. Neusner, Jacob, 1932– II. Sonn, Tamara, 1949–
III. Brockopp, Jonathan E., 1962–

BP173.J8J83 2000   99-34708
296.3'97—dc21

ISBN 0-415-21673-7 (hbk)
ISBN 0-415-21674-5 (pbk)

CONTENTS

PREFACE

Judaism and Islam are comparable in that they concur that God cares deeply not only about attitudes but actions, not only about what one says to God but how one conducts affairs at home and in the village. God aims at sanctifying the social order, not only private life. Both religions agree that God aims at the reconstruction of society in accord with norms of holiness and that God has in so many words, through revealed writings to the prophets, specified precisely the character of those norms. So the two great traditions bear much in common. That fact permits comparison – therefore also contrast. Why do so just now? Because this is an age in which, in the USA, Europe, and the Middle East, the monotheisms of law in the service of the All Merciful (as both call God) intersect once more, as they did a thousand years before. How the religions compare and contrast when, within the shared framework of convictions about the social, therefore legal, dimensions of theology, they speak in the same way about the same practical subjects defines the problem of this sourcebook.

Our goal is to provide readers with a direct encounter not only with the substance of the laws but also their language. That is why we set forth a sourcebook, in which lengthy abstracts allow close examination of Islamic and Judaic modes of expression and media of thought as much as the message of the religions concerning a subject they regard as critical to their respective accounts of the social order. We shall see that when we examine how Judaism and Islam portray the critical relationships that people maintain – between themselves and God, among themselves in the community of the faithful, and between that community and the outsider – we find a striking fact. It is that Judaism and Islam concur on a great many practical matters, using different language with the same result time and again. That does not mean the two are really saying the same thing and form a single religious tradition, divided in detail and perhaps in distinctive idiom – that is far from the fact. It does mean that Judaism and Islam, by reason of their concentric character and their concurring judgments about what matters between God and humanity, may undertake a sustained dialogue on issues of common concern. Out of the classical sources of each, we mean to construct the wherewithal of one such dialogue, the one concerning the practicalities of the religious life lived with God, conducted at home, and sustained in the face of difference beyond the circle of faith, home and family.

That aspiration to contribute to the common good explains the plan of the book. The three authors have chosen four areas, all of them critical to the life of piety and faith as actually practiced within the two faith-communities. They fall into three categories, defined by relationship, one covered by Chapter 1, the second, by Chapters 2 and 3, and the third by Chapter 4: between the believer and God, between and among believers, at home in marriage, outside the home in the community; and finally, between the faithful and the infidels (for Islam) or idolaters (for Judaism).

The first area of law addresses the life of the faithful with God and encompasses acts of piety in prayer, fasting, and ablutions. The second takes up the life of the faithful within their own community, both at home and in the fellowship of the faithful outside the walls of the household. The former involve relationships within the family – betrothal, marriage, inheritance and divorce – as these are topics deemed critical to the holy way of life under God's law by both Islam and Judaism in their classical, formative writings. The latter address the laws for the support of the poor, almsgiving and charity. The third category encompasses the laws regulating the relationship of the holy community to outsiders, in two aspects: first, defining who belongs to the community of the faithful; second, the matter of 'the Other' in Judaism and Islam. In this way we offer an encompassing portrait of the practicalities of the two religions of law and show their numerous points of concurrence, also underscoring where and how they differ.

We deal only with the initial, and everywhere authoritative, statements of the two religions, their classical formulations. So we portray the religions within the ideal type set forth in their respective bodies of classical law, Scripture as set forth by the Mishnah and Talmud, c. 200–600 CE, for Judaism, and the Quran and Sunna of the Prophet as set forth by the classic handbooks of Islamic jurisprudence, c. 700–1000 CE for Islam. We propose to state matters in their initial, canonical presentations, with which all later authorities concur, and to which all subsequent theologians and lawyers turn for normative rules. Since we claim to state the generative norms of the two theological–legal traditions and compare and contrast them in their ideal formulation, we do not take up questions of variation over time or space and among diverse interpreters of the common tradition. What we compare are the formulations of Judaism and Islam by their classical authorities: God's revelation to Moses as portrayed in Scripture and recapitulated in Oral Tradition by the rabbis who produced the Mishnah and the Talmud, God's revelation to Muhammad as portrayed in the Qur'an and the practice of his Prophet, and explained by the legal scholars who produced the classic handbooks of Islamic law. We intend to provide a picture that all subsequent generations of Judaism and

Islam to the present day will find accurate and familiar, even while taking account of later developments.

For Judaism, specifically, we portray the law and theology as set forth in the Hebrew scriptures of ancient Israel, with emphasis upon the Pentateuch, as those scriptures are interpreted and recapitulated by the Mishnah, a philosophical law code of *c.* 200 CE, the Tosefta, a compilation of supplementary laws of *c.* 300 CE, the Talmud of the Land of Israel, a commentary on thirty-nine of the Mishnah's sixty-two topical tractates, of *c.* 400 CE, and the Talmud of Babylonia, a commentary on thirty-seven of the Mishnah's tractates, of *c.* 600 CE. The abstracts take two forms. In some cases, the law is set forth in an English translation of the original Hebrew (or Aramaic, as the text dictates). In others, the law is presented in a different way. Here the Mishnah's statement is given, followed by the Tosefta's complement (or its independent ruling, amplifying the same topic but nothing that the Mishnah says about that topic), then by the discussion of the Talmud of the Land of Israel, and finally, by that of the Talmud of Babylonia. What we have is a reprise, in the sources' own language, but not a verbatim abstract of everything the classical sources say in their way of presenting matters. The former presentation brings readers into direct contact with the language as well as the substance of the sources. The latter provides a reprise of the sources, covering more ground in an efficient manner. Each type of presentation has its advantages.

For Islam we draw upon the classical sources, the authority of which all Muslims affirm. The absolute foundation of Islam is the Qur'an (which used to be spelled phonetically as Koran), Islam's sacred scripture. The Qur'an is believed to be the literal word of God, revealed through Prophet Muhammad, in the early seventh century CE in Arabia. (The Arabic word *qur'an* means 'recitation'.) But the Qur'an is not a law book. Of its 114 chapters (known as suras), only a few deal with specific legislation, such as those prohibiting female infanticide, usury, and gambling; those imposing dietary restrictions (the prohibition of alcohol and pork); and those specifying family law on issues such as inheritance, dower, and arbitration in divorce. The majority of the Qur'an's verses deal with theological teachings, such as the oneness of God, and moral themes, establishing general standards for virtue and justice. What is more, they were revealed gradually, over some twenty-two years. Over that period, many of the themes developed, some made more specific, some exemplified by the Prophet's words and example. Those words and examples, though not part of the Qur'an itself, are considered essential to a full understanding of Scripture, since the Qur'an itself repeatedly says that the Prophet Muhammad set the best example of how to follow its teachings. Collectively known as the Sunna ('way' or normative practice; also spelled 'Sunnah') of the Prophet, reports (*ahadith*, singular: *hadith*) of these examples were originally transmitted orally from one generation to another. But within a century after the Prophet's death in 632 CE, scholars began to recognize the need to record them. They collected as many individual reports as possible, then carefully screened them for authenticity, organized, and codified them. By the third century after the Prophet (late ninth/early tenth century CE), there were six major collections of hadith reports for Sunni Muslims. (Sh'i or Shi'ite Muslims, a minority who differ from the Sunni on issues of community leadership, compiled older collections of hadith reports, and by the eleventh century CE had identified three major books of Sunna.) Two of the Sunni collections (those of ninth century scholars Muhammad al-Bukhari and Muslim ibn al-Hajjaj al-Naysaburi) were designated by the majority of scholars at the time as most authoritative. The hadith collections, and especially those of al-Bukhari and Muslim, are the basis of commentaries purporting to amplify the meaning of Qur'anic verses (*tafsir*), and provide essential precedents in Islamic legislation (*fiqh*). Islamic law (collectively known as Shari'a; also spelled Shari'ah) is the basis of Islamic life – personal and public. There are four major schools of Islamic law for Sunni Muslims, and another for Shi'i Muslims. Other, smaller groups of Muslims rely on other formulations of normative behavior. But all Muslims agree that the sources for knowledge of normative behavior are the Qur'an and the Sunna of the Prophet. They are, therefore, the sources used in the treatment of issues presented in this volume.

While this sourcebook stands on its own and can be read in its own terms and framework, it also serves as a supplement to another book produced by the first two of the three authors of this one (Neusner and Sonn). In the companion, *Comparing Religions Through Law: Judaism and Islam* (London: Routledge, 1999), the authors spell out their theory of how to compare Islam and Judaism as religions of law. There they introduce the authoritative documents of the faiths, the intellectual sources that animate the exploration of the law and its logic in particular, the institutions that (in theory) administer the law, and the kinds of religious authority that bear primary responsibility for administration. In the process of contrast, they identify areas of the law treated by both religions but emphasized, in proportion, by one more than by the other, and they point to categories unique to the one and ignored by the other. But in their exposition, they deal only lightly with areas of law treated in common and in roughly comparable proportions by Judaism and Islam; in the present sourcebook, the contrast between the systems of law and theology having been highlighted, and joined by the third author (to whom the original idea of the entire project belongs), they turn to the areas of comparability and commensurate importance.

One point requires clarification. Our intent is to deal solely with Judaism and Islam as religions, with special reference to the classical writings of each, representing Judaism through to the seventh, and Islam through the tenth century. We do not enter into contemporary problems of politics. At the same time, the language of Judaism and Islam includes words bearing meanings today that did not exist in the formative ages of the two faiths. A principal one of these is 'Israel,' which, in the liturgy of Judaism and in the laws refers to the holy people called into being by God to receive the Torah at Sinai. That represents a supernatural entity. Members of that holy people, in line with the usage of Scripture, are called 'Israelites.' The territory they received from God is called 'the Land of Israel.' These represent formulations that have no bearing upon present-day politics dealing with the State of Israel, Israelis as citizens of the State of Israel, and other contemporary subjects of contention. So 'Israel' in the liturgy of Judaism, cited at some length, speaks of the holy people of God, not the State of Israel of our own times.

Professor Brockopp expresses his thanks to Bard College for the opportunity to pursue his scholarly career under splendid conditions, and Professor Neusner, holding professorships at Bard College and the University of South Florida, expresses thanks to both centers of higher learning and scholarship.

Jacob Neusner
University of South Florida and Bard College

Tamara Sonn
College of William and Mary

Jonathan Brockopp
Bard College

1

BETWEEN THE FAITHFUL AND GOD

PRAYER, FASTING, ABLUTIONS

1 INTRODUCTION

Prayer, fasting, and ablutions convey to God the aspiration of the faithful to relate to him. In prayer, they speak through language, in fasting, through abstinence, and in ablutions through acts of purification. In both Judaism and Islam, these actions – prayer throughout the day, fasting at specified times, and ablutions before acts of service – come about not spontaneously, when the faithful want, but as expressions of submission and service: routine, not charismatic response, in secular categories. To many in the West, that concept will prove puzzling.

While in the Protestant parts of the West prayer takes place in spontaneous response to the working of the Holy Spirit, in Judaism and in Islam prayer is liturgy in the classic sense of the word, that is, labor: it is work to be done for God. People recite prayers because they are commanded to do so, out of religious duty, in Judaism. And to that conception, the notion that one prays when the spirit moves the person, or one invents or fabricates a prayer for the occasion, is alien.

True, the Judaic and Islamic liturgies make provision for informal and idiosyncratic prayer, even for individual prayer, outside the framework of the quorum representing the holy community of the faithful. But both Islam and Judaism concur that fixed obligations govern the recitation of prayer, and much law encases the performance of those obligations in set rules and definitions. Prayer conforms to a fixed text. It is carefully choreographed, body movements being specified. It takes place at set times, not merely whenever and wherever the faithful are moved, or, indeed, whether they are moved at all. It is an obligation that God has set, because God wants the prayers of humanity. And while Protestant spirituality judges that the letter convicts but the spirit revives, Muslim and Judaic faithful attest to the contrary: the requirement of regular, obligatory prayer provokes piety despite the recalcitrant human spirit.

2 PRAYER IN ISLAM

Ritual prayer is the most visible manifestation of Islam. Five times a day, Muslims demonstrate their submission to God by making two or more full prostrations to him, touching their foreheads to the ground. This prayer may be performed anywhere – home, office, or on the street – except for noon on Friday, when Muslims gather at a mosque for communal prayer. When the Islamic legal handbooks address prayer, they usually refer to this ritual prayer, but the prayer of the community is also important at other events, either at the two great festivals (at the end of Ramadan and the end of the pilgrimage to Mecca) or at times of disaster. Muslims also engage in various forms of personal prayer, including the mystical repetition of God's name, known as *dhikr*; the Qur'an often refers to the power of personal prayer, recording specific prayers by Noah, Zechariah and others. But personal – votive – prayer is not a religious duty done in God's service; obligatory prayer is.

As in Judaism, ritual prayer has both public and private elements in Islamic law. Each prayer, for instance, must begin with a public call, even if one is alone in the desert. One authoritative legal handbook devotes twelve chapters to the subject of prayer, interweaving public and private elements: the [five] times of prayer; the call to prayer; the description of required acts in prayer; leading prayer; miscellaneous injunctions; prostrating during Qur'an recitation; prayer while travelling; Friday communal prayer; the fear prayer; prayer on the two festivals; prayer at the lunar eclipse; and prayer for rain. The order of these chapters is in descending importance of that which every Muslim should know: when and how to pray is absolutely essential, while the precise method of praying in times of trouble is far less vital. By far the longest of these chapters is the one describing the actual bodily movements to be performed in prayer, down to the position of hands and feet; since prayer is a physical symbol of a Muslim's absolute submission to the 'Lord of the worlds,' there is no room for innovative style. These twelve chapters are then followed by chapters on funeral rites, in which prayer plays a major role. The Talmud presents, for Judaism, counterpart rules on the physical conduct of a person at prayer: where one kneels, how one enunciates, and the like.

In prayer, the Qur'an takes its role as a liturgical document. Qur'an in Arabic literally means recitation, and Muslims must recite at least part of the Qur'an, in Arabic, during their prayer. Muslims from all over the world have memorized the first chapter for this ritual use, and it is sometimes referred to as the Mother of the Book:

> In the Name of God, the Merciful, the Compassionate.
> Praise belongs to God, Lord of the worlds,
> the Merciful, the Compassionate,

Master of the day of faith.
It is you that we serve and to you we pray for aid.
Guide us in the straight path,
the path of those for whom you have made the way smooth,
not of those against whom you are angry,
nor of those who are astray.

(The Qur'an, 1:1–9)

The message of this chapter exemplifies the focus of Muslim prayer. After invoking God's name and his characteristic mercy and compassion, it describes him as both Creator and judge of creation. It then proclaims the rightful position of Muslims as utterly dependent on God for help, guidance, and protection from hell.

The Qur'an constantly refers to prayer, and along with the giving of alms the command to pray is the injunction most commonly found in it. But while ritual prayer is described in the Qur'an, neither the number of daily prayers nor the order of movements are specified. For example, the following verses mention prostration and standing, two of the key elements in ritual prayer, but there is no systematic injunction:

The servants of the Merciful are those who walk the earth in tranquility,
   and who, when the ignorant speak to them, say, 'Peace;'
who pass the night prostrating and standing before their Lord;
who say, 'O our Lord, turn away the torture of hell from us; surely its
   torture seems inevitable;
it would be evil as a house or resting-place.'

(Ibid., 25:63–66)

This verse includes elements from ritual prayer, from the supererogatory night vigil, and from personal prayer against the horrors of hell. Another example is similarly unclear, though reference is made to a common ritual performed by the believers:

Muhammad is God's messenger, and those who are with him are hard
on unbelievers, but compassionate among themselves. You can see them
bowing, prostrating, and desiring that God bless them and be pleased
with them. Their mark on their faces is from the trace of prostrations.

(Ibid., 48:29)

The mark mentioned in this verse is an impression visible on the forehead of those who have spent their lives performing the prayer five times a day. But although the specific movements and times of prayer are not in the Qur'an, neither are they defined merely on Prophetic authority: rather, Islam holds that this ritual was established by God. Two hadith are of key importance in defining the parameters of ritual prayer: the first occurred during the Prophet's night journey into the presence of God and establishes that prayer is five times a day; the second establishes the specific times of these prayers and was sent down along the same path as the Qur'an itself, through the intermediary of the Angel Gabriel.

> When Gabriel took [Muhammad] up to each of the heavens and asked permission to enter, he had to say whom he had brought and whether he had received a mission and they would say 'God grant him life, brother and friend!' until they reached the seventh heaven and his Lord. There the duty of fifty prayers a day was laid upon him. The apostle said: 'On my return I passed by Moses and what a fine friend of yours he was! He asked me how many prayers had been laid upon me and when I told him fifty he said, "Prayer is a weighty matter and your people are weak, so go back to your Lord and ask him to reduce the number for you and your community." I did so and he took off ten. Again I passed by Moses and he said the same again; and so it went on until only five prayers for the whole day and night were left. Moses again gave me the same advice. I replied that I had been back to my Lord and asked him to reduce the number until I was ashamed, and I would not do it again. He of you who performs them in faith and trust will have the reward of fifty prayers.'[1]

Once the number of prayers was fixed at five, it remained to determine the times of these prayers. Interestingly, Islamic law does not designate specific times for each prayer (6 a.m., 1 p.m., and so on), but rather defines periods within which each prayer may be performed. Naturally, the exact time of these periods changes with the seasons. In this second hadith, Gabriel makes this distinction clear:

> When prayer was laid upon the apostle, Gabriel came to him and prayed the noon prayer when the sun declined. Then he prayed the evening prayer when his shadow equaled his own length. Then he prayed the sunset prayer when the sun set. Then he prayed the last night prayer when the twilight had disappeared. Then he prayed with him the morning prayer when the dawn rose. Then he came to him and prayed the noon prayer on the morrow when his shadow equaled his height. Then he prayed the evening prayer when his shadow equaled the height of both of them. Then he prayed the sunset prayer when the sun set at the time it had the day before. Then he prayed with him the last night prayer when the first third of the night had passed. Then he prayed the dawn prayer when it was clear but the sun was not shining. Then he said: 'O Muhammad, prayer is in what is between your prayer today and your prayer yesterday.'[2]

As detailed as these hadith are, they were seen as only some among many authorities as to the proper times and forms of prayer. Typically, collections of hadith were more concerned with including all sound, authoritative traditions than with providing a single source of authority for believers, and choosing one or two for demonstration purposes would misrepresent the variety of voices found in them. This selection from one of the earliest collections makes this variety of opinion quite apparent.

> Ata' b. Yasar said that a man came to the Messenger of God – may Allah bless him and grant him peace – and asked him about the time of the morning prayer: 'The Messenger of God was quiet and did not answer him, but in the morning he prayed when the dawn had just broken. On the following morning he performed the prayer when the sky was already yellow. Then he said, 'Where is the one who was asking about the time of the prayer?' 'Here I am, O Messenger of God,' he said; so the Prophet replied: 'The time is between these two.'

> Aisha, the wife of the Prophet, said, 'The Messenger of God – may God bless him and grant him peace – used to pray the morning prayer while it was still so dark the women could not be recognized when they would leave wrapped in their garments.'

> Umar b. al-Khattab wrote to his governors, saying: 'The most important of your affairs in my view is prayer. Whoever heeds this and maintains the prayer maintains his faith, but whoever is negligent about it will be even more negligent about other things.' [...] He also wrote: 'Pray the morning prayer when the stars are just beginning to fade.'[3]

Any one of these hadith might be taken by the community as authoritative; but what is important here is the way in which stories about key figures in the early community – the Prophet, his wife, his companion Umar – provide an explanation for regional differences in selection of time for prayer and in the ritual movements. In general, the classical handbooks of law discard this ambiguity as too confusing for the average believer, so instead of quoting all relevant Qur'an and hadith, they merely state the facts of prayer in their common interpretation. This selection from Ibn Abi Zayd al-Qayrawani (died in 996) represents one of the four orthodox interpretations for prayer time.

> As for the *subh* or morning prayer, it is the middle prayer according to the people of Medina; it is the prayer of dawn. The time at which it may be first performed is at the breaking of the dawn on the horizon with light at the easternmost point, running from the direction of prayer westward and making the whole horizon clear. The end of the prayer time is when the clear yellow of the tip of the sun is seen by

those who are completing their prayer. There is a long period between these two times, but it is preferred to pray at the beginning of this period.

> The time of the mid-day prayer, *zuhr*, begins when the sun has reached the center of the sky and shadows just start to lengthen. It is desirable to delay this prayer in the summer until shadows reach a quarter of the length of things above the normal shadow cast by the sun at mid-day. Some say, however, that it is preferred for the mosques to delay a bit when they are waiting for people to come to prayer, but when a man is by himself, the beginning of the prayer time is better. Others say, however, that in the heat of the day it is better for him to wait till it is cooler, even if by himself. This is according to the saying of the Prophet – may God bless him and grant him peace – 'Be cool in prayer, for blasts of heat are from the furnaces of Hell.' The end of the mid-day prayer is when the length of shadows equals the height of things beyond the normal mid-day shadow.

Note that although the actual times of prayer are fixed, and no debate concerning these times is considered, there is some question about when within those times is best to pray. A Prophetic hadith is used to address this disputed point, but the dispute is allowed to stand without resolving the issue. Al-Qayrawani continues with the remaining times of prayer:

> The beginning of the *asr*, or afternoon prayer is the end of the zuhr prayer; the end of the afternoon prayer is when the length of shadows is twice the height of things beyond the normal mid-day shadow. Some say, if you can gaze directly into the sun while facing in the sun's direction, while standing straight without your head bowed down or tilted up, the time has come. But if you do not see the sun, the time has not yet come. If the sun enters your field of vision, the time of prayer has certainly come. As for the way Malik – may God show him compassion – described the time, it is while the sun is still so high that it is not yet yellow.

> As for the time of the evening prayer, *maghrib*, it is the prayer of the settled, meaning that the traveler may not shorten it as with other prayers. Rather, the traveler prays it just like the prayer of one settled at home. Its period is from the setting of the sun as soon as the sun is hidden. It is required that this prayer not be delayed, as there is only one time for it which may not be deferred.

> The time of the evening prayer – also called *atama*, but the preferred name is *isha'* – is at the disappearance of twilight, that is the redness

remaining in the west from the last rays of the sun. If there is no yellow or red remaining in the west, then the time has come, but do not wait for all light to disappear from the west. This is the time until the first third of the night for those who wish to wait for prayer until after work or some other excuse, but doing it earlier is better. There is no fault in delaying the prayer a bit in order for the people to gather at a mosque. Sleeping before the evening prayer is reprehensible, as is engaging in idle gossip afterwards.[4]

In this passage, dissent from well-known hadith, and with other schools of law, is not mentioned, rather the times are laid out as if they were applicable for all Muslims. In fact, however, al-Qayrawani speaks about concerns well-known to his North African students: how to deal with the heat of the mid-day sun, and that the sun rises in same direction as Mecca, which is true for those in North Africa but not for other parts of the world. Finally, al-Qayrawani's concern with the exact times of prayer demonstrates the way that prayer forms a matrix of time for Muslims around which other events, such as work and sleep, must revolve. The same form is adopted for the rules of movement during prayer, which are far more detailed than Gabriel's demonstration above. This is al-Qayrawani's longest chapter, and it includes specific formulas and prayers for each of the five daily periods; the section for the morning prayer is included here.

At the beginning of prayer, it is required that you say, 'God is most great (Allahu akbar)'; no other formula is acceptable. Raise your hands to the level of your shoulders or below and then recite verses from the Qur'an.

If you are praying the morning prayer recite the first sura of the Qur'an. Do not begin with 'In the name of God, the Merciful, the Compassionate,' nor should you use this formula with the second sura. When you reach the last line, 'nor of those who are astray,' say 'Amen' if you are by yourself or praying behind a prayer leader. However, you should omit the amen if the leader does not say it aloud, or if he says it to himself. There is a difference of opinion as to what the leader is supposed to include in what he says aloud.

Thereafter, recite a sura the length of a section; if you recite more, that is commendable, depending on how much time is left before sunrise. Recite the sura aloud, and when you complete the sura, say, 'Allahu akbar' as you bow in prayer. Place your hands on your knees and keep your back straight without raising your head or tilting it, and do not hunch your shoulders. By your bowing and prostration, you demonstrate your obedience to God.

Do not make individual prayer while bowing, but if you wish, say: 'Glory be to my Lord, the Almighty, and to him be praise.' There is no time limit for these statements, nor is there a fixed period for this type of delay in the prayer. Then raise your head, and if you are by yourself, say: 'God listens to the one who praises him' and 'O God, our Lord, to you be praise.' The prayer leader and those praying with a leader do not say: 'God listens to the one who praises him,' but he does say: 'O God, our Lord, to you be praise.'

You then straighten to a standing position in a serene and submissive state,[5] then go down to a full prostration, without sitting in between. Prostrate yourself again while saying 'Allahu akbar' as you move down in prostration and touch your forehead and nose to the ground. Your hands should be directly on the ground with your fingers spread out, pointing toward Mecca, and placed to either side of your ears or below. These directions are to be interpreted as general advice, but do not rest your forearm on the ground and do not squeeze your upper arms against your body, rather hold them in the middle as wings.

Your feet should remain perpendicular to the ground in your prostration with the bottom of your big toes facing the ground. If you wish, you may say: 'Glory be to you, my Lord. I have wronged myself and done evil, so forgive me' or something similar to this in your prostration. You may also make personal prayer while prostrating, and there is no time limit for this portion. It should, however, be at least long enough for your body to rest calmly.

Then raise your head while saying: 'Allahu akbar' and move to a seated position. Between the two prostrations, fold your left leg under you while sitting and cover it with your right one, with the bottom of your big toe pointed to the ground. Lift your hands from the ground to your knees. You then prostrate yourself once again as you did the first time.

Then lift yourself up from the ground on your hands and knees, without returning to a sitting position so as to stand up from there, rather as I have just described to you. Say 'Allahu Akbar' as you are rising; you may either recite from the Qur'an just as you recited in the beginning of your prayer, or something less than this recitation. You continue with the prayer directly, without standing in submission after this cycle of movements. If you wish, you may stand in submission before bowing, but after completing the recitation. The statement said while standing in submission is as follows: 'O God, surely we request your help and your forgiveness; we trust in you, depend on you, submit to you; we denounce and shun those who do not believe in you. O God, you we serve and to

8

you we pray and prostrate ourselves; we serve you readily. We hope for your compassion and fear your earnest anger; surely your anger is descended against the unbelievers.'

Then you continue with the prostration and the sitting as described previously. If you sit down after two prostrations, cover your right leg with your left one, with the bottom of your toes pointed toward the ground; fold your left leg and finish with your buttocks to the ground. Do not sit on your left leg.[6]

These rules are removed from their theological context, and seem almost mechanical in their rigidity. Yet in following these movements, a Muslim is continuing a practice of some 1400 years, going back to the Prophet and ultimately to the Angel Gabriel himself. Still, it is important not to focus too heavily on the actions of ritual prayer to the exclusion of the words said by Muslims during this time; the actions, after all, are soon memorized leaving the mind free to focus on God.

Ritual prayer also has an intensely communal aspect, both in the weekly prayer on Friday and in the very call to prayer itself, which rings out from every mosque. In major cities, the effect of hundreds of muezzins chanting the same words from hundreds of mosques is a clear symbol of a whole city moving through the cycles of prayer. Here is how al-Qayrawani describes the call to prayer:

The call to prayer is required of Friday mosques and other places of prayer. As for a man who prays alone and by himself, if he gives the call to prayer, that is praiseworthy, but the call of starting is required of him. As for a woman who is praying alone, if she gives the call of starting, that is praiseworthy; if not, then there is no objection. The call to prayer should not be before the time of prayer, except for the morning prayer; there is no fault in calling for the morning prayer in the last sixth of the night.

The call is: 'God is most great, God is most great; I bear witness that there is no god but God, I bear witness that there is no god but God; I bear witness that Muhammad is the Prophet of God, I bear witness that Muhammad is the Prophet of God.' You chant this in your loudest voice one time and repeat the words of testimony, saying: 'I bear witness that there is no god but God, I bear witness that there is no god but God; I bear witness that Muhammad is the Prophet of God, I bear witness that Muhammad is the Prophet of God. Come to prayer, come to prayer; come to salvation, come to salvation.' If you are calling for the morning prayer, add here: 'Prayer is better than sleep, prayer is better than sleep.' Do not include this for any time other than morning.

And then: 'God is most great, God is most great; there is no god but God' just once.

The call of starting is always the same: 'God is most great, God is most great; I bear witness that there is no god but God; I bear witness that Muhammad is the Prophet of God; come to prayer; come to salvation; prayer is about to start. God is most great, God is most great; there is no god but God.'[7]

Ritual prayer is the same every day except Friday, when Muslims gather in mosques (the word is from Arabic, *masjid*, the place of prostration) for the mid-day prayer. This short service includes a hortative address by the prayer leader as well as the normal mid-day prayer. But as mentioned above, ritual prayer is only one form of Muslim prayer. Muslim mystics invoke a special form of prayer, known as the *dhikr* and involving repetition of a phrase or word. Dhikr means both remembrance and repetition: while the mystic adepts were repeating the name of God (Allah) or the statement 'there is no god but God' (*la ilaha illa Allah*), they were also remembering God's goodness and mercy, according to the Qur'anic command. Al-Qayrawani accepts a limited usage of the dhikr within daily prayer:

It is desirable to perform dhikr directly after ritual prayer in the following manner: say the formula 'Glory be to God' thirty-three times, then 'Praise be to God' thirty-three times, then 'God is most great' thirty-three times. One completes the hundred by saying: 'there is no god but God alone, and he has no companion. His is the kingdom and his is the praise, and he is above all things most powerful.'[8]

This form of repetitive prayer is very common, and Muslims often carry rosaries with thirty-three beads for counting off these formulas.

The prayers at times of particular celebration or despair are all variations of ritual prayer, although the role of the prayer leader is increasingly important. In the prayers for communal celebrations there is no separate call to prayer, and the prayer leader gives a special message. In case of an eclipse, the prayer leader makes an exceptional recitation of one of the longest suras; for the prayer for rain, the prayer leader may take off his cloak and put in on backwards. In all these cases, the normal ritual prayer is also performed as a community.

The theology of prayer in Islam can therefore be seen as having two main components. On the one hand each individual Muslim engages in recognizable submission to God – just as all creation submits naturally to his will, so humankind must do so intentionally. Not only is the bowing and prostration a visible sign of this submission, the fact that these complex movements become 'second nature' over time is a symbol of humanity re-learning its natural relationship with God. On the other hand, ritual prayer is itself a powerful representation of the whole Muslim community and of God's interaction with that community. Though one person may err, the whole community will never be led astray. In this way, prayer represents submission of the individual to the community as submission to God.

3 PRAYER IN JUDAISM

The halakhah, or law, encompasses the circumstance, timing, language, and gestures of prayer, and it speaks explicitly about the obligations imposed upon the faithful to pray. The law of prayer in Judaism presents the matter following obligations triggered through the natural sequence of the day, from formal worship, to conduct in connection with eating, to other occasions of worship. In Mishnah-tractate Berakhot, 'blessings,' statutory prayer covers five components: (1) recitation of the creed, (2) the Prayer (also called the Eighteen Benedictions), (3) blessings said before and after eating food (4) other rules for public worship at the table, and (5) blessings said on other occasions. So that organizing category of the law, then, sets forth a handbook of practical piety.

The creed, called the *Shema'* from the opening word, '*Hear,* O Israel, the Lord is our God, the one God,' is made up of Deut. 6:4–9 ('You shall love the Lord your God with all your heart, with all your soul, with all your might'), Deut. 11:13–21 ('If you will earnestly heed the commandments that I give you this day to love the Lord your God and to serve him with all your heart and with all your soul, then I will favor your land with rain at the proper season'), and Num. 15:37–41 ('Tell the children of Israel that throughout their generations they shall make fringes on the corners of their garments ... when you look upon these fringes, you will be reminded of all the commandments of the Lord and fulfil them'). The creed is set forth, furthermore, with paragraphs fore and aft, which pertain to creation and revelation (fore) and redemption (after); so the entire theological system of Judaism is set forth in that part of the daily worship, recited twice daily, morning and night.

When the law of Judaism refers to 'the Prayer,' it speaks of the shank of worship, private and public, a set of blessings, recited silently, and then, in public worship, repeated by the prayer leader. The Prayer, also called 'the Eighteen Benedictions,' or 'the prayer said standing,' is made up (in fact) of nineteen blessings, the shank of which shifts in accord with the occasion: an ordinary day, a Sabbath, a festival, and the like. Each individual prays by and for himself or herself, but together with other silent, praying individuals. The Eighteen Benedictions are then repeated aloud by the prayer leader, for prayer is both private and public, individual and collective. To contemplate the meaning of these prayers one should imagine a room full of people, all standing by themselves yet in close proximity, some swaying this way and that, all addressing themselves directly and intimately to God in a whisper or in a low tone. They do not move their feet, for they are now standing before the King of Kings, and it is not meet to shift and shuffle. If spoken to, they will not answer. Their attention is fixed upon the words of supplication, praise, and gratitude. When they begin, they bend their knees – so too toward the end – and at the conclusion they step back and withdraw from the presence. On ordinary days, though not Sabbaths, festivals or other specified holy times, these are the words they say:

> *Wisdom–Repentance*
> You graciously endow man with intelligence;
> You teach him knowledge and understanding.
> Grant us knowledge, discernment, and wisdom.
> Praised are you, O Lord, for the gift of knowledge.
> *Our Father, bring us back to your Torah;*
> Our King, draw us near to your service;
> Lead us back to you truly repentant.
> Praised are you, O Lord who welcomes repentance.
> *Forgiveness–Redemption*
> Our Father, forgive us, for we have sinned;
> Our King, pardon us, for we have transgressed;
> You forgive sin and pardon transgression.
> Praised are you, gracious and forgiving Lord.
> *Behold our affliction and deliver us.*
> Redeem us soon for the sake of your name,
> For you are the mighty Redeemer.
> Praised are you, O Lord, Redeemer of Israel.
> *Heal us–Bless our years*
> Heal us, O Lord, and we shall be healed;
> Help us and save us, for you are our glory.
> Grant perfect healing for all our afflictions,
> O faithful and merciful God of healing.
> Praised are you, O Lord, healer of his people.
> O Lord our God! Make this a blessed year;
> May its varied produce bring us happiness.
> Bring blessing upon the whole earth.
> Bless the year with your abounding goodness.
> Praised are you, O Lord, who blesses our years.
> *Gather our exiles–Reign over us*
> Sound the great shofar to herald [our] freedom;
> Raise high the banner to gather all exiles;
> Gather the dispersed from the corners of the earth.
> Praised are you, O Lord, who gathers our exiles.
> Restore our judges as in days of old;
> Restore our counsellors as in former times;

Remove from us sorrow and anguish.
Reign over us alone with loving kindness;
With justice and mercy sustain our cause.
Praised are you, O Lord, King who loves justice.
Humble the arrogant–sustain the righteous
Frustrate the hopes of those who malign us;
Let all evil very soon disappear;
Let all your enemies be speedily destroyed.
May you quickly uproot and crush the arrogant;
May you subdue and humble them in our time.
Praised are you, O Lord, who humbles the arrogant.
Let your tender mercies, O Lord God, be stirred
For the righteous, the pious, the leaders of Israel,
Toward devoted scholars and faithful proselytes.
Be merciful to us of the house of Israel;
Reward all who trust in you;
Cast our lot with those who are faithful to you.
May we never come to despair, for our trust is in you.
Praised are you, O Lord, who sustains the righteous.
Favor your city and your people
Have mercy, O Lord, and return to Jerusalem, your city;
May your Presence dwell there as you promised.
Re-build it now, in our days and for all time;
Re-establish there the majesty of David, your servant.
Praised are you, O Lord, who rebuilds Jerusalem.
Bring to flower the shoot of your servant David.
Hasten the advent of the Messianic redemption;
Each and every day we hope for your deliverance.
Praised are you, O Lord, who assures our deliverance.
O Lord, our God, hear our cry!
Have compassion upon us and pity us;
Accept our prayer with loving favor.
You, O God, listen to entreaty and prayer.
O King, do not turn us away unanswered,
For you mercifully heed your people's supplication.
Praised are you, O Lord, who is attentive to prayer.
O Lord, Our God, favor your people Israel;
Accept with love Israel's offering of prayer;
May our worship be ever acceptable to you.
May our eyes witness your return in mercy to Zion.
Praised are you, O Lord, whose Presence returns to Zion.
Our thankfulness
We thank you, O Lord our God and God of our fathers,
Defender of our lives, shield of our safety;

Through all generations we thank you and praise you.
Our lives are in your hands, our souls in your charge.
We thank you for the miracles which daily attend us,
For your wonders and favor morning, noon, and night.
You are beneficent with boundless mercy and love.
From of old we have always placed our hope in you.
For all these blessings, O our King,
We shall ever praise and exalt you.
Every living creature thanks you, and praises you in truth.
O God, you are our deliverance and our help. Selah!
Praised are you, O Lord, for your goodness and your glory.
Peace and well-being
Grant peace and well-being to the whole house of Israel;
Give us of your grace, your love, and your mercy.
Bless us all, O our Father, with the light of your presence.
It is your light that revealed to us your life-giving Torah,
And taught us love and tenderness, justice, mercy, and peace.
May it please you to bless your people in every season,
To bless them at all times with your light of peace.
Praised are you, O Lord, who blesses Israel with peace.[9]

The Prayer is recited three times a day, morning, dusk, and night. Other worship takes place before and after meals.

So much for obligatory prayer. What about the recitation of blessings? When the faithful eat, they are required to recite blessings over their food, reciting a further blessing afterwards for the entire meal. The grace after meals also reviews the main points of the creed: creation, revelation, and redemption, now in the setting of nourishment with special reference to the produce of the Holy Land. Finally, other occasions for reciting blessings are specified.

How do the writings of formative Judaism set forth the exposition of the law of praying? In the Mishnah and the Talmuds, halakhah, or law, defines the correct way to recite the Shema', the Prayer, the grace after meals, and other important daily liturgies. These are the five principal topics of the halakhah of prayer. An outline of the way in which the Mishnah presents the matter, together with the opening line of each passage, followed by the Tosefta's complement to the Mishnah's rules, provides a perspective on the way in which normative Judaism defines obligatory prayer. We then turn to the first Talmud's amplification of the same matter. In the following, M. = Mishnah; T. = Tosefta; Y. = Yerushalmi, and B. = Bavli – then come numbers signifying the chapter and paragraph of the entry. We present the opening sentence of each rule, to show the flow of the exposition and the topics that are covered, all in a logical and systematic manner.

I The Declaration of the Creed [the Shema']

A Reciting the Shema': Evening and Morning

M.1:1 From what time do they recite the Shema' in the evening?

M.1:2 From what time do they recite the Shema' in the morning?

M.1:3 The position in which one recites the Shema'.

M.1:4 In the morning one recites two [blessings] before it and one blessing after it. And in the evening two blessings before it and two blessings after it.

M.1:5 A detail in the same regard: They mention the exodus from Egypt at night.

T.2:1 A. One who recites the Shema' must mention the exodus from Egypt [cf. M. Ber. 1:5] in [the benediction following the Shema' which begins] 'True and firm.'

Here is how the Yerushalmi, or Talmud of the Land of Israel, explains the choice of the passages of Scripture that constitute the Shema', the creed of Judaism:

> Y.1:5 I:2 Why do they recite these two passages [Deut. 6:4–9 and Deut. 11:13–21] each day? R. Levi and R. Simon [disputed this question]. R. Simon said, 'Because in them we find mention of lying down and rising up [in Deut. 6:7 and Deut. 11:19. These are allusions to the beginning and end of each day when the Shema' is recited].' R. Levi said. 'Because the ten commandments are embodied in the [paragraphs of the Shema' as follows:]' [1] 'I am the Lord your God' [Exod. 20:2], [is implied by the phrase], 'Hear, O Israel the Lord our God' [Deut. 6:4]. [2] 'You shall have no other Gods before me' [Exod. 20:3], [is implied by the phrase], 'One Lord' [Deut. 6:4]. [3] 'You shall not take the name of the Lord your God in vain' [Exod. 20:7], [is implied by the phrase], 'And you shall love the Lord your God' [Deut. 6:5]. [How so?] One who loves the king does not swear falsely in his name. [4] 'Remember the Sabbath day, to keep it holy' [Exod. 20:8], [is implied by the phrase], 'So that you shall remember [and do all my commandments]' [Num. 15:40]. [5] 'Honor your father and your mother [that your days in the land may be long]' [Exod. 20:12], [is

implied by the phrase], 'That your days and the days of your children may be multiplied' [Deut. 11:21]. [The reference to a long life is an allusion to the reward for honoring one's parents.] [6] 'You shall not murder' [Exod. 20:13], [is implied by the phrase], 'And you [shall] perish quickly' [Deut. 11:17]. [This implies that] whoever murders, will be killed. [7] 'You shall not commit adultery' [Exod. 20:14], [is implied by the phrase], '[And remember ...] not to follow after your own heart and your own eyes' [Num. 15:39]. [8] 'You shall not steal' [Exod. 20: 15], is implied by the phrase], 'That you may gather in your grain [and your wine and oil]' [Deut. 11:14]. [Your grain implies that you may gather only yours] and not the grain of your fellow. [9] 'You shall not bear false witness against your neighbor' [Exod. 20:16], [is implied by the phrase] 'I am the Lord your God' [Num. 15:41]. [This is followed in the liturgy of the blessings of the Shema' by the word 'true.' Just as God is true, so should a person tell the truth.] [10] 'You shall not covet your neighbor's house' [Exod. 20:17], [is implied by the phrase], 'And you shall write them on the doorposts of your house' [Deut. 6:9]. [Write them on, 'Your house' and not on those of your friend's house. Do not covet your neighbor's house.]

The emphasis upon reciting one's prayers with the proper attitude should be understood. When an individual recites the words of the Shema', it must be with the intent of carrying out his obligation to do so, morning and night, as God requires in the Torah. If one recites those words with no intention of honoring the obligation, then the obligatory prayer has not been carried out.

B The Attitude And the Manner in Which One Recites the Shema': To Carry Out One's Obligation to Do So

M.2:1 As to one who was reading the verses of the Shema' in the Torah and the time for the recitation of the Shema' arrived: if he directed his heart to read in order to carry out his obligation to recite the Shema', he fulfiled his obligation to recite the Shema'. And if he did not, he has not fulfiled his obligation.

M.2:2 Said R. Joshua b. Qorha, 'Why does Shema' precede "And it shall come to pass" in the order of this liturgy? So that one should first accept upon himself the yoke of the kingdom of heaven and afterwards accept the yoke of the commandments. [Why does] "And it shall come to pass" [precede]: "And the Lord said"? For "And it shall come to pass" is customarily recited by both day and night. And "And the Lord said" is customarily recited only by day.'

M.2:3 One who recites the Shema' but did not recite it audibly – [still] has fulfiled his obligation. One who recited and did not articulate the letters precisely – One who recites in improper order has not fulfiled his obligation. One who recited and erred [in the recitation, later realizing his error] should return to the place where he erred [and continue reciting from there to the conclusion].

M.2:4–5 Craftsmen recite the Shema' while atop a tree or a scaffold, something which they are not permitted to do with respect to the Prayer [i.e. the eighteen benedictions]. A bridegroom is exempt from the recitation of the Shema' on the first night [after the wedding] until after the Sabbath [following the wedding], if he did not yet consummate the marriage.

T.1:3 Bridegrooms and all those engaged in [the performance of] commandments are exempt from [the obligation of] reciting the Shema' and the Prayer [cf. M. Ber. 2:5A],

T.2:6 Those who write [Torah] scrolls, phylacteries, and mezzuzot interrupt [their work] to recite the Shema', but do not interrupt for the Prayer.

C Those Exempt from the Obligation to Recite the Shema' and certain other obligatory Prayers

M.3:1–2 He whose deceased relative is lying before him [before burial of the body] is exempt from [1] the recitation of the Shema', [2] from the Prayer, [3] and from [wearing] phylacteries, and from all religious duties listed in the Torah.

M.3:3 Women, and slaves, and minors are exempt from the recitation of the Shema' [and from [the obligation of wearing] phylacteries, but are obligated [to recite] the Prayer, and [are obligated to post] the mezuzah and to recite Grace after meals.

Now we come to the Prayer, also known as the Eighteen Benedictions, and we see how the halakhah defines the proper manner of reciting that silent devotion:

II Reciting the Prayer

A Reciting the Prayer: Morning and Evening

M.4:1 The Prayer [Eighteen Benedictions] to be offered in the morning [may be recited] until mid-day. The afternoon recitation of the Prayer [may be done] until the evening. The recitation of the Prayer in the evening has no fixed rule. And [the recitation] of the additional Prayers [on Sabbath and festival days] [may be done] throughout the day.

M.4:3 The Prayer consists of Eighteen Benedictions, or an abbreviation thereof.

M.4:6 One should recite the Prayer facing the Holy of Holies of the Temple in Jerusalem.

M.4:7 [Like the Prayer,] the Additional Prayer [on Sabbaths and Festivals] may be said in private, not necessarily in a quorum.

B The Correct Attitude for Reciting The Prayer

M.5:1 One rises to recite 'The Prayer' only in a solemn frame of mind. [If one was praying], even if the king greets him, he may not respond. And even if a serpent is entwined around his heel, he may not interrupt [his prayer].

T.3:21A. One does not rise to recite the Prayer while conversing, while laughing, nor out of levity, but rather after words of wisdom. And so one should not take leave of his fellow while conversing, while laughing, nor out of levity, but rather after words of wisdom.

The Prayer encompasses special passages for various occasions such as the seasons of the year, and the law specifies where, in the liturgy, these special passages are inserted.

C Inclusion of Prayers for Special Occasions in the Recitation of The Prayer

M.5:2 They mention the 'power of the rain' in [the blessing concerning] 'the resurrection of the dead,' [the second blessing in the

Eighteen Benedictions]. And they ask for rain in the blessing of the years [the ninth blessing]. And [they insert] Prayer of Division [Habdalah, i.e. the blessing that marks the end of the Sabbath or festival] in [the blessing concluding] 'who graciously gives knowledge,' [the fourth blessing].

T.3:9A. If one did not mention the mightiness of [God's deeds in causing] the rains [to fall] in [the second benediction of the Prayer, which deals with] the resurrection of the dead, or if one did not petition for rainfall in the benediction for the years [viz., the ninth benediction of the Prayer, the petition for a fruitful and prosperous year], they make him begin [reciting the entire Prayer] again. If he did not recite Habdalah ['separation,' acknowledging the distinctiveness and sanctity of the people Israel and the Sabbath day] in [the fourth benediction, which concludes,] 'gracious giver of knowledge,' he may recite it over a cup [of wine; cf. M. Ber. 5:2]. If he did not recite it [even at that time], they make him begin [the Prayer] again.

There also is space for the individual and his or her votive prayers. The law has no intent of creating robots, who simply go through motions.

D Inclusion of Votive Prayers in the Recitation of The Prayer and Errors in its Recitation

M.5:3 He who says, 'May your mercy extend to the nest of a bird,' or 'For goodness may your name be invoked,' [or] 'We give thanks, we give thanks' [two times] – they silence him.

M.5:3–4 He who came before the ark [to recite the prayers] and erred – they replace him with another. And one may not be stubborn at this time [if asked to serve as replacement for the one who errs]. One who goes before the ark [to lead the prayer] shall not answer 'Amen' after the [blessing of the] priests because of [possible] confusion [which might arise].

In addition to the statutory, obligatory Shema' and Prayer, the faithful Israelite is required to say a blessing (Hebrew: *berakhah*) on the occasion of enjoying benefits of creation, for example, eating food or drinking water. These blessings are recited prior to the enjoyment of the food.

III Blessings Recited on the Occasion of Enjoying the Benefits of Creation

A The Requirement to Recite Blessings

T.4:1 One may not taste anything until he recites a blessing. It is written, 'The earth and all therein is the Lord's' [Ps. 24:1]. One who derives any benefit from the world without first reciting a blessing, has committed a sacrilege. He may not derive any benefit until he fulfils all the obligations that permit him [to derive benefit, i.e. recites the proper blessings].

M.6:7 This is the general rule: as to any primary [food] accompanied by a secondary [food], one says a blessing over the primary and exempts the secondary. [If] they brought before him a salted relish first and with it, a loaf [of bread], he says a blessing over the salted relish and [thereby] exempts the loaf, for the loaf is secondary to it.

Y.6:4 I:3 If one had before him several foods of the seven kinds, over which does he recite the blessing? [What is the order of priority among the foods of the seven kinds?] There [in Babylonia] they said, 'Whichever appears first in Scripture [in Deut. 8:8, 'A land of wheat and barley, of vines and fig trees and pomegranates, a land of olive trees and honey'] takes priority [with regard to the rule] for reciting a blessing [over these foods].' And [the following exception applies to this rule:] those foods mentioned after the word 'land' in the verse [i.e. wheat and olives] take priority over the other foods.' [Wheat and olives, take priority over foods made from barley, grapes, figs, and pomegranates.]

B Appropriate Blessings for Various Edibles

M.6:1 What blessings do they recite over produce? Over produce of the tree he says, '[Blessed art thou, O Lord our God, King of the Universe,] Creator of the fruit of the tree.' Except for wine, for over wine he says, '[Blessed art thou, O Lord our God, King of the Universe] Creator of the fruit of the vine. Over vegetables [produce which grows in ground] he says, '[Blessed art thou, O Lord our God, King of the Universe] Creator of the fruit of the ground.' Except for bread, for over bread he says, '[Blessed art thou, O Lord our God, King of the Universe] who brings forth bread from the earth.' And over [salad] greens he says, 'Creator of the fruit of the ground.'

T.4:3 'Over wine when it is in its natural state [thick, undiluted] they recite, "Blessed [art thou, O Lord our God, King of the Universe] Creator of the fruit of the tree." And they may not wash their hands with it. Once the wine has been diluted, they say over it, "Blessed [art thou, O Lord our God, King of the Universe] Creator of the fruit of the vine." And they may wash their hands with it,' the words of R. Eliezer. And sages say, 'Both over natural [thick wine] and over diluted [wine] they say, "Blessed [art thou, O Lord our God, King of the Universe] Creator of the fruit of the vine." And they may wash their hands with it'.

T.4:15 [When several kinds of breadstuff are eaten at the same meal], one recites a benediction over that breadstuff which is of the best quality. How so? [If] a whole fine loaf [i.e. one made from fine flour] and a whole homemade loaf [were to be eaten], he recites the benediction over the whole fine loaf. [If] a piece of fine loaf and a whole homemade loaf [were to be eaten], he recites the benediction over the whole homemade loaf. [If] a loaf of wheat bread and a loaf of barley bread [were to be eaten], he recites the benediction over the one of wheat.

M.6:2 If one has recited the blessing over the produce of the trees, 'Who creates the fruit of the ground,' he has fulfiled his obligation [to say a blessing]. But if he said the blessing over the produce of the ground, 'Who creates the fruit of the tree,' he has not fulfiled his obligation [to say a blessing over the fruit of the ground, since the produce of the ground by definition does not grow on trees]. And as to everything, if one has recited the blessing, 'By whose word all things come into being,' he has in any event carried out his obligation.

M.6:3 And over something that does not grow from the ground one says, 'By whose word all things come into being.' Over vinegar, unripe fruit, and edible locusts one says, 'By whose word all things come into being.'

M.6:5 If one said a blessing over the wine before the meal, he thereby exempts the wine after the meal [that is, need not say another blessing]. If one said a blessing over the appetizer before the meal, he exempts the appetizer after the meal. If one said a blessing over the loaf [of bread], he exempts the appetizer. [If one said a blessing] over the appetizer, he does not exempt the loaf.

When adult Israelites have eaten together, they recite the grace after meals as a group. The principal parts of the liturgy are as follows:

Blessed art thou, Lord our God, King of the Universe, who nourishes all the world by his goodness, in grace, in mercy, and in compassion: he gives bread to all flesh, for his mercy is everlasting. And because of his great goodness we have never lacked, and so may we never lack, sustenance – for the sake of his great Name. For he nourishes and feeds everyone, is good to all, and provides food for each one of the creatures he created.

Blessed art thou, O Lord, who feeds everyone.

We thank thee, Lord our God, for having given our fathers as a heritage a pleasant, a good and spacious land; for having taken us out of the land of Egypt, for having redeemed us from the house of bondage; for thy covenant, which thou hast set as a seal in our flesh, for thy Torah which thou has taught us, for thy statutes which thou hast made known to us, for the life of grace and mercy thou hast graciously bestowed upon us, and for the nourishment with which thou dost nourish us and feed us always, every day, in every season, and every hour.

For all these things, Lord our God, we thank and praise thee; may thy praises continually be in the mouth of every living thing, as it is written, and thou shalt eat and be satisfied, and bless the Lord thy God for the good land which he hath given thee.

Blessed art thou, O Lord, for the land and its food.

O Lord our God, have pity on thy people Israel, on thy city Jerusalem, on Zion the place of thy glory, on the royal house of David thy Messiah, and on the great and holy house which is called by thy Name. Our God, our Father, feed us and speed us, nourish us and make us flourish, unstintingly, O Lord our God, speedily free us from all distress.

And let us not, O Lord our God, find ourselves in need of gifts from flesh and blood, or of a loan from anyone save from thy full, generous, abundant, wide-open hand; so we may never be humiliated, or put to shame.

O re-build Jerusalem, the holy city, speedily in our day. Blessed art thou, Lord, who in mercy will rebuild Jerusalem. Amen.

Blessed art thou, Lord our God, King of the Universe, thou God, who art our Father, our powerful king, our Creator and redeemer, who made us, our holy one, the holy one of Jacob, our shepherd, shepherd of

Israel, the good king, who visits his goodness upon all; for every single day he has brought good, he does bring good, he will bring good upon us; he has rewarded us, does regard, and will always reward us, with grace, mercy and compassion, amplitude, deliverance and prosperity, blessing and salvation, comfort, and a living, sustenance, pity and peace, and all good – let us not want any manner of good whatever.[10]

Grace after meals is recited whether one is alone or in a group. But if three or more Israelites are gathered, then one of them calls on all present to form a praying entity for the recitation of the grace, and the others respond: the community that has been brought into being for the common meal then recites it, very often out loud and in unison.

IV Communal Meals and their Protocol

A Establishing the Communal Character of a Meal: Private and Public Gatherings and the Recitation of Blessings

M.6:6 When they are sitting [together prior to a meal], each person recites the blessings for himself. When they have reclined [on couches at the meal together], one person recites the blessings for all of them. When they have brought to them wine during the meal, each person recites the blessing for himself [because they drink by themselves]. [When they have brought to them wine] after the meal, one person recites the blessing for all of them [because they drink together]. And [that person] says the blessing over the incense, even though they bring out the incense only after dinner.

T.4:8A. What is the order of the meal [at a communal meal]? As the guests enter, they are seated on benches or chairs while all [the guests] assemble [and are seated together]. Once all have assembled [and] they [the attendants] have given them [water] for their hands, each [guest] washes one hand. [When] they [the attendants] have mixed for them the cup [of wine], each one recites the benediction [over wine] for himself. [When] they have brought before them appetizers, each one recites the benediction [over appetizers] for himself. [When] they have arisen [from the benches or seats] and reclined [to the second stage of the meal], and they [the attendants] have [again] given them [water] for their hands, even though each has already washed one hand, he now must wash both hands. When they [the attendants] have [again] mixed for them the cup, even though each has recited a benediction over the first [cup], he recites a benediction over the second [also]. When they [the attendants] have brought before them appetizers, even though each

23

has recited a benediction over the first [appetizers], he recites a benediction over the second, and one person recites the benediction for all of them [at this stage of the meal]. One who arrives after three [courses of] appetizers [have been served] is not allowed to enter [to join the meal].

B Declaring a Quorum for the Recitation of Grace: Special Problems

M.7:1 Three who ate together are obligated to [appoint one] to invite [the others to recite the blessings over the meal]. One who ate produce about which there is a doubt whether or not it was tithed, or first tithe from which heave offering [of the title] was taken, or who ate second tithe or [produce which had been] dedicated [to the Temple] and then redeemed, or a servant who ate an olive's bulk [of food], or a Samaritan – these may invite others [to say the blessings over the meal] on their account. But one who ate produce which is subject to the separation of tithes but not yet tithed, or who ate first tithe from which heave offering [of the tithe] has not yet been taken, or [who ate] second tithe or [produce which had been] dedicated [to the Temple] but which was not redeemed, or a servant who ate less than an olive's bulk, or the Gentile – they may not invite others [to say the blessing after the meal] on their account.

M.7:2 Women, slaves or minors [who ate together with adult Israelite males] – they may not invite others to recite grace on their account.

M.7:3 How do they invite [others to join in the blessing after the meal]? For three [who ate together, the leader] says, 'Let us bless.' For three [others] and himself [i.e. four], he says, '[All of you] bless.' For ten he says, 'Let us bless our God.' For ten and himself he says, '[All of you] bless.' The same [rule applies for] ten and for ten thousand.

M.7:4–5 Three who ate together may not divide up. And so too four, and so too five. Six to ten may divide up [into two or three groups]. And ten may not divide up – up to twenty. Two eating associations which were eating in one room – when some [members] of each group face one another, lo, they may combine as an invited group [i.e. a single group which together says the blessing over the meal]. And if not, each invites [members of its own group to bless] for themselves.

C Special Problems Debated by the Houses of Shammai and Hillel in Regard to the Protocol of Blessings at Table: The Normative Law

M.8:1 In reciting the sequence of blessings for wine and the Sabbath, one blesses over the wine, and afterward one blesses over the day.

T.5:25 The reason is that it is [the presence of the cup of] wine [at the table] that provides the occasion for the Sanctification of the Day to be recited. The benediction over the wine is usual, while the benediction for the day is not usual [and that which is usual takes precedence over that which is infrequent].

M.8:5 The sequence of blessings at the end of the Sabbath is: light, and spices, and food, and Habdalah.

M.8:6 In reciting the Habdalah prayer, they do not bless over the light or the spices of Gentiles, nor the light or the spices of the dead, nor the light or the spices which are before an idol. And they do not bless over the light until they make use of its illumination.

M.8:7: He who ate and forgot and did not bless [say grace] – should bless in the place in which he remembered. Until when does he bless? Until the food has been digested in his bowels.

In addition to the routine occasions of prayer – sunrise and sunset for the recitation of the Shema', the Prayer, and prayers at meals, blessings are also recited on special occasions, and those occasions are defined not by eating but by other events altogether. The halakhah describes these in the following way.

V Blessings on Exceptional Occasions

A Blessings For Evil as Much as For Good

M.9:5 One is obligated to say a blessing on the occasion of evil as one says a blessing on the occasion of good.

B. Blessings in Commemoration of Miracles or Other Exceptional Events

M.9:1 One who sees a place where miracles were performed for Israel says, 'Blessed is he who performed miracles for our fathers in this place.'

25

[One who sees] a place from which idolatry was uprooted says, 'Blessed is he who uprooted idolatry from our land.'

T.6:2 He who sees a statue of Mercury says, 'Blessed is he who has granted patience to those who violate his will.' He who sees a place from which an idol has been uprooted says, 'Blessed is he who uprooted idolatry from our land. And just as it has been uprooted from this place, so may it be uprooted from all of the places in which Israel dwells. And return the hearts of those who serve them to your service.' And abroad it is not necessary to say, 'And return the hearts of those that serve them to your service,' because the majority of the people there are idolaters anyhow.

Here is how the Talmud of the Land of Israel expresses the same matter:

Y.9:1 II:1 If idolatry was uprooted from one location and established in another, when one comes to the place to which it was located, he says, 'Blessed [art thou, O Lord, our God, King of the Universe,] who is patient.' And when one comes to the place from which it was uprooted, he says, 'Blessed [art thou, O Lord, our God, King of the Universe,] who uprooted idolatry from this place. May it be thy will, Lord our God, God of our fathers, that just as you uprooted it from this place, so shall you uproot it from all other places. And you shall return the hearts of those who worship it, to worship thee, and no more shall there be found [in the Land] any worshipper of idolatry' [outside of the Land of Israel one need not say this prayer because the majority of the inhabitants are Gentiles].

Y.9:1 I:2 One who sees Babylonia must recite five blessings: When he sees the Euphrates river he says, 'Blessed [art thou, O Lord, our God, King of the Universe] who carries out the works of creation.' When he sees the statue of Mercury he says, 'Blessed [art thou, O Lord, our God, King of the Universe] who is patient.' When he sees [the ruins of] the palace of Nebuchadnezzar he says, 'Blessed [art thou, O Lord, our God, King of the Universe] who destroyed this wicked one's house.' When he sees the place of the fiery furnace and the lion's den [associated with the narratives in Dan. 3 and 6] he says, 'Blessed [art thou, O Lord, our God, King of the Universe] who performed miracles for our forefathers in this place.' When he sees the place from which they quarry gravel [for idolatrous purposes], he says, 'Blessed is he who speaks and acts; Blessed is he who decrees and upholds his word.' When one sees Babylonia he [further] says, 'I will sweep it with the broom of destruction' [Isa. 14:23].

Phenomena of nature are covered as well:

> M.9:2 For meteors, earth tremors, lightning, thunder, and wind, one says, 'Blessed ... whose power and might fill the world.' For mountains, hills, seas, rivers, and deserts, he says, 'Blessed ... the maker of [all of] creation.' For the rain and for good tidings, he says, 'Blessed ... who is good and does good.' And for bad tidings he says, 'Blessed ... the true judge.'

> T.6:4 One who sees attractive people or attractive trees says, 'Praised be he who has [made] such attractive creations.'

> T.6:5 One who sees a rainbow in the clouds says, 'Praised [be thou, O Lord ...] who is faithful to his covenant, who remembers the covenant.' 6:6A. One who was walking between graves [in a cemetery] says, 'Praised [be thou, O Lord ...] ... who knows your number. He will judge you and he will resurrect you to judgment. Praised [be thou, O Lord ...] whose word is trustworthy, who resurrects the dead.' One who sees the sun, or the moon, or the stars, or the constellations says, 'Praised [be thou, O Lord ...] who made creation.'

> Y.9:1 II:8 One who sees a crowd says, 'Blessed [art thou, O Lord, our God, King of the Universe,] who knows the secrets. Just as their faces are different one from the other, so are their opinions different one from the other.'

> B.9:1–5 II.5 One who sees Israelite sages says, 'Blessed is he who has given a share of his wisdom to those who fear him.' [He who sees] Gentile sages says, 'Blessed is he who has given some of his wisdom to those whom he has created.' He who sees Israelite kings says, 'Blessed be he who has given some of his honor to those who fear him.' [If he sees] Gentile kings, he says, 'Blessed is he who has given some of his honor to those who fear him.'

> M.9:3 One who built a new house, or bought new clothes says, 'Blessed ... [who kept us alive and] brought us to this occasion.' One [who] blesses over evil [with the blessing used] for good, or [who blesses] over good [with the blessing used] for evil [or] one who cries out about the past – lo, this is a vain prayer. If one was coming along the road and he heard a noise of crying in the city and he said, 'May it be thy will that those [who are crying] are not members of my household' – lo, this is a vain prayer.

C Prayers and Protocol in Connection With Entering a Given Location: A Town or the Temple in Jerusalem

M.9:4 One who enters a town prays two [prayers] – one upon his entry and one upon his exit.

M.9:6 One should not act lightheadedly while facing the Eastern Gate [of the Temple in Jerusalem] for it faces toward the Chamber of the Holy of Holies. One should not enter the Temple Mount with his walking stick, his shoes, his money bag, or with dust on his feet. And one should not use [the Temple Mount] for a shortcut. And spitting [there likewise is forbidden, as is proven by an argument] *a minori ad majus*.

Here we see the role of law in the formulation of the religious life. The halakhah takes up the conditions of ordinary life and defines in detail where and how Israel meets God in its everyday existence: it does not define the media of the encounter; these are taken for granted. Rather, the halakhah concerns itself with the mode and method of that same encounter. A massive theology is encompassed within the topic. The Shema', the Prayer, the grace after meals – these obligatory prayers contain the creedal principles of the faith: God's unity and dominion, the Torah as God's plan, the categories – creation, revelation, redemption – as these organize holy Israel's existence. The Prayer then brings about direct address to God conducted in his concrete presence.

The law self-evidently serves as a principal medium of theological discourse in classical Judaism. What, then, are the main theological points contained within the halakhah? Within the detail of the laws is embedded a major statement about the relationship between God and Israel.

1. God takes a constant and intense interest in Israelite attitudes and opinions. He cares that Israel affirms his unity and declares his dominion, through the recitation of the Shema' and related acts of prayer. He waits for the expression of love, he hears, and he responds. That is why he pays close attention to the manner in which the obligation to do so is carried out, noting that it is done in a correct and respectful way. How else is a merely formal gesture to be distinguished from a truly sincere, intentional one? What is important is that when the correct words are spoken, they are spoken with the attitude of acknowledging God's dominion, as an explicit act of accepting the government of Heaven and the discipline ('yoke') of the commandments. That is what is meant in the laws covering reciting the blessings, for instance, *Blessed are you … who …*, or *Blessed are you, who has sanctified us by his commandments and commanded us to … .* God values these words of acknowledgement and thanks.

28

The halakhah rests on the premise that God further hears and responds to the praise, supplication, and thanks of Israel, as these are set forth in the Prayer. Reciting the Prayer while facing Jerusalem's Temple and the Holy of Holies, the Israelite directs the Prayer to the place in which God's presence once came and will one day come again to rest. The attitude of the Israelite in reciting the Prayer acutely concerns God, and that must be an attitude of solemnity; the one who says the Prayer must conduct himself or herself as in the very presence of God, in the model of the rules of conduct before the emperor.

How does God respond to Israel's acknowledgement, thanks, and above all, acceptance of his dominion? God sees to it that life is sustained, with special reference to food, and prayers that acknowledge the gift of life through food must respond with precision to the specificities of the gift: what particular class of food is involved? When Israel is embodied in a quorum of Israelites, God's presence, not only his gifts, is to be noted properly in a call to attend upon the shared rite. Finally, God intervenes at all times, past, present, future, and in all circumstances, however humble and personal, and God's intervention is to be watched for and acknowledged. So when the aggadah insists that all Israel – everyone who accepts the rule of the one and only God – will rise from the grave to eternal life, while the Gentiles, defined by their idolatry and rejection of God, are destined to death, that point of insistence bears more than abstract interest. God is intimately involved in the ongoing life of Israel, sustaining that life in the here and now, not only at Judgment and in the world to come. At every act of breathing, on every occasion of nourishment, God renews the promise of the creation of life and confirms the promise of restoration at the end.

2. If God immediately engages with Israel, then for its part Israel, all together and one by one, seeks that engagement. That is because Israel lives and acts under God's perpetual gaze. In the morning the Israelite accepts God's dominion in an act of personal submission, then explicitly undertakes to carry out God's commandments, in all their concrete specificity. In exchange, the Israelite recognizes that whatever happens expresses a chapter in God's plan for creation, a paragraph – perhaps only a sentence, a word, a mere letter – of God's intention for that particular person. That fact forms the premise of the Prayer, with its systematic, personal program of praise, supplication, and thanks. More broadly still, the very fact that the individual lives attests to God's will, by which every person lives or dies that very moment through the course of life.

Life depends on food, the point of intersection, then, between God and humanity, the moment of special and appropriate acknowledgement of the gift of life: nourishment by this means provokes these words, by that means, those. Since God pays such close and continuing attention to what each person says and how it is said, what an individual does and why he or she does it, none need find surprising God's intervention or humanity's specific and

response. That is why the correct formula of acknowledgement
response to all miracles, both the routine and the extraordinary,
ly God's intervention. Throughout, there is no distinguishing
bly people from the Israelite: what affects the whole obligates the
one, what happens to the one forms the destiny of all. In the halakhah sages
instruct Israel on what it means to take God personally.

4 FASTING IN ISLAM

Fasting in the month of Ramadan is one of the central events of the Muslim
calendar. For an entire month, Muslims take neither food nor drink during
the hours of daylight. Sexual intercourse and food-like substances such as ciga-
rettes are also forbidden. The discipline of denying oneself sustenance during
the day helps Muslims to focus on God as the real source of that sustenance.
Nevertheless, this denial is to be kept within certain boundaries, and those
who are sick, travelling or pregnant are not required to fast. The theological
focus of fasting is stated directly in the Qur'an: it is the month when the Scriptures were first revealed to Muhammad, therefore Muslims are instructed to
fast in order to 'praise God for that to which he has guided you' (2:185).

In Islamic countries, life's rhythms adjust to this rigor, and people rest
during the day and feast during the night. It is also common to recite the
Qur'an, or listen to recitation, during this month, and the Qur'an has been
separated into thirty sections for just this purpose. By denying themselves the
basic food and water needed to survive, believers are reminded of their absolute dependence on God. Nightfall brings life to the cities once again, however. After the breaking of the fast at sunset, the streets fill with shoppers and
shops re-open. Ramadan is also considered a time to remember God's mercy;
shopkeepers set up tables on the street, inviting strangers to break the fast with
them, and people make a special effort to see that no one goes hungry. Thus,
night becomes day and day becomes night in Ramadan, an inversion of time
which changes the believer's focus from the mundane to the divine.

The chapters on fasting in the legal handbooks are uncharacteristically
short; al-Qayrawani's text contains only two chapters: one on fasting in
Ramadan and another on fasting during spiritual retreat, a distinction which
corresponds to the two types of fasting in Judaism – obligatory and votive.
The cursory treatment in the lawbooks may be a result of the extraordinary
detail on fasting found in the Qur'an itself. Fasting in the Qur'an also fits in
two categories, but these are not the same as those addressed in legal handbooks: the prescriptions for the ritual fast in Ramadan; and fasting in atonement for a sin. The first category is covered in five verses; the first three of these
cover the main provisions in some detail:

O those of you who believe, the fast is prescribed for you, even as it was prescribed for those that were before you; perhaps you will be godfearing.

These are the numbered days, though for those among you who are sick or travelling, then a number of other days; and for those who would have been able to fast, redemption by giving food to a poor person. As for the one who willingly does good, that is better, but better yet is that you should fast, if you only knew.

The month of Ramadan is that in which the Qur'an was sent down, as a guide for the people and as clear signs of guidance and salvation. The one who witnesses this month must fast it, but the one who is sick or on a journey, should fast a number of other days. God desires ease for you, not hardship. You must complete the number, and praise God for that to which he has guided you; perhaps you will be thankful.

(The Qur'an, 2:183–185)

These verses stipulate the month of the fast, the reasons for fasting, and also distinguish between those who cannot fast through no fault of their own (because of illness or the need to travel) and those who do not fast even though they could have. Persons in both categories are instructed as to how they are to make up for their lapses. Of particular interest is the reference in the first verse to 'those that were before you,' as the Qur'an is explicitly modifying the religious practices of other peoples. This series of legal prescriptions continues, separated by verse 186 which makes an important theological statement:

When my servants ask you about me: Surely, I am near. I answer the cry of the one who cries out, when they cry unto me. They must seek answers from me, and believe in me, perhaps then they will be rightly guided.

During the nights of the fast it is allowed for you to go in to your women; they are a vestment for you and you are a vestment for them. God knows that you had been betraying yourselves, and has now turned to you and forgiven you. Now you may make love to them and in so doing seek what God has prescribed for you. Eat and drink, until you can distinguish the white thread from the black thread at the dawn; then complete the fast until nighttime. Do not make love to them while you are taking spiritual retreat in the mosques. Those are God's bounds – do not transgress them. In this way God makes his signs clear to people; perhaps they will be godfearing.

(Ibid., 2:186–187)

Of particular importance in this passage is the mention of spiritual retreat, the Muslim version of votive fasting; this verse will be referred to by al-Qayrawani in his chapter on the subject. The other occasion for fasting according to the Qur'an is in atonement for specific transgressions. The prescriptions are short and somewhat inconsistent. For example, the following verse addresses the recompense required for breaking an oath which is used to seal a contract:

> God will not hold you accountable for thoughtlessness in your oaths; but He will hold you accountable for that which you contract by means of an oath. The expiation is to feed ten poor persons with the same amount of food you serve to your families, or to clothe them, or to set free a slave. As for someone who finds not the means: fasting for three days. That is the expiation of the oaths which you swear – but keep your oaths! In this way God makes his signs clear to you; perhaps you will be thankful.
>
> (Ibid., 5:89)

As with fasting in Ramadan, fasting in expiation for a transgression is seen as a means of appealing to God for forgiveness and of remembering his characteristic mercy. In this way, the two types of fasting are intimately connected in their theological implications. The Islamic legal handbooks do not fail to address fasting as a way of atoning for specific transgressions, but they tend to do so in separate chapters devoted to those transgressions, so the prescription of fasting in atonement for using a reprehensible curse in the divorce formula is found in the chapter on divorce. Similarly, fasting during the pilgrimage is addressed in the chapter on pilgrimage.

With the main outlines of the Ramadan fast made clear in the Qur'an, al-Qayrawani limits his chapter to addressing some specific problems which may arise in carrying out the fast. As with the sages of Judaism, Islamic legal scholars tend to bring their own agenda to bear on these questions. In the beginning of his chapter on the Ramadan fast, al-Qayrawani turns immediately to the old question of external factors preventing the believer from carrying out well-intended actions. First, what if you cannot see the new moon which signals the beginning of the fast?

> Fasting in the month of Ramadan is a religious duty. One fasts at the sight of the new moon's crescent and breaks fast at the sight of the crescent of the next new moon, whether this ends up being thirty or only twenty-nine days. If the new moon is hidden by clouds when the fast is to begin, then one counts thirty days from the first day of the last month and begins fasting on that day; the same is done if the moon is hidden when the fast is to be broken.[11]

The practical concerns mentioned in the Qur'an are not addressed here, nor is the Qur'an cited. Rather, al-Qayrawani continues with his own agenda concerning specific cases where the right action is not entirely clear.

> One may intend to fast during the first night of Ramadan, but not the remaining nights. The fast is completed at nightfall. It is commonly accepted (*sunna*) to break the fast in the evening as soon as possible and delay the final meal of the night, before beginning the daily fast, until the last moment. If there is doubt as to exactly when sunrise is, one should not eat; nor does one fast on a day if there is doubt as to whether it is part of Ramadan – this is in order to prevent Ramadan from encompassing doubt. As for one who fasts on such a day, it does not count for him as fasting in Ramadan, even if he thought it was part of Ramadan. If someone still wishes to fast on such a day voluntarily, this is accepted.

> But as for the person who arises in the morning, and does not eat and does not drink, but only thereafter is it made clear that that was a day of Ramadan, it does not count. Such a person must refrain from food for the remainder of the month and complete an additional day of fasting.

> If the traveler arrives having broken the fast, or the menstruating woman cleanses herself on the day when her period is over, they are given food for the remaining part of that day. As for someone who breaks the fast intentionally, or who travels during Ramadan and breaks the fast for the duration of the trip, the days missed must be made up on another occasion. If one breaks the fast inadvertently, those days are not made up for this lapse in one's religious duty.

> There is no fault in the use of a toothpick during the entire fast, nor is cupping disapproved, unless one fears it would render a person too weak to continue fasting. As for one who is overcome by vomiting during Ramadan, it is not required that such a day be made up merely because of food being in the mouth. But if one purposefully induces vomiting, and then vomits, this day must be made up. If a pregnant woman is concerned about that which is in her womb, then she breaks the fast but is not required to feed sixty poor persons in compensation for purposefully breaking the fast. Others say she is required to feed sixty poor.

As in the Qur'an, al-Qayrawani distinguishes between those who break the fast through no fault of their own and those who break the fast intentionally. The last two cases illustrate this point nicely. In the first, someone who vomits during the day, perhaps because they ate their dawn meal too quickly, could be considered to have food in their mouths, thereby breaking the fast. As always, an individual's intentions are key here, and the distinction between voluntary and involuntary vomiting clarifies matters. But in the case of the pregnant woman, she breaks her fast voluntarily, and al-Qayrawani feels compelled to include a dissenting opinion that she must atone for this lapse, even though he feels that her action is not entirely voluntary. The dissenting opinion appears to be based on a Qur'anic verse (58:4), which demands the feeding of sixty poor persons or fasting for two months in expiation for a false oath.

As with the rules on prayer, al-Qayrawani's list of required actions may seem like a cold mechanistic view of the law, especially in comparison with the Qur'anic verses which include refrains about being godfearing and thankful. But al-Qayrawani is also aware of the importance of maintaining a worshipful frame of mind during this month.

> It is appropriate for those who are fasting to guard their tongues and control their gestures in order to magnify during the month of Ramadan that which God – Glory be to him; he is most high – magnified. Those who fast do not approach women, either for sex, flirting or amorous kisses during the days of Ramadan, though these things are not forbidden at night. There is no fault in arising early in the morning in a state of ritual impurity due to sexual intercourse at night.[12]

The second category for fasting in the legal handbooks concerns a practice only briefly mentioned in the Qur'an: spiritual retreat. Such a retreat is among the actions performed by the Prophet, but not seen as an absolute requirement of all Muslims. The rules for fasting are the same as in Ramadan, and in fact, spiritual retreat is often performed in conjunction with the Ramadan fast. Since the person undergoing such a retreat remains in the central mosque for the duration, no sexual intercourse is allowed, either during the day or night. Al-Qayrawani begins his chapter on this practice with reference to the etymology of the word *akafa*, which suggests clinging on to God or to the mosque itself. Most of the Qur'an's references to this practice speak of such retreats in connection with pre-Islamic polytheistic practices of clinging to idols and their places of worship.

> Spiritual retreat is among works of supererogation done for the good of the believer. The word itself denotes clinging to something. There can be no spiritual retreat without fasting, without a specific period of consecutive days, and without retreating to a mosque, just as God – Glory be to him; he is most high – says in the Qur'an: '... while you are taking spiritual retreat in mosques.' (2:183) If retreat is taken in a town where there are specific mosques designated for Friday prayer, then retreat must be taken in one of these mosques, except if the one

retreating vows that the days on which retreat is taken will not include a Friday. We prefer, however, that the minimum number of days be ten. These rules are incumbent on someone who vows to undertake a retreat for one or more days. As for someone who vows a retreat for a night, both the day and the night are incumbent upon them.

As for someone who intentionally breaks fast while in retreat, they must begin the retreat once again; the same applies for someone who engages in sexual intercourse during the day or night, whether intentionally or out of forgetfulness. If the one in retreat becomes sick, they return to their house. When they are well again, they continue the retreat where they left off; the same applies to the woman who begins menstruating during retreat. For both these cases, the bodily taboos of spiritual retreat remain incumbent upon them, whether sick or menstruating. As soon as the menstruating woman finishes her monthly course and cleanses herself – or the sick person is rehabilitated – they return to the mosque in that very hour, whether day or night.

The person undergoing retreat does not leave the place of retreat except for human necessities. On the first day of retreat, one enters the place of retreat before sundown on the evening of the first days of retreat. One does not visit the sick, pray over the dead at funerals or leave the mosque to engage in trade during this time. No conditions may be made on a vow of retreat.

There is no fault in the prayer leader of a mosque undergoing retreat – a person in retreat may still marry and engage a marriage contract for another.

As for someone who undertakes spiritual retreat during the month of Ramadan, whether at the beginning or middle of it, they leave their retreat after the setting of the sun on the last day of the month, even if the time for which they vowed retreat would have included that day on which the fast of Ramadan is broken. Such a person stays in the mosque on the night when the fast has ended up to the point when all the Muslims go to the prayer grounds to celebrate the end of the fast.

This last paragraph shows the importance of the pious individual joining the entire community of believers on the days of breaking the fast. As one of the two most important feast days in Islam, this moment of celebration must take precedence over individual acts of self-deprivation. This emphasis on fasting as a social act thus pervades the Islamic perspective. From the very beginning of the fast, individuals are urged to refrain from fasting before the official declaration of the beginning of the month in order to keep the community

ually, spiritual retreat is to be undertaken in the public mosques,
home or in isolation. Finally, the fast is broken in common, with
inity joining together at the prayer grounds when the next new
ghted.

5 FASTING IN JUDAISM

In Judaism, fasts – meaning, abstinence from food, drink, sex, and other plea-
sures for a specified period of time, usually a day – are of two kinds, obligatory
and votive. The Day of Atonement, Yom Kippur, stands for the former; fasting is required as a form of repentance for sin. The halakhah defines the rule as
follows:

A. On the Day of Atonement it is forbidden to (1) eat, (2) drink,
(3) bathe, (4) put on any sort of oil, (5) put on a sandal, (6) or engage
in sexual relations.

B. But a king and a bride wash their faces.

(Mishnah-tractate YOMA, 8:1)

In general, the theory of fasting in the halakhah treats fasting as a mode of sacrifice – one's own flesh and blood being diminished in the process – and therefore, given the theory of the sacrifice that predominates in Judaism, as a
medium of atonement for sin.

The governing theology does not permit us to predict, however, the character of the halakhah that will define the matter. Rather, as we already have
noted, the halakhah brings to a given topic a fixed agenda of questions. The
result is that, once a topic comes into view, the halakhah tends to find the same
thing to say about many issues. Here, for example, a recurrent interest in the
joining of quantities that constitute a forbidden amount of a named substance
is given expression, as in the following:

A. He who eats a large date's bulk [of food], inclusive of its pit —

B. [or] he who drinks the equivalent in liquids to a mouthful

C. is liable.

D. All sorts of foods join together to form the volume of the date's
bulk,

E. and all sorts of liquids join together to form the volume of a mouthful.

F. He who eats and he who drinks —

G. [these prohibited volumes] do not join together [to impose liability for eating or for drinking, respectively].

(Ibid., 8:2)

Another familiar issue, raised here as in numerous other contexts, concerns intentionality; if one performs many actions within a single spell of inadvertence, the entire set of actions is deemed to form one set, requiring one act of atonement (a sin offering, brought on account of inadvertent sin). If one performed acts of two categories, these are treated as disjoined:

A. [If] one ate and drank in a single act of inadvertence, he is liable only for a single sin offering.

B. [If] he ate and did a prohibited act of labor, he is liable for two sin offerings.

C. [If] he ate foods which are not suitable for eating,

D. or drank liquids which are not 'suitable for drinking —

E. [if] he drank brine or fish brine —

F. he is exempt.

(Ibid., 8:3)

The law, as is its way, attends also to special cases, that is, to issues particular to the topic under discussion:

A. As to children, they do not impose a fast on them on the Day of Atonement.

B. But they educate them a year or two in advance, so that they will be used to doing the religious duties.

(Ibid., 8:4)

A. A pregnant woman who smelled food [and grew faint] – they feed her until her spirits are restored.

B. A sick person – they feed him on the instruction of experts.

C. If there are no experts available, they feed him on his own instructions,

D. until he says, 'Enough.'

(Ibid., 8:5)

So much for obligatory fasting. The calendar encompasses other obligatory fast days, commemorating historical tragedies: for example, the 9th of Ab (early August), marking the destruction of the first Temple in 586 BCE, and the second in 70 CE. The halakhah requires such fasting for the specified purpose, part of the halakhah's larger construction of the sacrificial system centered on cultic rites.

Votive fasting in the halakhah of classical Judaism takes place in times of crisis, as an act of penitence for the sin that has brought about drought or some other calamity by way of punishment. Votive fasting is communal and focused upon the public act of collective penitence.

A. The manner of fasting: how [was it done]?

B. They bring forth the ark into the street of the town and put wood ashes on the ark, on the head of the patriarch, and on the head of the head of the court.

C. And each person puts [ashes] on his head.

D. The eldest among them makes a speech of admonition: 'Our brothers, concerning the people of Nineveh it is not said, "And God saw their sackcloth and their fasting," but, "And God saw their deeds, for they repented from their evil way" ' (Jonah 3:10).

E. 'And in prophetic tradition it is said, "Rend your heart and not your garments" ' (Joel 2:13).

(Mishnah-tractate Taanit, 2:1)

F. They arise for prayer.

G. They bring down before the ark an experienced elder, who has children, and whose cupboard [house] is empty, so that his heart should be wholly in the prayer.

H. And he says before them twenty-four blessings:

I. the eighteen said every day, and he adds six more to them.

J. And these are they:

K. Remembrance verses, shofar verses,

L. 'In my distress I cried to the Lord and he answered me ...' (Ps. 120),

M. and, 'I will lift up my eyes to the hills ...' (Ps. 121),

N. and, 'Out of the depths I have cried to you, O Lord ...' (Ps. 130),

O. and 'A prayer of the afflicted when he is overwhelmed' (Ps. 102).
(Ibid., 2:2)

P. And he concludes each of them with its appropriate ending.'
(Ibid., 2:3)

Q. For the first [ending] he says, 'He who answered Abraham on Mount Moriah will answer you and hear the sound of your cry this day. Blessed are you, O Lord, redeemer of Israel.'
(Ibid., 2:4)

R. For the second he says, 'He who answered our fathers at the Red Sea will answer you and hear the sound of your cry this day. Blessed are you, O Lord, who remembers forgotten things.'
(Ibid., 2:5)

S. For the third he says, 'He who answered Joshua at Gilgal will answer you and hear the sound of your cry thus day. Blessed are you, O Lord who hears the sound of the shofar.'
(Ibid., 2:6)

T. For the fourth he says, 'He who answered Samuel at Mizpah will answer you and hear the sound of your cry this day. Blessed are you, O Lord, who hears a cry.'
(Ibid., 2:7)

U. For the fifth he says, 'He who answered Elijah at Mount Carmel will answer you and hear the sound of your cry this day. Blessed are you, O Lord, who hears prayer.'
(Ibid., 2:8)

V. For the sixth he says, 'He who answered Jonah in the belly of the fish will answer you and hear the sound of your cry this day. Blessed are you, O Lord, who answers prayer in a time of trouble.'

W. For the seventh he says, 'He who answered David and Solomon, his son, in Jerusalem, will answer you and hear the sound of your cry this day. Blessed are you, O Lord, who has mercy on the land.'

(Ibid., 2:9)

While communities, as distinct from 'all Israel' in the Temple, may fast, they are not required to do so. Individuals may also accept upon themselves the discipline of a fast, for example, by taking a vow. The halakhah contains rules on carrying out a vow of abstinence of one sort of another. Fasting represents a means of atonement for sin, in which the faithful give up food and drink as a sacrifice and as a gesture of uncoerced submission to God's will.

6 ABLUTIONS IN ISLAM

In the Islamic legal handbooks, ablution usually has pride of place as the first chapter, just before prayer. This arrangement is sensible, since prayer without being ritually clean has no effect. As with other actions in Islamic law, however, the point of ablution is not actual cleanliness, but the intention to begin prayer in the right state of mind. In the case of ablution in countries where pure water is a scarce commodity, allowances are made for symbolic washing with pure dirt or pebbles. As in Jewish law, ablution is a cultic practice which leads to a state of ritual cleanliness. Al-Qayrawani's handbook separates the practice of ablution into the following six chapters: that which requires ritual ablution and washing; the purity of water; the description of ritual cleansing; washing; a description of cleansing with sand; and the wiping of shoes.

As is the case with prayer, the Qur'an says little on the subject of ritual ablution, and does not even contain reference to the technical term *wudu*; two brief passages mention washing before prayer, however, and reference to women washing after menstruation is also found (see 2:222). It is worth noting that the larger issue of purity receives significant treatment in the Qur'an, but not as a practical concern of separating pure from impure food, for instance. Several references are made to God purifying his prophets, or the hearts of believers. For instance, in speaking directly to the Prophet's wives, the Qur'an says:

Women of the Prophet, you are not like any other women. If you are in awe of God, do not humble others with your words, so that he in whose heart is sickness desires you; but speak honorable words.

Abide in your apartments; and do not display yourselves in the ignorant fashion of old. Arise for prayer, give alms and obey God and his messenger.

People of the house, God only desires to put away from you abomination and to purify you.

(The Qur'an, 33:32–33)

Although the context of these commands is quite different from the simple command to perform ritual ablution, the theological basis ('God desires ... to purify you') is the same:

O believers, when you stand up to pray wash your faces, and your hands up to the elbows, and wipe your heads, and your feet up to the ankles. If you are defiled, purify yourselves; but if you are sick or on a journey, or if any of you comes from the privy, or you have touched women, and you can find no water, then have recourse to wholesome dust and wipe your faces and your hands with it. God does not desire to make any impediment for you; but he desires to purify you, and that he may complete his blessing upon you; perhaps you will be thankful.

(Ibid., 5:6)

This simple statement is remarkably compact, distinguishing between washing for prayer and purifying after specific defilements: being sick, coming from a journey, and having sexual intercourse. Provision for ritual cleansing without water is also included.

There are many hadith on the subject of ritual ablution, many of which address minute questions which are left unanswered in the Qur'an. Some of these hadith also include further theological explanation of the purpose of ablution before prayer. First, as with the times of daily prayer, one famous hadith shows the Angel Gabriel demonstrating the precise movement of ablution and prayer to the Prophet, who, in turn, shows his wife Khadija.

A learned person told me that when prayer was laid on the apostle Gabriel came to him while he was on the heights of Mecca and dug a hole for him with his heel in the side of the valley from which a fountain gushed forth, and Gabriel performed the ritual ablution as the apostle watched him. This was in order to show him how to purify himself before prayer. Then the apostle performed the ritual ablution as he had seen Gabriel do it. Then Gabriel said a prayer with him while the apostle prayed with his prayer. Then Gabriel left him. The apostle came to Khadija and performed the ritual for her as Gabriel had done for him, and she copied him. Then he prayed with her as Gabriel had prayed with him, and she prayed his prayer.[13]

Other hadith are more explicit about the salvific effects of ablution. Here are

41

two separate hadith, transmitted by two different companions of the Prophet, which contain a similar message.

> Abd Allah al-Sanabihi said that the Messenger of God – may God bless him and grant him peace – said: 'When the believing worshipper performs ritual ablution and rinses, the sins leave the mouth. When the worshipper ejects water from his nostrils, the sins leave the nose. When the worshipper washes the face, the sins leave the face, even from underneath the lashes of the eyes. When the worshipper washes the hands, the sins leave them, even from underneath the nails of the fingers. When the worshipper wipes the head, the sins leave the head, even from the ears. When the worshipper washes the feet, the sins leave them, even from underneath the nails of the toes.' He said: 'Thereafter, walking to the mosque and prayer are like a supererogatory action for the worshipper.'

> Abu Hurayra said that the Messenger of God – may God bless him and grant him peace – said: 'When the Muslim worshippers, or the believing worshippers, perform ritual ablution, as they wash their faces every sin they have seen with their eyes leaves with the water or with the last drop of water. When they wash their hands, every sin which their hands have done leaves with the water or with the last drop of water. When they wash their feet, every sin which their feet have walked leaves with the water or with the last drop of water, until they go out cleansed of their sins.'[14]

Note that although the specific parts of the body mentioned in the two hadith are different, the order of ablution – face, hands, head, feet – is the same as that found in the Qur'anic verse. Such an order would seem to suggest that the hands are not the primary source of uncleanliness in Islam, since they are used to wash the face before they themselves are washed. The legal handbooks, however, insist on the washing of hands three times before beginning the process of ritual ablution. Since the order of ablution is fixed in the Qur'an, it should not be surprising that al-Qayrawani begins his discussion of ritual ablution with other questions, only turning to the process of the actual act of ablution in the third of his six chapters. In that chapter he will distinguish between ritual ablution before prayer (wudu') and full washing after defilement (ghusl), a distinction intimated, but not expressed, in the Qur'an.

First, however, al-Qayrawani addresses the question of precisely what causes a person to lose a state of purity and thereby require ablution:

> Ritual ablution is required when urine, feces, or air is excreted from one of the two places of excretion; when *madhi* is excreted from the penis it must be washed entirely in addition to ablution. Madhi is the limpid

white fluid which is secreted at the enjoyment of sexual excitement while caressing or while remembering such caresses. As for *wady*, it is the viscous white fluid secreted when urinating and which is categorized as urine for the purposes of ablution. As for *mani*, it is the fluid of ejaculation which is secreted at orgasm during sex; its odor is like the smell of the palm flower. The fluid secreted by women is a limpid yellowish fluid which requires purification of the entire body, just as required for the menstrual cycle. As for the blood which comes from menstruation, ritual ablution is required. Due to the possible release of urine or blood of menstruation, it is recommended to perform ritual ablution for each prayer.

With five daily prayers, the time between one prayer and another might be very short, and a person who does not have an emission of the sorts listed above would not need to perform ritual ablution before the next prayer, though al-Qayrawani recommends it just to be sure. He continues with other situations which might necessitate ritual ablution.

Ritual ablution is required at the loss of consciousness in deep sleep, or fainting, or drunkenness, or insanity. Ablution is also required for amorous touching, amorous fondling of the body, or amorous kissing, also for touching of the penis. There is a difference of opinion on whether a woman is required to perform ritual ablution for the touching of her vagina.

As we have mentioned, cleansing is required when one ejaculates during sleep or while awake – both men and women – or: at the end of the menstrual period; or during menstruation; or postnatal bleeding; or hiding of the glans of the penis by the vagina. Even if there is no ejaculation, the hiding of the glans by the vagina necessitates full washing (*ghusl*), just as it necessitates: punishment in the case of unlawful intercourse; repayment of the bridal dower in consummation of marriage; and marital status. It also enables divorce by threefold statement for the one who wishes to divorce his wife; further it renders the state of purity in pilgrimage and the fast invalid.[15]

In this last section, al-Qayrawani is explicit about which act of sex renders one in need of ablution and is also concerned to draw the analogy with the other legal effects of this same act. In the next section, he turns his attention to the identification of water as pure enough to effect ablution. In this short excerpt, the main concern is with standing water, since running water is understood to be pure.

Those who pray confide in their Lord, and it is necessary for them to be

43

prepared for this either by ritual ablution or purification if purification
is required. This is done with pure water, not mixed with filth nor with
water which has just changed its color because of something which
mixed with it, whether filthy or pure, except for water which has
changed color because of the earth from the marsh, or the mud, or
something like this. Water from rain, springs, wells or from the sea is
fine; it is both pure and purifies.[16]

As this chapter continues, al-Qayrawani covers the process of purifying the
place of prayer and details minimum clothing requirements for men and
women in order to perform the prayer. Finally, after several pages,
al-Qayrawani gives his description of the ablution itself in the same order as
the Qur'an: face, hands, head, feet. The first two of these are covered in the
following excerpt:

Among the traditional acts of ritual ablution are: washing of the hands
before inserting them into the basin of water to be used for ablution;
the rinsing of the mouth; the snuffing of water up the nostrils and the
forceful expulsion of that water; and the wiping of the ears. These acts
are traditionally required (*sunna*), while the rest of the actions are
requirements of faith.

As for someone who arises from sleep, or from elsewhere, to perform
the ablution, some of the Learned say that he begins by invoking God,
while others say that this invocation is not among the accepted acts.
The basin is placed to the right, within reach, and he begins by washing
his hands three times before inserting them in the basin – if he had just
urinated or defecated, that is washed away first and then the ablution is
begun. He inserts his hands in the basin, gathers up some water and
rinses his mouth three times, either with a single handful of water or
three separate handfuls. If he cleans the mouth with his fingers, that is
fine.

Thereafter, he snuffs water up his nostrils and forcefully expels it three
times, covering his nose as if blowing it. It is allowed to rinse or snuff
less than three times, and all of this may be done with a single handful
of water. However, more is better.

Then he takes water in both hands, or if he wishes with the right hand
first and then spreading the water to both hands, and brings the water
up to his face, dousing it and washing it with both hands beginning at
the top of the forehead to the hairline, to the side his beard: all around
his face from his jawbone to his temples. He passes his hands over the
hollows of his eyes, over the ridge of his forehead and under the flexible

part of his nose. He washes his face three times in this fashi⟨
up water each time. He shakes his beard with his hands wh⟨
his face in order to allow water to enter it, since water norm
right off a beard, but according to Malik's dicta he is not r⟨
comb it during ablution, only to runs his hands over it up to the end.

Then he washes his right hand three times, or twice, pouring water over
it and rubbing with his left hand; he interlaces his fingers and passes
one hand through the other and then washes his left hand in the same
manner. He washes up to the elbows, inserting the elbows into the
water as he is washing. Some say the elbows are the limit and it is not
necessary to insert them into the water, but inserting them is more
prudent to alleviate the burden of determining the exact limit.[17]

The instructions attending to washing of the head and feet are even more
detailed, as al-Qayrawani seeks to provide an exact description of the proper
acts of ablution for his disciples. The remaining chapters cover a description of
the full washing required after major defilements, such as sexual intercourse or
menstruation, and ritual cleansing using wholesome dust when no water is
available.

It is particularly this last category which makes clear that ablution in Islam is
primarily a cultic act in which the point is not to be hygienic, but to be prepared for acts of worship. The reason that such ritual actions can have the
effect of making a person clean before God is found in the Qur'anic verse
which clarifies that God is the one who is purifying the believer. In this way,
human action serves as God's instrument. The power of this symbolic action is
expanded in the image of sins falling away from various parts of the body –
hands, face, feet – as the water of ablution runs off.

7 ABLUTIONS IN JUDAISM

Ablutions form a central concern for the halakhah of classical Judaism.
Immersion in a suitable body of water, which has been collected naturally and
not through human activity, is declared by Scripture to begin the process of
removing uncleanness, with sunset marking the recovery of cleanness. But
bodily immersion, for example, after the advent of an excretion signifying
death or the intervention of what is not going to propagate life (Lev. 15), is not
the only form of purification; one may pour water on the hands to clean them,
and they are deemed an area of the body distinct, for the present purpose,
from the rest of the body.

Ablutions are required for diverse occasions and take various forms. The
main points are two. First, before eating bread, the hands are washed for reasons of purification. That should not be confused with hand-washing for

hygienic purposes. Second, as Scripture specifies at Leviticus 15, after her menstrual period a woman has to immerse to re-enter the status of cleanness, and only when it is clear that her period has ended and she has immersed may she resume sexual relations. Not only so, but it is customary to immerse after seminal emissions. Because Islam takes special interest in what Judaism would term hand-washing, however, we shall concentrate on the law that pertains to that aspect of purification through ablutions; that is, hand-washing before meals.

What is at issue is washing the hands just as the priests of the Temple are required to wash their hands before the conduct of the sacred rites. The hands are deemed perpetually unclean, a realm of uncleanness – fingertips to wrist – distinct from the rest of the body. That is why the hands are seen as a distinct source of uncleanness among the animate sources, and also why the hands are subject to their own rite of purification, the area from the wrists to the finger-tips forming a separate area not only for contracting uncleanness but also for removing it. In addition to immersion for known encounters with unclean-ness that have taken place during the day, hand-washing is required for cultic cleanness prior to eating a meal; and that has no bearing on whether or not the sun has set or when the meal takes place. The hands are deemed constantly active, whether or not the person is aware of that activity, and so are assigned a position in the second remove of uncleanness. That is to say, even though the person may know what he or she may or may not have touched, the person cannot know with what the things the hands have touched have themselves had contact – thus the second remove. Accordingly, the hands form a distinct realm of uncleanness and require their own rite of purification.

Just as the uncleanness of hands derives from the designated sources of uncleanness, which may or may not be dirty in the conventional sense, so purifying the hands has no bearing on whether or not they are actually free of dirt. What is required is a cultically prescribed action to respond to a cultically designated source of uncleanness. Accordingly, the required hand-washing in the halakhah has no bearing on hygienic cleanliness. To state matters simply: it is performed in accord with cultic rules. It constitutes an act of cultic purifica-tion of a demarcated part of the body. The hands, up to the wrist, are restored to cleanness not through immersion in an immersion pool but through rins-ing. The water that hits the hands affects but is affected by them, and that water too requires a rinsing – hence, as we shall see, a cultic purification through a repeated act of rinsing. Further, how the water is collected and administered defines a rite of purification for a component of the person that bears its own traits of cultic uncleanness. The human being's hands then con-stitute an animate source of uncleanness. Scripture is explicit that priests in the tabernacle 'sanctify' (= wash) their hands and feet before performing priestly functions at the altar (Exod. 30:19–21, 40:12, 31–32): 'Command the priests that they shall wash their hands and feet lest they die' (Exod. 30:21). Hand-washings punctuate the high priest's conduct of the rite on the Day of

Atonement (Lev. 16). But the ablutions with which we now deal are required everyday of ordinary people. Here are the principal rules as laid out in the Mishnah and the Tosefta.

I Washing Hands: A Repertoire of Rules

M.1:1 [To render hands clean] a quarter-log of water do they pour for hands, for one, also for two. A half-log [is to be used] for three or four. A log [is to be used] for five and for ten and for a hundred. They add [to the water used] for the second [pouring], but they do not add [to the water used] for the first [pouring of water over the hands].

T.1:1 [To render hands clean], a quarter-log of water do they pour for one, but not for two. A quarter-log of water do they pour for hands, even for two, and a half a log for three, even for four, a log for five and ten and a hundred.

T.1:2 They add to the second but they do not add to the first – How so? [If] one poured the first [water] and rubbed off [his hands] and went and poured the second, and it [the water] is not sufficient to reach the wrist, lo, this one adds to it. All the same is one who washes one of his hands and one who washes two of his hands, [all the same is] the hand of a large person and the hand of a small one – he must pour out a quarter-log [of water]. How so? [If] two people washed their two hands with a quarter-log, the second one should not go and wash his hands with what is left of the quarter-log.

T.1:5 He who washes his hands [for unconsecrated food prepared in accord with cleanness required for] Holy Things must pour out a quarter-log of water. And as to the sanctification [washing] of hands and feet, there is no fixed measure.

M.1:2 With all sorts of utensils do they pour [water] for hands, even with utensils made of dung, utensils made of stone, utensils made of [unbaked] clay. They do not pour [water] for hands either with the sides of [broken] utensils, or the bottom of a ladling jar, or with the plug of a barrel. Nor should a man pour [water] for his fellow with his cupped hands. For they draw, and they mix [water with the ash of the red cow], and they sprinkle purification water, and they pour [water] for hands only with a utensil. And only utensils afford protection with a tightly fitted cover, and nothing affords protection from the power of a clay utensil [in the tent of a corpse] except utensils.

47

T.1:6 A stopper which one made for a utensil – they pour out water from it for hands. The water-skin and the tub, even though they are broken down – they pour out from them water for hands. The sack and the basket, even though they hold [liquid] – they do not pour out water from them for the hands. A chest, box, and cupboard, when they hold [requisite measure to be insusceptible to uncleanness], even though they are not deemed as tents – they do not pour out water from them for hands.

T.1:7 Priests sanctify in the sanctuary only with a utensil. And they force the suspected wife to drink, and they purify a person afflicted with the skin-ailment of Lev. 13 [only with a utensil]. The sides of a wooden utensil and a bone utensil and glass utensil – they do not pour out from them water for hands. If one smoothed them, sanded them, and made them into utensils and they can hold a quarter-log of water, they do pour out water from them for hands.

T.1:8 Sherds of earthenware utensils which can hold a quarter-log of water – they pour out from them water for hands. Sherds of metal utensils, even though they can hold a quarter-log of water – they do not pour out from them water for hands.

T.1:9 He who hews out a water-channel and made in it a receptacle, even though the water uprooted it and attached it – they do not draw with it water for the purification-rite and they do not mix in it, and they do not sprinkle from it [purification water onto someone made unclean by the corpse], and it does not require a tightly sealed cover, and they do not pour out water for hands from it. [If] one uprooted it and affixed it and gave thought to it to make use of it as a utensil after its uprooting – they do draw with it, and they do mix in it, and they do sprinkle from it, and it does require a tightly sealed cover [in the tent of the corpse], and they do pour water for hands from it.

M.1:3 Water which was unfit for cattle to drink [when it is located] in utensils, is unfit. [When it is located] on the ground, it is fit. [If] there fell into it ink, gum, or copperas, and its color changed, it is unfit. [If] one did work with it, or if he soaked his bread in it, it is unfit.

T.1:10 Water which has been made unfit for cattle to drink – [If] it is on the ground, they immerse [in it], but they do not pour from it water for hands. Water which is before the baker, even though its color has not changed – they do not pour from it water for hands. And when he takes it with his hands and pours it on loaves, if its color changes, it is unfit. And if not, it is fit.

M.1:4 [If] he rinsed utensils in it, or scrubbed measures in it, it is unfit. [If] he rinsed in it vessels which had already been rinsed, or new [vessels], it is fit.

M.1:5 The water in which the baker dips loaves of fine bread is unfit. And when he rinses his hands in it, it is fit. All are fit to pour water on hands, even a deaf-mute, an imbecile, or a minor. One places the jar between his knees and pours [out water on his hands]. One sets the jar on its side and pours [out water]. And the ape pours water for hands.

T.1:11 Water which is before the smith, even though its color has not changed – they do not pour from it water for hands, for it is certain that work has been done in it. Water which is before the scribe, if its color has changed, is unfit, and if not, is fit.

T.1:12 All are fit to pour out water for hands, even a person unclean by reason of corpse contamination, even a man who has had intercourse with a menstruating woman. Whoever does not impart uncleanness to water when he carries it is fit to pour out water for hands.

T.1:13 [If] the one who takes the water intends and the one who pours out the water does not intend [that by his act the water will clean the hands], [if] the one who pours out the water intends, and the one who takes the water does not intend [that the water should clean the hands] his hands are deemed clean.

T.1:14 [If] one broke open the cauldron and poured out water for hands from a pipe which contains a place capable of containing a quarter-log of water – his hands are clean.

II Washing Hands: The Status and Condition of the Water (First and Second Pourings)

M.2:1 [If] one poured water for one hand with a single rinsing, his hand is clean. [If he poured water] for two hands with a single rinsing – [if] a loaf of heave offering fell [on the water a quarter-log in quantity which has been poured on the hands in a single rinsing], it is clean.

T.1:3 One who pours water on his hands must rub his hands off. [If] he rubbed one hand on the other, it is unclean. [If he rubbed it] on his head or on the wall, it is clean. [If] he went and touched them, it is unclean.

M.2:2 [If] one poured out the first [water] in one place and the second in another place, and a loaf of heave offering fell on the first, it is unclean. And [if it fell] on the second, it is clean. [If] he poured out the first [water] and the second in one place, and a loaf of heave offering fell [on it], it is unclean. [If] he poured out the first [water], and a splinter or pebble was found on his hands, his hands are unclean, for the second water cleans only the water which is on the hand.

T.1:4 Whatever interposes in the case of the body interposes in the case of the hands, with reference to the sanctification of the hands and feet for the Temple House.

T.2:3 He who pours out water on his hands, if he had proper intention, his hands are clean, and if not, his hands are unclean. But he who immerses his hands, one way or the other – his hands are clean.

T.2:5 [If] one poured out the first water, and one of his hands was made unclean, lo, this one pours out the second water on the second hand and does not scruple in the matter. [If] he poured out the first water, and it flowed beyond the wrist, and then he poured out the second water on it, and a loaf of bread fell from the wrist and inward, it is unclean. [If it fell] from the wrist and outward, it is clean.

T.2:6 [If] he poured out the first water and the second water beyond the wrist, and a loaf of heave offering bread fell, it is unclean. But logic requires that it be clean: Now if the (first) [rain] water, which does not impart cleanness to water which is on the hand, imparts cleanness to water which is on the ground, the second water, which does impart cleanness to the water which is on the hand, logically should impart cleanness to water which is on the ground.

M.2:3 The hands are susceptible to uncleanness and are rendered clean up to the wrist. How so? [If] one poured the first [water] up to the wrist, and the second beyond the wrist and it went back to the hand – it is clean. [If] he poured out the first and the second [pouring of water] beyond the wrist and it went back to the hand, it is unclean. [If] he poured out the first water onto one hand, and was reminded and poured out the second [water] on to both hands, they are unclean. [If] he poured out the first water on to both hands and was reminded and poured out the second [water] on to one hand, his hand [which has been washed twice] is clean. [If] he poured out water on to one hand and rubbed it on the other, it is unclean. [If he rubbed his hand] on his head or on the wall, it is clean. They pour out [water on the hands of] four or five people side by side, or above one another, J. on condition that they [the hands] lie loosely so that the water will flow among them.

T.2:1 The priests sanctify in the sanctuary, in regard to the hand, up to the wrist, and in regard to the foot, up to the calf. He who pours out water on his hands should not say, 'Since the first [water] is unclean [anyway], lo, I shall pour out unclean [water to begin with].' If he did so, lo, he must dry off his hands. He who pours out water on his hands must dry his hands. But he who immerses his hands does not have to dry off his hands.

T.2:2 He who pours water on his hands must raise his hands so that the water does not flow beyond the wrist and go back and render his hands unclean. But he who immerses his hands does not have to raise his hands.

T.2:4 He who pours water on his hands – if the water goes up to the wrist, his hands are clean, and if not, his hands are unclean. [If] he poured out the first water on this [hand] by itself and changed his mind and poured out the second water on both hands simultaneously, they render one another unclean. [If] he poured out the first water on both hands and changed his mind and poured out the second [water], this on this hand by itself and that on that hand by itself, if he had proper intention in the matter, his hands are clean, and if not, his hands are unclean.

T.2:7 They pour out water for four or five people, one beside the other, and they do not scruple on account of four things: lest it be made unclean; lest work have been done with it; lest it not be poured from a utensil; and lest a quarter-log not be poured out on a hand. But he who takes and he who pours out for his fellow with his cupped hands – his [the fellow's] hands are unclean, for in the first place the water has not been poured from a utensil.

T.2:8 Two who poured out water for two hands, this one from [a measure of] an eighth of a log, and this one from an eighth of a log, even though it goes and is mixed together in a spout – their hands are unclean. For in the first place [the water] was not poured from a quarter-log.

M.2:4 [If it is in] doubt that work has or has not been done with it, [if it is in] doubt that they contain or do not contain the requisite measure, [if it is in] doubt whether it is unclean or clean – a matter of doubt concerning it is clean. For they have said: A matter of doubt concerning the hands, whether [they are] unclean, or whether [they are deemed] to have imparted uncleanness, or whether [they are deemed] to have been made clean, is resolved as clean. How so? [If] his hands were clean, and before him were two unclean loaves of bread, [if it is in] doubt whether or not he touched them – [if] his hands were unclean, and before him were two clean loaves of bread, [if] one of his hands was unclean and one of his hands was clean and before him were two clean loaves of bread, [and if] he touched one of them, [if it is in] doubt whether he touched with the unclean or whether he touched with the clean [hand] – [if] his hands were clean, and before him were two loaves of bread, one of them unclean and one of them clean, [and if] he touched one of them, [if it is in] doubt whether he touched the unclean or whether he touched the clean [loaf of bread] – [if] one of his hands was unclean and one was clean, and before him were two loaves [of bread], one of them unclean and one of them clean, [if] he touched both of them, [if it is in] doubt whether the unclean [hand touched] the unclean [loaf of bread] and the clean [hand touched] the clean [loaf of bread], or [whether] the clean [hand touched] the unclean [loaf of bread] and the unclean [hand touched] the clean [loaf of bread] – the hands remain as they were before [in their former status], and the loaves of bread as they were before [in their former status].

T.1:15 [If] there were before him two glasses [of water] – with one of them work had been done, and with one of them work had not been done – [if] he poured [water] from one of them onto both of his hands and prepared foods requiring cleanness – they are held in suspense. [If he poured out water] from the second and prepared [foods requiring cleanness], they are clean. [If he poured out water] from the first and did not prepare foods requiring cleanness, [and if he then poured out water] from the second and prepared [foods requiring cleanness], they are clean. [If he poured out water] from the first and prepared from the second [if] these and those are lying [before him] these and those are clean.

T.1:16 [If] one poured out [water] from one of them on to one of his hands and prepared foods requiring cleanness, they are held in suspense. [If he did so] from the second and prepared [foods requiring cleanness], they are clean. [If he did so] from the first and did not prepare from the second and did prepare [foods requiring cleanness], they are clean. [If he poured out water] from the first and prepared from the second and prepared [if] these and those are lying [before him], these and those are clean.

T.1:17 [If] there were before him two glasses [of water], one unclean and one clean, and he poured out [water] from one of them for one of his hands and prepared foods requiring cleanness they are held in suspense. [If he did so] from the second and prepared [foods requiring cleanness], they are clean. [If he did so] from the first and did not prepare from the second and prepared [they are clean]. (If he did so) from the first and prepared, from the second and prepared] – [if] these and those are lying before him lo, they determine [the status of one another]. [If] he ate the first [foods which he prepared], or they were made unclean, or they were lost, before the second [foods requiring cleanness] were prepared, they are clean. [If this took place] after the second were prepared, the second are kept in a state of suspense. [If] he poured out water from one of them on to one of his hands and prepared things requiring foods requiring cleanness, they are kept in suspense. [If he poured out] the second and prepared [foods requiring cleanness], they are clean. [If he did so] with the first and did not prepare, with the second and did prepare, [if] these and those are lying [before him], [supply: lo, they determine (the status of one another).]

T.1:18 [If] one of his hands was unclean, and one of his hands was clean, and before him were two glasses, one unclean and one clean, and he poured out water from one of them on to both his hands and prepared foods requiring cleanness, they are kept in a state of suspense. [If] one of his hands was unclean, and one was clean, and before him were two loaves of bread, one unclean and one clean, and [if] his two hands touched one loaf, whether simultaneously or in succession, or one of his hands touched both of the loaves, in succession the hands and the loaves are kept in a state of suspense. [If] one of his hands touched the two loaves simultaneously, the hands remain as they were, and the loaves of bread are to be burned.

The hands are deemed a cogent area, so that what affects part of them affects the entirety of them. What affects the hands does not contaminate the rest of the body and vice versa (M.3:1). The uncleanness affecting them exhibits other distinctive traits as well. The hands never enter the first remove of uncleanness. They are made unclean only by a Father of uncleanness, not by an Offspring, such as food and utensils that have been made unclean by liquids. They are deemed unclean in the second remove, affecting heave offering. The hands are susceptible to uncleanness and are rendered clean up to the wrist. This theory of purification is constructed in the model of the one that governs in the Temple: the priests 'sanctify' – that is, wash hands – in the sanctuary, in regard to the hand, up to the wrist, and in regard to the foot, up to the calf. Consequently, when pouring water on the hands for cultic cleanness, one has to hold the hands up, so that the water will not flow beyond the wrist and then flow back and render the hands unclean again. So too the analogy is explicitly drawn: whatever interposes in the case of the body interposes in the case of the hands, with reference to the sanctification of the hands and feet for the Temple House.

Then, in the two washings, water may touch one part of the hands at the first, another at the second, and the process is fully valid. This conception is expressed in the following language: if one poured out the first water, and one of his hands was made unclean, lo, this one pours out the second water on the second hand and does not scruple in the matter. The result is as follows: if one poured out the first water in one place and the second in another place, and a loaf of heave offering fell on the first, it is unclean. And if it fell on the second, it is clean. But if the first and second rinsings fall on the ground together, a loaf of bread in the status of heave offering that afterward falls on the puddle is unclean; the second water cleans the first water – only when the first water is located on the hands, but first water situated elsewhere than on the hands is not cleaned by the second water. What interposes on the hands prevents them from being cleaned: for the second water cleans only the water which is on the hand. Interposition involves uncleanness of the first water removed by the second water. The second water does not clean the interposing object or the first water that is located on it.

Water used for sanctification involves human agency and intentionality, and water used for purification from uncleanness (but not sanctification) does not – a huge difference signaled by a small distinction. Since the hands are not immersed in water but rather water is poured out on to the hands, human agency is required in the use, not only the preparation of the water. Human agency, by contrast, would spoil the water for the immersion pool, which must be collected naturally; human agency is demanded for water used for the purification rite. What statement emerges from the facts now adduced: (1) that the hands are deemed always just one remove away from corpse contamination, and (2) it is through water analogous to that used for preparing purification water for the removal of corpse uncleanness that the hands are sanctified (not merely cleansed of uncleanness, with sunset required to complete the process of purification) even for eating food in the status of priestly rations? What I hear from the halakhah is the statement that death – the principal source of uncleanness in the halakhah – is ever-present, if not in what is touched, then in what has touched what is touched. So the hands are always in the second remove of uncleanness, meaning, death is always just a step or two away from contact with what is meant to be kept holy, clear of death. And that is – in the context of the hands and when they are sanctified – food for the nourishment of Israel. But death and all that death overspreads can be kept beyond the boundary of the household table by deliberate action defined by perpetual concern: the right intention, especially for the meal. So with that first bite of bread at the meal, the stakes are very high indeed.

What about ablutions for bodily uncleanness, as distinct from ablutions of the hands? For purifying the human being the principal medium is the use of water – but water in different venues served different purposes. The ideal venue was the immersion pool, requiring sufficient water to cover the entire body, forty seah-measures. The water could not be drawn but had to have been collected naturally, for example, rain water collected in a pond. The hands are rendered cultically clean prior to meals by pouring a small quantity of drawn-water over them, so Mishnah-tractate Yadayim 1:1–2: '[To render hands clean] a quarter-log of water do they pour for hands, for one, also for two. A half-log [is to be used] for three or four. A log [is to be used] for five and for ten and for a hundred. With all sorts of utensils do they pour [water] for hands, even with utensils made of dung, utensils made of stone, utensils made of [unbaked] clay.' Furthermore, those who suffered an involuntary sexual emission had to immerse in a regular immersion pool:

A. A man who has produced a flux [in line with Lev. 15] who then had a seminal emission,

B. a menstruating woman who discharged semen,

C. and a woman who during sexual relations produced menstrual blood [all of whom by definition are unclean without respect to the presence of semen],

D. must immerse [in a proper ritual pool].

(Mishnah-tractate Berakhot, 3:6)

On the other hand, after sexual relations one could not recite the Shema' and other prayers right away; he was restored to cleanness through having nine qabs of water poured over his body:

C. One who had a seminal discharge [on account of illness] upon whom one poured nine qabs of water is clean.

Behold he recites [cf. M. Ber. 3:4] for what purpose?

D. For himself. But he cannot exempt others from their obligation [to recite the Shema'] unless he first immerses himself in [a pool of] forty seahs [of water].

E. R. Judah says, '[He must immerse himself in] forty seahs in all cases [whether to recite the Shema' for himself or to exempt others from the recitation]'.

(Tosefta-tractate Berakhot, 2:12)

As the classical statement of Judaism defines matters, it follows that ablutions form a principal part of the life with God that is lived by the pious Israelite.

8 CONCLUSIONS

Prayer, fasting and ablutions form a distinctive category in the laws of Judaism and Islam as they concern acts which define the believer's relationship to God. Through worship, sacrifice and purification, the practitioner submits to a complex set of rules which function symbolically on a number of levels. Prayer emphasizes both the personal relationship with God but also the connections between the individual and the community. Fasting is an intentional denial of daily sustenance in order to remember God's gifts, but also to atone for sins. Finally, ablution is undertaken not for hygienic cleansing, but for cultic preparation. Thus the categories are defined, and these structural similarities demonstrate that these religions share fundamental notions of how a believer is to relate to God. It is in the ways that Jewish and Islamic law diverge, however, that we gain the most from our work of comparison. This is true both for understanding the import of what each religion describes for its own adherents, as well as for the contributions this comparison makes to the study of religion as a whole.

Both religions agree that prayer is a time for petitions to God, and on the personal level, one might well imagine that these petitions are quite similar: health, long life, success. The differences in petitions on the communal level, however, are striking. In Judaism, petitions are replete with specific historical and institutional references (Jerusalem, judges, exiles, etc.), both defining the community and its relationship to God. As we noted, prayer in Judaism is public and communal. The act of prayer itself is validated by God's revelation to Israel; without that revelation, prayer has no more standing than learned mumbling. In contrast, Islamic petitions are much less specific, appealing rather for general concepts, like guidance and compassion. But this difference is fixed and will characterize other categories treated in these pages. Judaism is the religion of that group in humanity that knows God. The Torah does not contemplate the possibility that God is made known other than through the Torah, and the Torah's teachings then form the context and the model for all relationships with God. Islam, for its part, comes at the end of a long process, encompassing not only Judaism but Christianity, by which God has made himself known to humanity. Islam accords full recognition to those that came before, finding in the Prophet the seal of prophecy and meeting no difficulty in recognizing precursors. In that context, Islam speaks to a humanity that has met God, if not so reliably or truly, before. Judaism, from the perspective of Scripture, speaks to a humanity that just now, only here, meets God. That difference helps us to understand the specificity of Israelite prayer in Judaism, the universal reference point of Islamic prayer then forming a striking contrast.

A second contrast regarding prayer concerns the communal/individual duality, which both religions share. The communal aspect of prayer in Judaism is reflected in the recital of the Eighteen Benedictions by the leader, but the communal aspect of prayer in Islam is found in the call to prayer broadcast from the minaret. One religion sees community primarily existing within the synagogue, while the other sees community extending beyond the walls of the mosque, reflecting, perhaps, Islam's greater commitment to proselytization. The 'call to worship' then travels through the streets and marketplaces of a corporate community. But within the framework of synagogue worship, Judaism too knows a call to worship, addressed to the community at prayer. The different circumstances in which each religious community lives out its life – the one master of half the world, the other scarcely begrudged a place anywhere – accounts for the striking distance in how the faithful are called to prayer. Where Jews live in large numbers and in coherent neighborhoods, in Jerusalem for example, the advent of the Sabbath is announced in a public way, and there, in times of peace, the music of the two faiths hangs in the air, forming a song that only God may hear.

It should be noted that both religions insist that God's name be mentioned over food (as well as many other times), but the law of Judaism classifies this as part of prayer, while the law of Islam does not. This difference can be accounted for by the distinct place of the name of God within Judaism. Whereas Muslims are commanded to invoke God's name throughout the day (using Qur'anic phrases such as 'if God so wills' and 'praise belongs to God'), Jews take the commandment not to take God's name in vain to mean, one may refer to God constantly, but invoke his name only with great trepidation.

There is overwhelming agreement, similarly, in terms of the categories and logic of fasting in the law of both Judaism and Islam. For these religions, fasting can be understood as a type of sacrifice, and therefore it does the work of atonement for certain sins. The discipline of fasting over a longer period of time – ten days in Judaism; a month in Islam – helps to focus the believer on God's great gifts of life, food and water. Islam extends fasting to another realm, however, in turning time on its head; night in Ramadan is for eating and reciting the Qur'an, while day is consigned to the restrictions of the fast. This inversion of time is a divinely ordained interruption of normal human activity and is a fitting symbol for remembering the month in which God interrupted Muhammad's life by revealing the Qur'an.

Finally, ablutions play a central role in the laws of both Judaism and Islam. Both traditions have gender-based rules, singling out the bleeding of menstruation and childbirth as requiring special washing for women and the emission of semen requiring ablution for men. This focus on blood and semen does not mean that Judaism and Islam see childbirth and sexual intercourse as sinful; rather, it has to do with a fundamental awe of life, shared by both traditions. As another example, consider that the law of both Judaism and Islam explicitly demands that the blood of a slaughtered animal run directly into the ground.

In this way the life-blood of the animal is returned to its Creator and is not consumed by Muslims and Jews. Just as blood is a symbol of life, so bleeding is related to dying. This then explains Judaism's focus on washing as a symbol for separating the living person from death, since death is seen as the principal source of uncleanness.

Perhaps the most important distinction between the two religions, however, is the fact that while ablution is recommended before each prayer in Islam, it is not required; it is possible to maintain a state of ritual purity for hours, even days. Judaism, however, demands ablution before each eating of bread, since the hands are deemed perpetually unclean. This distinction points to a difference in the ultimate goal of ablutions in these two religions: whereas Judaism is primarily interested in ablution to gain freedom from uncleanness, Islam is primarily interested in ablution as an instrument of God's desire to purify the hearts of his believers. In this detail a large difference may lurk: Islam treats as symbolic what for Judaism is immediate and practical. For the one, the here and now is a metaphor; for the other, the immediate embodies the divine encounter.

2

AMONG THE FAITHFUL [I]

BETROTHAL, MARRIAGE,
INHERITANCE, DIVORCE:
HOW THE FAMILY IS REGULATED

1 INTRODUCTION

Both the Islamic and Judaic systems of law take for granted that the family forms a critical focus of Godly concern. That is because the family is one focus of sanctification, the woman to the man in particular, and sexuality is a principal medium for the sanctification of life. Arrangements made by man accord with God's wishes or violate them. God confirms and sustains the right ones, condemns the wrong. Central to these systems is the status of a woman, who ordinarily is not left out of relationship with a man but is assigned to the protection of her father (and brothers) before marriage, her husband afterward. Provision of valid rites of betrothal, marriage, and divorce, as the case requires, validate in the eyes of God arrangements that, lacking such provision, would otherwise constitute sin. Specifically, when a woman passes from the domain of her father (or, lacking a father, her widowed mother and brothers) to the domain of her husband, particular rites, (for example, documents) must mark the change in her status, through its stages. In the absence of such rites or documents, the woman's actions constitute license. The same actions, properly validated, accord with God's will and plan. So rites of betrothal and marriage, on the one hand, and divorce, on the other, classify a given action involving a woman's status; properly done these are an occasion for celebration, improperly done, for sanction. That other dimension of the family – the preservation and transmission of property from generation to generation –enters into this same framework. In the case of both Judaism and Islam, law frames a theology of family life that fits well into the larger religious system set forth by the respective revelations.

2 BETROTHAL IN JUDAISM

The transformation of the status of a woman from daughter to wife takes place in two stages: betrothal, at which point the woman is designated, or sanctified, to a particular man, and marriage, at which point the relationship is sexually consummated under the marriage canopy, or *huppah* (which lends its name to the entire transaction). In the law of Judaism a father may betroth and marry off his daughter if she is a minor, but when she reaches maturity, at the age of twelve, she may without penalty reject the arrangement and leave the arranged marriage. From maturity, moreover, a young woman may enter into a betrothal on her own account. Betrothal has the legal force of marriage, in that should the arrangement fall apart, a proper rite of divorce is required.

The change in the woman's status, from free agent to designated for a particular man, takes place through a rite that transfers her – by which is meant, responsibility for the woman – from her father to her prospective husband. This may be done through the prospective husband giving her – and the woman willingly accepting – a token money-payment; through the provision of a writ of betrothal, properly witnessed and delivered; or through a sexual act. The law of Judaism takes for granted that a man does not wantonly commit such an action, to which the woman acquiesces (otherwise a charge of rape would be entered), but only with the intent of acquiring the woman for himself, and therefore assumes that the intent of both parties is to effect a betrothal. These three media for the transfer of title hardly compare; the woman's (or her father's in the case of a minor) acceptance of a token being different from the provision of a legal document, and a legal document hardly comparing to a change in the physical relationship of the couple. All, however, produce the same effect. The same passage covers the dissolution of the relationship. 'The woman acquires herself,' meaning, regains the status of free agent, no longer sanctified to a given man, by receiving a writ of divorce – matching the document that inaugurates the relationship – or by reason of the husband's death. The other two means of effecting the relationship, her acceptance of a token or the act of sexual relations, produce no counterpart, for example, returning the token or severing the sexual bond. The paragraphing delineates secondary amplification of the main point:

A. A woman is acquired [as a betrothed wife] in three ways, and acquires [freedom for] herself [to be a free agent] in two ways.

B. She is acquired through money, a writ, and sexual intercourse.

C. Through money:

60

D. The House of Shammai say, 'For a denar or what is worth a denar'

E. And the House of Hillel say, 'For a perutah or what is worth a perutah.'

F. And how much is a perutah?

G. One eighth of an Italian issar

H. And she acquires herself through a writ of divorce and through the husband's death.

(Mishnah-tractate Qiddushin, 1:1)

The Houses are law-schools assumed to have flourished in the first century BCE and CE, Shammai and Hillel being listed in the chain of tradition from Sinai forward. That the betrothal takes effect only when the woman agrees to accept the token of betrothal or its counterparts accords the woman equality in the transaction. That means, just as a man may send an agent, so a woman may participate through her designated representative.

A. A man effects betrothal on his own or through his agent.

B. A woman becomes betrothed on her own or through her agent.

C. A man betroths his daughter when she is a girl on his own or through his agent.

(Ibid., 2:1)

The law, further, takes account of the implications of language that is used, deeming the language, like a document, the effective instrument of transformation of the woman's status. In the continuation of the rule at hand, we note the difference between language that is partitive, that is, that distinguishes one thing from another, and language that is inclusive, that is, that joins one thing to another. At D–E, the language refers to one thing or to another, at F–G, the language implies that the several things that are handed over are treated as a single entity, and the rest follows.

D. He who says to a woman, 'Be betrothed to me for this date, be betrothed to me with this,'

E. if [either] one of them is of the value of a perutah, she is betrothed, and if not, she is not betrothed.

61

F. 'By this, and by this, and by this' —

G. if all of them together are worth a perutah, she is betrothed, and if not, she is not betrothed.

H. [If] she was eating them one by one, she is not betrothed,

I. unless one of them is worth a perutah.'

(Ibid., 2:1)

Finally, we deal with conditional betrothals. If the man specifies the thing that he intends to serve as the token of betrothal, what he says is interpreted as a condition that, in the woman's mind, is operative; if that condition is not met, the betrothal is null.

A. 'Be betrothed to me for this cup of wine,' and it turns out to be honey —

B. '... of honey,' and it turns out to be of wine,

C. '... with this silver denar,' and it turns out to be gold,

D. '... with this gold one,' and it turns out to be silver —

E. '... on condition that I am rich,' and he turns out to be poor,

F. '... on condition that I am poor,' and he turns out to be rich —

G. she is not betrothed.

H. R. Simeon says, 'If he deceived her to [her] advantage, she is betrothed.'

2:3 A. '... on condition that I am a priest,' and he turns out to be a Levite,

B. '... on condition that I am a Levite,' and he turns out to be a priest,

C. '... a netin,' and he turns out to be a mamzer,

D. '... a mamzer,' and he turns out to be a netin,

E. '... a town dweller,' and he turns out to be a villager,

F. '… a villager,' and he turns out to be a town dweller,

G. '… on condition that my house is near the bath,' and it turns out to be far away,

H. '… far,' and it turns out to be near:

I. '… on condition that I have a daughter or a servant girl who is a hairdresser' and he has none,

J. '… on condition that I have none,' and he has one;

K. '… on condition that I have no children,' and he has;

L. '… on condition that he has,' and he has none —

M. in the case of all of them, even though she says, 'In my heart I wanted to become betrothed to him despite that fact,' she is not betrothed.

N. And so is the rule if she deceived him.

(Ibid., 2:2)

What we see in this elaborate passage is how the legal system transforms a given topic into an exercise in a broader principle of the law. In this case, the law in general takes account of deceit in contracts and wishes to say that if one party has deceived the other, the agreement is null. That principle is then translated into the case at hand, and in an elaborate way at that. That is a fine example of what happens when a religious conviction, resting on a theological principle, is set forth in law rather than in a religious rite or even a theological statement. The law now makes the principle concrete and shows how the principle may apply to a broad variety of cases.

3 BETROTHAL IN ISLAM

Islamic law distinguishes between three acts within the process of getting married: betrothal, the marriage contract, and consummation of the marriage. However, the legal effects of betrothal are disputed, and it may be done away with entirely. Moreover, betrothal is not a legal obligation, and so it does not receive a separate chapter in the legal handbooks. At the beginning of his chapter on marriage, al-Qayrawani simply states: 'There is no marriage without: an agent, marriage present, and two trustworthy witnesses.' His concern is with issues central to the contract, and betrothal is hardly addressed. Nor is betrothal the subject of extensive discussion in the Qur'an. In fact, when it comes to matters of preparation for marriage, the Qur'an's primary concern is with those men who may not have sufficient funds to pay the marriage present, suggesting either that they remain abstinent (4:25 and 24:30) or that they should marry slaves (2:221, 4:24, and 24:32), for whom no particular gift is required.

Although betrothal is not a legal act, it may have legal effects, including permitting the prospective groom to see his fiancée and giving the prospective groom priority over other suitors. Either party may break off the engagement, but any presents given to the bride are considered gifts and not returned. No statement of divorce is, however, required. A number of hadith demonstrate both the process and principals of betrothal:

> Yahya told me on Malik's authority from Nafi from Abdullah ibn Umar that the Messenger of God, may God bless him and grant him peace, said, 'One of you should not make an engagement upon the engagement of his brother.'

> Malik said: The explanation of the statement of the Messenger of God, may God bless him and grant him peace, according to what we think – but God knows best – is that 'One of you should not make an engagement upon the engagement of his brother.' This means that when a man is engaged to a woman, and she trusts him, and they have agreed on an honorable marriage present, with which they are satisfied, and she has made this a condition for herself, that this is that which is forbidden: that another man makes an engagement upon this engagement of his brother.

> It does not mean that when a man has made an engagement with a woman, and his suit does not agree with her and she does not trust him, that no one else may seek an engagement with her. That would be a door to immorality for the people.

> Yahya told me on Malik's authority from Abd al-Rahman ibn al-Qasim that his father said about God's word, he is blessed and most high: 'There is no harm in the betrothal you offer to women, or hide in yourselves. God knows that you will remember them; but do not make secret promises to them without honorable words' (Qur'an, 2:235). This is when a man says to a woman, while she was still in her waiting period after the death of her husband, 'You are precious to me, and I am desirous of you. May God cause goodness and wealth to flow to you!' and words such as these.[18]

The first two hadith nicely demonstrate the careful reasoning of Islamic jurists. Taken literally, the words of the Prophet could be interpreted to forbid both concurrent suits and consecutive ones! The second hadith forms a commentary on one of the few Qur'anic verses on the subject of proposals. In the classical handbooks of Islamic law, this story is simply summed up as follows: 'A woman may not be betrothed during her waiting period, but there is no fault in honorable expressions of intent.'[19] This, in fact, is the only statement on betrothal in all of al-Qayrawani's handbook.

One important aspect of the law of betrothal, however, is that an engagement may only be arranged between two people who would normally be allowed to marry. Following the Qur'an, the Muslim jurists legislate extensively on whom a man may marry in the first place, forbidding marriage to close family. Interestingly, both blood and milk form the ties that bind the Muslim family together. That is to say, if a boy and a girl are suckled by the same woman – even if they are not related by blood – they may not marry one another. The Qur'an begins with this list.

> Do not marry women such as those your fathers married, unless it was a marriage from before; such a marriage is an abomination and abhorrent, an evil path.
>
> Forbidden for you to marry are your mothers and daughters, sisters, aunts on both sides, the daughters of your brothers and sisters, milk-mothers, milk-sisters, mothers-in-law, stepdaughters who are in your care – that is, born of wives with whom you have had sexual intercourse, but if you have not yet consummated the marriage, then there is no harm – or women belonging to your actual sons; it is also forbidden to have intercourse with two sisters together, unless this was from before.
>
> (The Qur'an, 4:22–23)

In his handbook, al-Qayrawani quotes this passage and then extends the same pattern of reasoning, referring to a hadith from the Prophet. Here the law makes explicit what the Qur'an implies, that all marital relations forbidden because of blood ties are also forbidden if connected by milk.

> The Prophet – may God bless him and grant him peace – forbade relations by milk all who were forbidden by blood. He also refused to marry a woman due to her relationship as an aunt [of the groom]. As for someone who marries a woman, his father, grandfather and sons are forbidden from marrying her by the contract itself, even before she is touched [by sexual intercourse]; and her mother and grandmother are forbidden to the groom. However, her daughters [from previous marriages] are not forbidden to him until he has sexual intercourse with their mother, or enjoys sexual pleasure whether by right of marriage,

65

ownership [in the case of concubines], or something similar. The woman normally permitted to a man is not rendered impermissible by adultery [with, for instance, her sister].[20]

That milk should form a family bond in Islamic law suggests that mother's milk is categorized with blood as a life-giving substance, but also that Muslim family boundaries are not established by blood alone. In fact, slaves are also considered a part of the family, so while a man may have sexual intercourse with the female slave that he personally owns, he may not have intercourse with his wife's female slave. Nor may he take as concubines his female slave and her daughter, even though he owns them both. In this manner, al-Qayrawani extends the logic of his discussion to include forbidden relationships with female slaves, unbelievers, and Jews and Christians, known collectively as 'People of the Book.'

> God – may he be praised – forbade sexual intercourse, whether by right of marriage or ownership, with unbelievers who are not of the People of the Book. But he did allow sexual intercourse with females of the People of the Book by right of ownership, and he did allow marrying free women of the People of the Book. However, he did not allow right of sexual intercourse with their female servants, nor did he allow marriage to them, whether free or slave.

> A free woman may not marry her slave, or the slave of her child. Nor may a man marry his female slave, nor the female slave of his child. He may, however, marry the female slave of his father or the female slave of his mother; he may also marry the daughter of one of his father's women who was born of another father. Similarly, a woman may marry the son of her father's wife who was born of another father.

> It is permitted for both the free male and the slave to marry up to four: for the free male, four free women, whether Muslim or of the People of the Book; for the male slave, four female Muslim slaves. A free man may also marry female slaves if he fears fornication [because he cannot marry a free woman and he cannot remain abstinent].[21]

This last sentence offers some explanation for the bond of marriage within Islam. The ordering of the family is the very basis of the ordering of society, and fornication – sex outside the legal boundaries of marriage – is emblematic of a disordered society. Yet Islamic law does not see marriage between a free man and a female slave as a comparable example of disorder; further, al-Qayrawani makes clear that the only way a man may marry a female slave is for this slave to belong to another man. This is a marriage of lowly status, yet it is more conducive to a well-ordered society than the alternative.

This concern with order is reflected in other Qur'anic injunctions on marriage, for while the legal handbooks concentrate solely on the negative commands – whom one is not allowed to marry – the Qur'an also provides positive commands, bidding Muslims to marry widows, slaves and orphans in order to provide for them.

> Marry those among you who have no husbands, and those of your male and female slaves that are righteous; if they are poor, God will enrich them by his grace; God is generous, wise.
>
> (The Qur'an, 24:32)

> Give the orphans their assets, and do not exchange the hateful for the good; and do not consume their assets as your assets; this is a great crime.

> If you fear you will not act justly toward the orphans, then marry women who seem good to you: two, three, or four.
>
> (Ibid., 4:2–3)

In this way, marriage can be seen as an institution to bring these marginalized persons, widows and orphans, back into the family structure.

4 MARRIAGE IN JUDAISM

Marriage takes place through a second rite, after that of betrothal. (In contemporary Judaism the rite of betrothal and that of marriage take place on the same occasion, the whole rite under the marriage canopy or huppah.) That is the point at which the couple live together as man and wife. The rite involves the provision of a critical document, called a *ketubah*. That document specifies the settlement that will take place if the husband divorces the wife and provides for at least a year of alimony, during which time it is assumed the divorcée will remarry. It takes effect when witnessed and attests to the husband's commitment to support the wife even at the cost of the shirt on his back. Without that protection the marriage cannot take place. The funds to which the ketubah attests vary: a virgin at marriage being allowed two hundred zuz, a widow or divorcée, one hundred. The law then provides for the husband's claim that his new wife, for whom the ketubah of a virgin has been provided, was not in fact a virgin:

1:1 A. A virgin is married on Wednesday, and a widow on Thursday.

B. For twice weekly are the courts in session in the towns, on Monday and on Thursday.

C. So if he [the husband] had a complaint as to virginity, he goes early to court.

(Mishnah-tractate Ketubot, 1:1)

1:2 A. A virgin – her marriage contract is two hundred [zuz].

B. And a widow, a maneh [one hundred zuz],

C. A virgin, widow, divorcée, and one who has severed the Levirate connection [described at Deut. 25:1–4] through a rite of halisah [which severs the Levirate connection as does a writ of divorce in an ordinary marriage]

D. at the stage of betrothal —

E. their marriage contract is two hundred [zuz].

F. And they are subject to the claim against their virginity.

G. A convert, a woman taken captive, and a servant girl who were redeemed or who converted or who were freed at an age of less than three years and one day —

H. their marriage contract is two hundred [zuz].

I. And they are subject to the claim against their virginity.

(Ibid.,1:2)

Once again, we see the result of a religion making its statement through law. The issues that arise are those that concern lawyers, even though the principles derive from religious convictions about the nature of relationships between the sexes as God has arranged them. The basic point is that marriage is a public transaction, a relationship of sanctification, in which God has a heavy stake as much as the participants.

Because of the nature of the transaction, however, involving as it does exchanges of property and not only the acquisition of persons, we should not be surprised to find a variety of concerns that we in the West should classify as conventionally legal, for example, rules of evidence and testimony. We proceed to the issue of evidence: what kind of claims are permitted, and what sort of evidence is required to sustain them?

1:6 A. He who marries a woman and did not find tokens of virginity —

B. she says, 'After you betrothed me, I was raped, and your field has been flooded,'

C. and he says, 'Not so, but it was before I betrothed you, and my purchase was a bargain made in error' —

D. Rabban Simeon b. Gamaliel and R. Eliezer say, 'She is believed.'

E. R. Joshua says, 'We do not depend on her testimony. But lo, she remains in the assumption of having had sexual relations before she was betrothed and of having deceived him, until she brings evidence to back up her [contrary] claim.'

(Ibid., 1:6)

1:7 A. She says, 'I was injured by a piece of wood,'

B. and he says, 'Not so, but you have been laid by a man' –

C. Rabban Simeon b. Gamaliel and R. Eliezer say, 'She is believed.'

D. And R. Joshua says, 'We do not depend on her testimony. But lo, she remains in the assumption of having been laid by a man, until she brings evidence to back up her claim.'

(Ibid.,1:7)

At issue in the positions attributed to the sages who flourished at the end of the first century is the weight of a woman's testimony as to her own status. Joshua demands evidence to sustain the woman's claim; Gamaliel and Eliezer accept the claim at face value. Joshua's position invokes the principle of commercial law, 'He who wishes to exact payment of a claim from another bears the burden of proof,' and since at issue here is the difference of one hundred zuz, the woman is in the position of such a claimant.

The same dispute extends to a woman's allegation as to the parentage of her unborn child in a case in which she is not wed. At stake is the child's status in the hierarchy of castes, priest, Levite, Israelite, netin (originally an indentured Temple worker), and mamzer (a person lacking a clear lineage). If the woman claims the child to be the offspring of a priest, then the child enjoys the status of a priest and may eat food that is reserved for priestly consumption and enjoy other perquisites of the priesthood of the Temple. It is a valuable claim. We note that the status of the offspring is not affected by the fact that the parents are not wed; if they are legally free to marry – the woman not being betrothed or married to some other man, for example – the child enjoys the status conferred upon him by the father's genealogy, and no stigma denies the child that status:

1:8 A. [If] they saw her [sexually] conversing with a man in the market,

B. [and] they said to her, 'What is the character of this one?'

C. [and she said,] 'It is Mr. So-and-so, and he is a priest' –

D. Rabban Simeon b. Gamaliel and R. Eliezer say, 'She is believed.'

E. [And] R. Joshua says, 'We do not depend on her testimony. But lo, she remains in the assumption of having had sexual relations with a netin or a mamzer, until she brings evidence to back up her claim.'

(Ibid., 1:8)

1:9 A. [If] she was pregnant, and they said to her, 'What is the character of this fetus?'

B. [and she said,] 'It is by Mr. So-and-so, and he is a priest' —

C. Rabban Simeon b. Gamaliel and R. Eliezer say, 'She is believed.'

D. [And] R. Joshua says, 'We do not depend on her testimony. But lo, she remains in the assumption of having been made pregnant by a netin or a mamzer,

E. 'until she brings evidence to back up her claim.'

(Ibid., 1:9)

Joshua's position in both cases remains consistent, even though here, the prospective claim of the offspring to the emoluments of the priesthood is not addressed to some specific party. If recognized as a priest, the child will get his share of the priestly rations, with the result that the rest of the priests get less, and that suffices to require the mother to prove the status of the child.

What about law covering the duration of the marriage, between marriage and either the death of one of the parties or the divorce by the husband of the wife? The law of Judaism legislates mainly for the point at which the woman's status changes, that is, the beginning and the end of the marriage: betrothal, marriage (marriage contract), and divorce. But in two aspects the law of Judaism is explicit in defining required conduct during the marriage. First, the woman must perform certain duties for her husband, and these concern the maintenance of the household and the care of children. Second, the husband and the wife must conduct a regular sexual life, neither denying the other a normal sexual relationship; that is a duty of marriage, not a favor, as we shall see. The basic philosophy that the law embodies is, however, that a woman must not be left idle and without purposeful, useful labor to perform.

5:5 A. These are the kinds of labor which a woman performs for her husband:

B. she (1) grinds flour, (2) bakes bread, (3) does laundry, (4) prepares meals, (5) feeds her child, (6) makes the bed, (7) works in wool.

C. [If] she brought with her a single servant girl, she does not (1) grind, (2) bake bread, or (3) do laundry.

D. [If she brought] two, she does not (4) prepare meals and does (5) not feed her child.

E. [If she brought] three, she does not (6) make the bed for him and does not (7) work in wool.

F. If she brought four, she sits on a throne.

G. R. Eliezer says, 'Even if she brought him a hundred servant girls, he forces her to work in wool,

H. 'for idleness leads to unchastity.'

I. Rabban Simeon b. Gamaliel says, 'Also: he who prohibits his wife by a vow from performing any labor puts her away and pays off her marriage contract.'

J. 'For idleness leads to boredom.'

(Ibid., 5:5)

The sages at the same time propose to take account of class differences – those with or without servants; but schismatic opinion is explicit that under all circumstances the woman must enjoy a useful role in life.

In this connection we should recall that the law of Judaism presupposes polygamy, so the provision is important in providing each wife regular access to her husband's sexual services, and that accounts for what follows. First, neither party may take a vow to Heaven not to engage in sexual relations with the other. Such a vow would violate the given of the marriage, and neither partner has the power to nullify the contract of the marriage. Such a vow must be nullified within a brief period.

5:6 A. He who takes a vow not to have sexual relations with his wife —

71

B. The House of Shammai say, '[He may allow this situation to continue] for two weeks.'

C. And the House of Hillel say, 'For one week.'

On the other hand, the law makes provision for the husbands to absent themselves from home for required periods of time, even though that deprives the wife of the husband's sexual services. The provision takes account of other physical obligations incumbent on the man, for example, workers on farms and in fields provide less, those who do not engage in heavy lifting, more; those who live at home, more, those who must travel, less:

D. Disciples go forth for Torah study without [the wife's] consent for thirty days.

E. Workers go out for one week.

F. 'The sexual duty of which the Torah speaks [Exod. 21:10]: (1) those without work [of independent means] – every day; (2) workers – twice a week; (3) ass-drivers – once a week; (4) camel-drivers – once in thirty days; (5) sailors – once in six months,' the words of R. Eliezer.

(Ibid., 5:6)

What happens if the woman denies her husband access to her bed? She is penalized by a fine, deducted from the marriage settlement, of one denar a day; that fine continues until the entire settlement has been used up. The husband has to pay a half-denar a day in the same circumstance.

5:7 A. She who rebels against her husband [declining to perform wifely services (M . 5:5)] —

B. they deduct from her marriage contract seven dinars a week.

C. R. Judah says, 'Seven tropaics.'

D. How long does one continue to deduct?

E. Until her entire marriage contract [has been voided].

F. R. Yosé says, 'He continues to deduct [even beyond the value of the marriage contract], for an inheritance may come [to her] from some other source, from which he will collect what is due him.'

G. And so is the rule for the man who rebels against his wife [declining to do the husband's duties (M. 5:4)] —

H. they add three dinars a week to her marriage contract.

I. R. Judah says, 'Three tropaics.'

(Ibid., 5:7)

Clearly, the marriage contract forms the legal contract, including provisions for enforcement of the contract, that defines the marital relationship. Its purpose, to protect a woman from divorce on a man's whim by making divorce costly and to provide for a woman during such time as she is not married to a man, is to the woman's advantage. But what if the woman forfeits her right to that advantage by violating the givens of the marriage, besides the sexual ones? Then she loses her marriage settlement entirely, making it easy for the husband to divorce her.

Such a gross penalty applies, in particular, when a woman violates the law of the Torah, and this is defined with some precision:

7:6 A. And those women go forth without the payment of the marriage contract at all:

B. She who transgresses against the law of Moses and Jewish law.

C. And what is the law of Moses [which she has transgressed]? [If] (1) she feeds him food which has not been tithed, or (2) has sexual relations with him while she is menstruating, or [if] (3) she does not cut off her dough offering, or (4) [if] she vows and does not carry out her vow.

D. And what is the Jewish law? If (1) she goes out with her hair flowing loose, or (2) she spins in the marketplace, or (3) she talks with just anybody,

E. Abba Saul says, 'Also: if she curses his parents in his presence.'

F. R. Tarfon says, 'Also: if she is a loudmouth.'

G. What is a loudmouth? When she talks in her own house, her neighbors can hear her voice.

(Ibid., 7:6)

The law of Moses involves four principal provisions: tithing food, refraining from sexual relations during the menstrual period (Lev. 15), setting apart dough offering, and not observing vows voluntarily undertaken. 'Jewish law' concerns feminine modesty; the woman must avoid any appearance of accessibility to any man other than her husband. The sages add matters of conduct of an other than sexual nature.

Now we come to a critical issue, the wife accused of adultery and how the law deals with such a case. How does Judaism in its classical statement deal with infidelity? The answer begins with Numbers 5, which lays out the rite of the drinking of bitter water by a wife whose husband accuses her of infidelity. In this connection, however, the halakhah of the Mishnah and Talmuds makes a statement on family life that we should not miss. It is that the injustice done to the innocent wife, required by the husband's whim to undergo the humiliating ordeal of the bitter water, serves as the halakhah's occasion to make its definitive statement that God's justice is perfect: the wicked get their exact punishment and the righteous their precise reward. For the sages that statement becomes possible only here, for in their view it is not enough to show that sin or crime provokes divine response, and that God penalizes evil-doers. Justice in the here and now counts only when the righteous also receive what is coming to them. Scripture's casual remark that the woman found innocent will bear more children provokes elaborate demonstration, out of the established facts of history that Scripture supplies, that both righteous and wicked are subject to God's flawless and exact justice.

The penalty must fit the crime, measure must match measure, and the more exact the result to the cause, the more compelling the proof of immediate and concrete justice as the building block of world order that the sages would put forth out of Scripture. That is the point at which justice is transformed from a vague generality – a mere sentiment – to a precise and measurable dimension of the actual social order of morality: how things hold together when subject to tension, at the pressure points of structure, not merely how they are arrayed in general. Here, in fact, is how God made the world: what is good about the creation that God pronounced good. And to make that point, the sages select a rite that reeks of injustice, the case of the wife accused of adultery and the ordeal to which she is subjected. Their presentation of the rite, in the setting of home and family, is framed so as to demonstrate God's perfect justice – not only in the public life of Israel's social order, but in the here and now of home and family. It is hard to find a less likely candidate for service in demonstrating that proposition than the subject before us. But, for reasons that are now clear, the sages identified the topic as the ideal occasion for saying just that. Here are the main points of the halakhah of the Mishnah (indicated by M.) and the Tosefta (marked by T.) on the rite that tests the wife accused of adultery.

I Invoking the Ordeal

M. 1:1–2 He who expresses jealousy to his wife [concerning her relations with another man (Num. 5:14)] how does he express jealousy to her? [If] he stated to her before two witnesses, 'Do not speak with Mr. So-and-so,' and she indeed spoke with him, she still is permitted to have sexual relations with her husband and is permitted to eat priestly rations. [If] she went with him to some private place and remained with him for sufficient time to become unclean, she is prohibited from having sexual relations with her husband and [if the husband is a priest,] she is prohibited from eating priestly rations. And if he [her husband] should die, she performs the rite of *halisah* [removing the shoe, which severs her relationship to the childless husband's surviving brother, in line with the law of Deut. 25:5–10] but is not taken into Levirate marriage.

T.1:2 What is the character of the first testimony [M. Sot.1:2]? This is the testimony concerning her going off alone [with such and such a person]. The second [testimony]? This is testimony concerning her having been made unclean. And how long is the time required for becoming unclean? Sufficient time to have sexual relations. And how much is sufficient time for having sexual relations? Sufficient time for sexual contact.

M.1:3 And these women [married to priests and accused of unfaithfulness] are prohibited from eating priestly rations: (1) She who says, 'I am unclean to you,' and (2) she against whom witnesses testified that she is unclean; and (3) she who says, 'I shall not drink the bitter water,' and (4) she whose husband will not force her to drink it; and (5) she whose husband has sexual relations with her on the way [up to Jerusalem for the rite of drinking the water]. What should he do in respect to her? He brings her to the court in that place [in which they live], and [the judges] hand over to him two disciples of sages, lest he have sexual relations with her on the way.

The sages amplify the law of the Torah at Numbers 5 by invoking a variety of juridical protections for the wife. Formal testimony is required before the woman is threatened with the loss of her property (non-payment of the marriage settlement). A variety of situations result in the nullification of the rite. In the narrative of the ordeal itself, we hear also from the Talmud of Babylonia (marked as B.), which amplifies the rite and enhances its drama.

II Narrative of the Ordeal

M.1:4 They would bring her up to the high court which is in Jerusalem and admonish her as they admonish witnesses in a capital crime. They say to her, 'My daughter, much is done by wine, much is done by joking around, much is done by kidding around, much is done by bad friends. For the sake of the great Name which is written in holiness, do it so that it will not be blotted out by water [Num. 5:23]' and they tell her things which neither she nor the family of her father's house should be hearing.

T.1:6 And just as the court admonishes her to repent [M. Sot. 1:4], so they admonish her not to repent. Therefore they say to her, 'Now my daughter, if it is perfectly clear to you that you are clean, stand your ground and drink. For these waters are only like a dry salve which is put on living flesh and does no harm. If there is a wound, it penetrates and goes through [the skin, and if there is no wound, it has no effect]. Two accused wives are not made to drink simultaneously, so that one not be shameless before the other.

B.1:4 III.1 7B And they tell her things ... [M. 1:4C]: He tells her lessons of narrative and events that took place [and are recorded] in the earlier writings [of the Pentateuch]. For example 'Which wise men have told and have not hid from their fathers [by confessing their sin]' (Job 15:18). Specifically: Judah confessed and was not ashamed to do so. What was his destiny? He inherited the world to come. Reuben confessed and was not ashamed to do so. What was his destiny? He inherited the world to come. What was their reward? What was their reward?! Rather, what was their reward in this world? 'To them alone the land was given, and no stranger passed among them' (Job 15:19).

M.1:5 [Now] if she said, 'I am unclean,' she gives a quittance for her marriage contract [which is not paid over to her], and goes forth [with a writ of divorce]. And if she said, 'I am clean,' they bring her up to the Eastern Gate, which is at the entrance of Nicanor's Gate. There it is that they force accused wives to drink the bitter water, and they purify women after childbirth and purify lepers. And a priest grabs her clothes – if they tear, they tear, and if they are ripped up, they are ripped up – until he bares her breast. And he tears her hair apart [Num. 5:18].

T.1:7 Priests cast lots among themselves. Whoever won the lottery, even a high priest, goes out and stands next to the accused wife. And a priest grabs her clothes – if they tear, they tear, and if they are ripped up, they are ripped up – until he bares her breast. And he tears her hair apart.

M.1:6 [If] she was clothed in white clothing, he puts black clothes on her. [If] she had gold jewelry, chains, nose-rings, and finger rings on, they take them away from her to put her to shame. Then he brings a rope made out of twigs and ties it above her breasts. And whoever wants to stare at her comes and stares, except for her boy-slaves and girl-slaves, since in any case she has no shame before them. And all women are allowed to stare at her, since it is said, that all women may be taught not to do after your lewdness (Ezek. 23:48).

Now comes the principal lesson that the sages wish to draw from the rite – which they described out of their imagination to begin with. It concerns the theological principle that animates Judaism (and Islam as well). God is just, what happens comes about by his will, and the punishment that a person receives matches the crime that has been committed. First the exposition deals with the case at hand, and then it generalizes.

> M.1:7 By that same measure by which a man metes out [to others], do they mete out to him: she primped herself for sin, the Omnipresent made her repulsive. She exposed herself for sin, the Omnipresent exposed her. With the thigh she began to sin, and afterward with the belly, therefore the thigh suffers the curse first, and afterward the belly. But the rest of the body does not escape [punishment].

> T.3:2 And so you find that with regard to the accused wife: with the measure with which she measured out, with that measure do they mete out to her. She stood before him so as to be pretty before him, therefore a priest stands her up in front of everybody to display her shame, as it is said, And the priest will set the woman before the Lord (Num. 5:18).

> T.3:3 She wrapped a beautiful scarf for him, therefore a priest takes her cap from her head and puts it under foot. She braided her hair for him, therefore a priest loosens it. She painted her face for him, therefore her face is made to turn yellow. She put blue on her eyes for him, therefore her eyes bulge out.

> T.3:4 She signaled to him with her finger, therefore her fingernails fall out. She showed him her flesh, therefore a priest tears her cloak and shows her shame in public. She tied on a belt for him, therefore a priest brings a rope of twigs and ties it above her breasts, and whoever wants to stare comes and stares at her [M. Sot. 1:6C–D]. She pushed her thigh at him, therefore her thigh falls. She took him on her belly, therefore her belly swells. She fed him goodies, therefore her meal offering is fit for a cow. She gave him the best wines to drink in elegant goblets, therefore the priest gives her the bitter water to drink in a clay pot.

T.4:1 I know only with regard to the measure of retribution that by that same measure by which a man metes out, they mete out to him [M. Sot. 1:7A]. How do I know that the same is so with the measure of goodness [M. Sot. 1:9A]? Thus do you say: 'The measure of goodness is five hundred times greater than the measure of retribution.' With regard to the measure of retribution it is written, Visiting the sin of the fathers on the sons and on the grandsons to the third and fourth generation (Exod. 20:5). And with regard to the measure of goodness it is written, And doing mercy for thousands (Exod. 20:6). You must therefore conclude that the measure of goodness is five hundred times greater than the measure of retribution.

The discussion now takes up other cases in which sinners are punished justly, and in a proportionate manner, for their sin.

M. 1:8 Samson followed his eyes [where they led him], therefore the Philistines put out his eyes, since it is said, And the Philistines laid hold on him and put out his eyes (Judg. 16:21). Absalom was proud of his hair, therefore he was hung by his hair [II Sam. 14:25–26]. And since he had sexual relations with ten concubines of his father, therefore they thrust ten spear heads into his body, since it is said, 'And ten young men that carried Jacob's armor surrounded and smote Absalom and killed him' (II Sam. 18:15). And since he stole three hearts – his father's, the court's, and the Israelite's – since it is said, 'And Absalom stole the heart of the men of Israel' (II Sam. 15:6) – therefore three darts were thrust into him, since it is said, 'And he took three darts in his hand and thrust them through the heart of Absalom' (II Sam. 18:14).

The halakhah reverts to a description of the rite, which from here onward is abbreviated.

M. 2:1 He [the husband (Num. 5:15)] would bring her meal offering in a basket of palm-twigs and lay it into her hands to tire her out. All meal offerings at the outset and at the end are in a utensil of service. But this one at the outset is in basket of palm-twigs, and [only] at the end is in a utensil of service. All meal offerings require oil and frankincense, But this one requires neither oil nor frankincense. All meal offerings derive from wheat. But this one derives from barley. As to the meal offering of the first sheaf (omer), even though it [too] derives from barley, it would derive from sifted flour. But this one derives from unsifted flour. Just as she acted like a cow, so her offering is food for a cow.

M.2:2 He [the husband] would bring a clay bowl and put in it a half-log of water from the laver. And he [the priest] goes into the hekhal and turns to his right. Now there was a place, an amah by an amah, with a marble flagstone, and a ring was attached to it. And when he raised it [the stone], he took the dirt from under it and put it [into the bowl of water], sufficient to be visible on the water, since it says, 'And of the dust that is on the floor of the tabernacle the priest shall take and put it into the water' (Num. 5:17).

M.2:3 He came to write the scroll. From what passage [in Scripture] did he write? From 'If no man has lain with thee ... but if thou hast gone aside with another instead of thy husband ...' (Num. 5:19f.). But he does not write, 'And the priest shall cause the woman to swear' (Num. 5:21). And he writes, 'The Lord make thee a curse and an oath among thy people... and this water that causeth the curse shall go into thy bowels and make thy belly to swell and thy thigh to fall away.' But he does not write, 'And the woman shall say, Amen, Amen!'

M.2:4 He writes (1) neither on a tablet, (2) nor on papyrus, (3) nor on unprepared hide, but only on [parchment] scroll, since it is written, in a book (Num. 5:23). And he writes (1) neither with gum, (2) nor with coppera, (3) nor with anything which makes a lasting impression [on the writing material], but only with ink, since it is written, And he will blot it out – writing which can be blotted out.

T.2:1 He would take her scroll and bring it into the Temple plaza. Now there was a gold flagstone set up there by the wall of the hekhal [sanctuary proper]. And it was visible from the ulam. At that point he sees it, and he writes, neither leaving out anything nor adding anything. He goes out and stands by the accused wife. He reads it aloud and explains it and spells out every detail of the pericope. And he says it to her in whatever language she understands, so that she will know for what she is drinking the bitter water and for what incident she is drinking it, on what account she is accused of being unclean, and under what circumstances she is accused of being unclean. And he says to her, 'I invoke an oath upon you – And may it come upon you.' 'And may they come upon you' – this is the curse. 'I invoke an oath upon you' – this is an oath.

M.2:5 To what does she say, Amen, Amen? (1) 'Amen to the curse' [Num. 5:21] (2) 'Amen to the oath' [Num. 5:19]. (3) 'Amen that it was not with this particular man'. (4) 'Amen that it was with no other man.' (5) 'Amen that I have not gone aside while betrothed, married, awaiting Levirate marriage, or wholly taken in Levirate marriage.' (6) 'Amen that

I was not made unclean, and if I was made unclean, may it [the bitter water] enter into me.'

M.2:6 All concur that he [the husband] may make no stipulation with her about anything which happened before she was betrothed or after she may be divorced. [If after she was put away], she went aside with some other man and became unclean, and afterward he [the first husband] took her back, he makes no stipulation with her [concerning such an event]. This is the general principle: Concerning any situation in which she may have sexual relations in such wise as not to be prohibited [to her husband], he [the husband] may make no stipulation whatsoever with her.

M.3:1 He would take her meal offering from the basket made of twigs and put it into a utensil of service and lay it into her hands. And a priest puts his hand under hers and waves it [the meal offering].

M.3:2 He waved it [Num. 5:25] and brought it near the altar. He took a handful [of the meal offering] and burned it up [on the altar]. And the residue is eaten by the priests. He would give her the water to drink. And [only] afterward he would offer up her meal offering.

M.3:3 [If] before the scroll is blotted out, she said, 'I am not going to drink the water,' her scroll is put away, and her meal offering is scattered on the ashes. But her scroll is not valid for the water ordeal of another accused wife. [If] her scroll was blotted out and then she said, 'I am not going to drink it,' they force her and make her drink it against her will.

T.2:2 He goes in and writes the scroll, comes out and blots it out. If before the scroll is blotted out, she says, 'I am not going to drink it' [M. Sot. 3:3A], or if she said, 'I am unclean,' or if witnesses came and testified that she is unclean, the water is poured out. And no sanctity adheres to it. And the scroll written for her is hidden under the hekhal, and her meal offering is scattered [M. Sot. 3:3A].

T.2:3 [If] the scroll is blotted out and she said, 'I am unclean,' the water is poured out, and her meal offering is scattered on the ashes. And her scroll is not valid for the water ordeal of another accused wife [M. Sot.3:3C, B]. If her scroll is blotted out and then she said, 'I am not going to drink it,' they force her and make her drink it against her will [M. Sot.3:3D].

M.3:4 She hardly sufficed to drink it before her face turns yellow, her eyes bulge out, and her veins swell. And they say, 'Take her away! Take her away!' so that the Temple Court will not be made unclean [by her corpse]. [But if nothing happened], if she had merit, she would attribute [her good fortune] to it. There is the possibility that merit suspends the curse for one year, and there is the possibility that merit suspends the curse for two years, and there is the possibility that merit suspends the curse for three years.

T.2:6 [If] witnesses came against her to testify that she was unclean, one way or the other the meal offering is prohibited. [If] they turned out to be conspiring witnesses, one way or the other her meal offering is treated as unconsecrated. In the case of any woman married to a priest, whether she is a priest-girl, or a Levite-girl, or an Israelite-girl, her meal offering is not eaten, for he has a share in it. But the offering is not wholly consumed in the fire, because she has a share in it. What should he do? The handful is offered by itself, and the residue is offered by itself. A priest stands and makes offerings at the altar, which is not the case of a priest-girl [cf. M. Sot. 3:7].

The halakhah proceeds to a variety of secondary points, but its portrayal of the rite is clear from what has been given.

The Written Torah at Numbers 5 appears superficially to have set forth the program of the Oral Torah's halakhah, but in fact, sages have redefined the entire program of the topic. First of all, the halakhah takes the ordeal and encases it in juridical procedures such as rules of evidence, guidelines meant to protect the woman from needless exposure to the ordeal to begin with. The halakhah radically revises the entire transaction when it says: if the husband expresses jealousy by instructing his wife not to speak with a specified person, and the wife spoke with the man, there is no juridical result – she still is permitted to have sexual relations with her husband. But if she went with him to some private place and remained with him for sufficient time to become unclean, she is prohibited from having sexual relations with her husband and if the husband is a priest, she is prohibited from eating priestly rations.

The halakhah thus conceives of a two-stage process, two kinds of testimony. In the first kind, she is warned not to get involved, but she is not then prohibited to the husband. In the second, witnesses attest that she can have committed adultery. Not only so, but the halakhah wants valid evidence if it is to deprive the wife of her marriage settlement. If a single witness to the act of intercourse is available, that does not suffice. People who ordinarily cannot testify against her do not have the power to deprive her of her property rights in the marriage, for example, her mother-in-law and the daughter of her mother-in-law, her co-wife, and the husband's brother's wife, and the daughter of her husband. She still collects her settlement. But because of their testimony, she does not undergo the rite; she is divorced in due course and the transaction concludes there.

Before the ordeal is invoked, the Oral Torah therefore wants some sort of solid evidence (1) of untoward sexual activity and also (2) of clear action on the part of the wife: at least the possibility, confirmed through a specific case, that adultery has taken place. Scripture leaves everything to the husband's whim, the 'spirit of jealousy.' So here if the husband gives his statement of jealousy and the wife responds by ignoring the statement, the ordeal does not apply. By her specific action the wife has to indicate the possibility that the husband is right. This is a far cry from Scripture's 'spirit of jealousy.' For the Written Torah, the ordeal settles all questions. For the Oral Torah, the ordeal takes effect only in carefully defined cases where (1) sufficient evidence exists to invoke the rite, but (2) insufficient evidence to make it unnecessary: well-established doubt, so to speak.

The halakhah of the Oral Torah introduces the further clarification that the marriage must be a valid one; if the marriage violates the law of the Torah, for example, the marriage of a widow to a high priest, the rite of the ordeal does not apply. The rite does not apply at the betrothal stage, only to a fully consummated marriage. If the fiancé expressed jealousy to the betrothed or the levir to the deceased childless brother's widow, no rite is inflicted. The sages severely limited its range of applicability: not only so, but the marriage may well be severed without the ordeal being inflicted, if the wife confesses, if there are witnesses to the act, if the wife declines to undergo the ordeal, if the husband declines to demand it, or if the husband has sexual relations with her en route to the performance of the ordeal – all these are reasons for not imposing the rite. In such cases the marital bond is called into question, so the wife loses her status as wife of a priest, should the husband be a priest. If in the preliminaries to the ordeal she confesses, she is given a writ of divorce, losing her marriage settlement. Only if she continues to plead purity is the ordeal imposed. The details of the rite are meant to match the sequence of actions that the unfaithful wife has taken with the paramour, beautifully expounded at M. 1:7 and its accompanying Tosefta-composite, cited in the interpretive section of this account.

The halakhah makes provision for the cancellation of the rite, down to the point at which the scroll is blotted out, with the divine names inscribed therein. At that point, the accused wife can no longer draw back from the ordeal. That moment matches, in effect, the moment of death for the sacrificer, when we have to dispose of the animals that he has sanctified for his offering. But if at that point she confesses, the water is poured out, and she loses her marriage settlement, but is otherwise left alone. So too, if witnesses come, or if she refuses to drink, or if the husband pulls out, the meal offering is burned. If we had to summarize in a single sentence the main thrust of the halakhah of Sotah, it is to create the conditions of perfect, unresolved doubt, so far as the husband is concerned, alongside perfect certainty of innocence, so far as the wife is concerned. Despite the humiliation that awaits, she is willing to place her marriage settlement on the line, so sure is she that she is innocent.

His doubt is well-founded, but remains a matter of doubt, so uncertain is he of her status. Then, and only then, the ordeal intervenes to resolve the exquisitely balanced scale of her certainty against his doubt.

As the sages re-present the ordeal imposed on the accused wife, they underscore the exact justice that the ordeal executes. The exposition of the topic in the Mishnah and the Tosefta, therefore also in the Talmuds, lays heavy emphasis upon how, measure for measure, the punishment fits the crime – but the reward matches the virtue as well. What the guilty wife has done, the law punishes appropriately; but they also point to cases in which acts of merit receive appropriate recognition and reward. In this way the sages make the point that, within the walls of the household, rules of justice prevail, with reward for goodness and punishment for evil the standard in the household as much as in public life. Why the sages have chosen the halakhah of the accused wife as the venue for their systematic exposition of the divine law of justice is not difficult to explain.

Here is the sages' account of God's justice, which is always commensurate, both for reward and punishment, in consequence of which the present permits us to peer into the future with certainty of what is going to happen (M. Sot. 1: 7ff). What is striking is the sages' identification of the precision of justice, the exact match of action and reaction, each step in the sin, each step in the response, and, above all, the immediacy of God's presence in the entire transaction. They draw general conclusions from the specifics of the law that Scripture sets forth, and that is where systematic thinking about governing principles takes over from exegetical learning about cases, or, in our own categories, philosophy from history, noted earlier.

A. By that same measure by which a man metes out [to others], do they mete out to him:

B. She primped herself for sin, the Omnipresent made her repulsive.

C. She exposed herself for sin, the Omnipresent exposed her.

(Mishnah-tractate Sotah 1:7)

We begin with the sages' own general observations based on the facts set forth in Scripture. The course of response of the woman accused of adultery to her drinking of the bitter water that is supposed to produce one result for the guilty, another for the innocent, is described in Scripture in this language: 'If no man has lain with you ... be free from this water of bitterness that brings the curse. But if you have gone astray ... then the Lord make you an execration ... when the Lord makes your thigh fall away and your body swell; may this water ... pass into your bowels and make your body swell and your thigh fall away' (Num. 5:20–22). This is amplified and expanded, extended to the entire rite, where the woman is disheveled; then the order, thigh, belly, shows the perfect precision of the penalty. What Scripture treats as a case, the sages transform into a generalization, so making Scripture yield governing rules. The same passage proceeds to further cases, which prove the same point: where the sin begins, there the punishment also commences; but also, where an act of virtue takes its point, there divine reward focuses as well. It is enough merely to list the following names, without spelling out details – the cognoscenti of Scripture will have understood that point: Samson, Absalom, Miriam, Joseph, and Moses. Knowing how Samson and Absalom match, and also Miriam, Joseph, and Moses, would then suffice to establish the paired and matched general principles.

Justice requires not only punishment of the sinner or the guilty but reward of the righteous and the good, and so the sages find ample, systematic evidence in Scripture for both sides of the equation of justice.

A. And so is it on the good side:

B. Miriam waited a while for Moses, since it is said, 'And his sister stood afar off' (Exod. 2:4), therefore, Israel waited on her seven days in the wilderness, since it is said, 'And the people did not travel on until Miriam was brought in again' (Num. 12:15).

(Ibid., 1:9)

A. Joseph had the merit of burying his father, and none of his brothers was greater than he, since it is said, 'And Joseph went up to bury his father … and there went up with him both chariots and horsemen' (Gen. 50:7, 9).

B. We have none so great as Joseph, for only Moses took care of his [bones].

C. Moses had the merit of burying the bones of Joseph, and none in Israel was greater than he, since it is said, 'And Moses took the bones of Joseph with him' (Exod. 13:19).

D. We have none so great as Moses, for only the Holy One blessed be he took care of his [bones], since it is said, 'And he buried him in the valley' (Deut. 34:6).

E. And not of Moses alone have they stated [this rule], but of all righteous people, since it is said, 'And your righteousness shall go before you. The glory of the Lord shall gather you [in death]' (Isa. 58:8).

(Ibid., 1:10)

Scripture provides the main probative evidence for the anticipation that when God judges, he will match the act of merit with an appropriate reward and the sin with an appropriate punishment. The proposition begins, however, with general observations as to how things are, M. 1:7, and not with specific allusions to proof-texts; the character of the law set forth in Scripture is reflected upon. The accumulated cases yield the generalization. What we see with great clarity in the law of the accused wife is the basic message of the Torah as sages propound it: God's perfect, proportionate justice.

5 MARRIAGE IN ISLAM

Islamic law assumes a world in which people marry, and so regulates the institution without explaining its origin or rationale. In the classical sharia handbooks, laws on marriage are grouped together before laws on business transactions and after laws on oaths. This placement is instructive as to the definition of the category 'marriage' within Islam. Marriage is not a sacrament over which a religious authority must preside, as in Catholicism; rather it is a contract between two parties: the man's family makes an offer, which the woman's family either accepts or refuses. Further it is an oath both between husband and wife and before God; it entails promises of fidelity and support, which may not be broken lightly. But just because Islamic marriage is better described as a contract rather than a sacrament, it does not follow that marriage in Islam is not 'religious.' Rather, as in Judaism, Islam sees all human interaction, including personal and economic spheres, as regulated by God through the religious law. By getting married, a man and a woman enter into God's intended order.

In the classical statement of Islamic law, it is assumed that marriage is a relation between unequal beings: men and women are different and have particular roles within the marriage. So men may have multiple wives, but women can have only one husband. Modern interpreters of Islamic law, however, argue that men and women are morally equal, differing only in rights and responsibilities, and some modernists have done away with gender-based privileges. Nevertheless, in the following verses from the Qur'an, differences between men and women are emphasized through the example of menstruation, and this biological model leads to women being compared to fertile fields plowed by the husband.

> They will question you about menstruation. Say: 'It is a trouble, so withdraw from women during their period, and do not go near them until they have purified themselves. When they have purified themselves, then come to them just as God commanded you.' God loves those who repent, and he loves those who purify themselves.

Your women are fields for you to plow, so come to your fields as you wish.

(The Qur'an, 2:222–223)

This passage seems to emphasize a woman's receptive role, both in terms of her body and in terms of her husband's desire for sex. Another verse is even more direct in addressing the differing status of women and men:

Men are in charge of women, in that God has preferred some over others, and in that men have expended their wealth. So righteous women are obedient, guarding the secret in the way that God guards.

(Ibid., 4:34)

Again, these verses are open to broad interpretation, but rules of marriage and inheritance are directed toward men, who are seen in the role of providing for women and protecting them. Men also make the offer of the marriage contract, which the woman may accept or reject, and men may divorce at will; further, they may take up to four wives in addition to an unlimited number of concubines. Within this framework, both men and women have specific rights and responsibilities. Al-Qayrawani's rules on the role of a woman's voice in the marriage contract reflect this uneven position.

There is no marriage without: an agent, marriage present, and two trustworthy witnesses – if they did not witness the actual contract then he may not have intercourse with her until they do witness the contract. The minimum marriage present is one-quarter dinar.

The father may marry off his virgin daughter without her permission, even if she has reached the age of reason. If he wishes, he may consult her. As for someone other than the father, whether authorized by the father or not, he may not marry her off until she reaches the age of reason and gives her permission. If she is silent, that is permission. As for the woman who is not a virgin [due to a previous marriage], neither the father nor any other person may marry her off except with her consent, and she gives her permission by word [not silence]. A woman may not marry herself off except with the permission of her guardian or someone of importance within her family, such as a man of her clan or the sultan.[22]

When al-Qayrawani refers to the contract, this does not mean that Islamic law demands a written contract of marriage. Unlike Judaism, both an oral contract of marriage and an oral oath of divorce are seen as sufficient in Islam. The agent mentioned above is the woman's representative in concluding the contract; this is normally her father or brother. The marriage present is a gift from the man to the woman, according to the Qur'anic statement: 'Give women their marriage present as a gift' (Qur'an 4:4). It is not paid to her father and so is not a 'bride price.' Finally, the witnesses are proof of the authenticity of this contract, which may be as simple as exchanging words of offer and acceptance; their oral testimony to this oral event is acceptable evidence within a Muslim court of law. Not included in this handbook is the assumption that men, whether of age or not, whether previously married or not, are assumed either to represent themselves at the contract or to have the right of consent in an arranged marriage.

Once the contract is completed, the couple is married and sexual intercourse is now considered licit, but both the contract and the act of sexual intercourse have specific legal effects. That is to say, a woman who only signed a contract of marriage is divorced differently than a woman who had both a contract and sexual intercourse. Al-Qayrawani covers these rules in the following manner.

> As for the woman who is divorced before consummation of the marriage, she retains half of the marriage present, unless she is a woman who has been previously married and she forgoes it. If she is a virgin, any decision to forego the marriage gift is up to her father. Similarly, if she is a female slave, the decision belongs to her master.

> As for someone who divorces, he ought to grant his divorced wife some gift. He is not forced to give a gift to a woman with whom he has not had sex; he allocates a share of inheritance to her, but does not give her a gift, nor does he give a gift to the woman divorced by *khul'* (a special form of divorce).

> If he dies and is survived by a woman to whom he had neither allocated a share of inheritance nor had intercourse, she receives an inheritance but not the marriage gift. If he had had intercourse with her, she also receives an appropriate marriage gift, unless she is satisfied with some other thing of value.[23]

The specifics of these rules are addressed in the section on divorce, but it is worth noting that when the marriage has been consummated the husband is considered to have greater financial responsibility, commensurate with his greater personal involvement. In practice, contract and consummation may occur in the same evening or years apart; likewise, one may be betrothed in marriage many years before actually marrying.

In his section on marriage, al-Qayrawani has made an exposition of the major rules of marriage, but to comprehend the logic of the Islamic law of marriage, we must turn to stories of exemplary individuals. As a religion that

sees the life of Prophet Muhammad to be a paradigm for all Muslims to emu-
late, Islam uses his marriages as a model for all believers. For instance, the
Prophet's wives, and particularly his favorite wife Aisha, are addressed directly
in the Qur'an, separated out from the rest of the believers and made into
examples. Known as the 'mothers of the believers,' Muhammad's wives played
important roles in the early community. When the Qur'an addresses the wives
of the Prophet, though, it admonishes them for not taking their roles seriously
enough.

> Women of the Prophet, you are not like any other women. If you are in
> awe of God, do not humble others with your words, so that he in whose
> heart is sickness desires you; but speak honorable words.

> Abide in your apartments; and do not display yourselves in the ignorant
> fashion of old. Arise for prayer, give alms and obey God and his
> messenger.
>
> (The Qur'an, 33:32–33)

In addition to serving as examples of pious obedience to God, these wives have
an extraordinary role in establishing the law of marriage in Islam. In particular,
the Prophet's favorite wife, Aisha bint Abi Bakr, is referred to as an authority
by the classical sources both for transmitting information about the Prophet's
actions and also for her own judgments on matters of marriage and divorce.
The following selections from Malik's *al-Muwatta* all refer to Aisha's authority

> Yahya told me on Malik's authority from Yahya ibn Said from al-Qasim
> ibn Muhammad that Aisha, the wife of the Prophet, may God bless him
> and grant him peace, was asked about a man who had divorced his wife
> conclusively. Another man had then married her after him and divorced
> her without touching her – would it be amenable for her first husband
> to marry her again? Aisha answered: 'Not until he has tasted her honey.'[24]

> Yahya told me on Malik's authority from Abd al-Rahman ibn
> al-Qasim from his father that Aisha, the mother of the believers,
> proposed to Qurayba bint Abi Umayya on behalf of Abd al-Rahman
> ibn Abi Bakr. They married her to him, but then they found fault
> with Abd al-Rahman, saying: 'We only married for Aisha's sake.' So
> Aisha sent for Abd al-Rahman and told him about it, and he put the
> matter in Qurayba's hand. She chose her husband and there was no
> divorce.

> Yahya told me on Malik's authority from Abd al-Rahman ibn al-Qasim
> from his father that Aisha, the wife of the Prophet, may God bless him
> and grant him peace, married Hafsa bint Abd al-Rahman to

al-Mundhir ibn al-Zubayr while Abd al-Rahman was away in Syria. When Abd al-Rahman arrived, he said, 'Does someone like me have this done to him? Is someone like me to be undermined?' So Aisha spoke to al-Mundhir ibn al-Zubayr, and al-Mundhir said, 'It is in the hands of Abd al-Rahman.' But Abd al-Rahman said, 'I will not take back something which is already passed.' So Hafsa was confirmed with al-Mundhir, and there was no divorce.[25]

Yahya told me on Malik's authority from Rabia ibn Abi Abd al-Rahman from al-Qasim ibn Muhammad that Aisha, the mother of the believers, said: 'There were three rules (*sunan*) established in connection with Barira. The first of the three traditions was that when she was emancipated she was given the choice concerning her husband. Also, the Messenger of God, may God bless him and grant him peace, said: 'Clientage belongs to the one who emancipates.' Also, the Messenger of God, may God bless him and grant him peace, entered when there was a pot with meat on the fire, but bread and food were brought to him from the food of the house. So the Messenger of God, may God bless him and grant him peace, said: 'Did I not see a pot with meat in it?' They said, 'Yes, Messenger of God, but this meat was given as alms for Barira, and you do not eat alms.' But the Messenger of God, may God bless him and grant him peace, said: 'It is alms for her, but it is a gift for us.'[26]

In the each of these accounts, Aisha actually defines the law through her words and actions. In the first case, Aisha is referring to a rule that a man may not simply divorce and remarry a woman at will. It is possible, however, that if she marries someone else after the divorce, and then divorces this other person, that the first husband can marry her once again. To prevent this intermediate marriage from merely being one of convenience, however, Aisha rules that the marriage must have both contract and consummation. In the second and third accounts, Aisha acts as the agent of both a man and another woman in securing marriages; the third case is particularly impressive, as she acts while the father of the bride is out of the country.

The final case is more complicated, as Aisha summarizes three complex stories by relating the rule (*sunna*) which resulted from them. In the first, the female slave Barira had been married to another slave, but she was then emancipated while her husband remained in bondage. Since her new status might make her former marriage to a slave onerous, she was given the choice of breaking the marriage or remaining married to this slave. The second rule refers to the fact that although Barira was owned by another family, it was Aisha who put up the money for her emancipation; the rule then declares that Barira's family loyalties are with Aisha, not her former owners. Finally, the Prophet declares that charitable gifts can serve more than one function.

But Aisha's most famous role in establishing the Islamic law of marriage has to do with a story known as 'The Affair of the Lie,' when she was falsely accused of an adulterous affair. As in Judaism, adultery is the most flagrant transgression against the laws of marriage, and since marriage is the emblem of an ordered society, it is not surprising that the punishment of the adulterer is harsh; in al-Qayrawani's words:

> Someone who commits adultery with a free, 'sheltered' woman, is stoned until he dies. 'Sheltered' is defined as a woman who is in an actual marriage and another man actually has sex with her. If she is not sheltered, he is given one hundred lashes and the sultan banishes him to another country where he is imprisoned for one year. As for the slave who commits adultery: fifty lashes; the same goes for the female slave, even if one of them was married at the time. Banishment is not required for slaves, nor for a woman.[27]

However, these harsh rules are somewhat mitigated by the fact that an accusation of adultery is almost impossible to prove, unless, of course, a woman is suddenly, inexplicably pregnant.

> The adulterer is only punished if proven guilty by confession, visible pregnancy or testimony of four free, male, trustworthy eyewitnesses who see the act just as one sees the kohl-stick inside of the kohl-bottle. They must all witness the act at the same time. If one of them does not fulfil this description, the other three men who made the accusation are punished.[28]

These strict rules of evidence come directly from a set of Qur'an verses which are traditionally associated with 'The Affair of the Lie.' It seems that when Aisha was about fifteen, she fell behind a caravan returning to Medina and became lost. When she eventually got back to town, it was in the company of a handsome young man. Tongues began to wag, and many people questioned her honor. An early source relates the story in Aisha's own voice.

> I [left the caravan] for a certain purpose, having a string of Zafar beads on my neck. When I had finished, it slipped from my neck without my knowledge, and when I returned to the camel I went feeling my neck for it but could not find it. Meanwhile the main body had already moved off. I went back to the place where I had been and looked for the necklace until I found it. The men who were saddling the camel for me came up to the place I had just left and having finished the saddling they took hold of the howdah thinking that I was in it as I normally was, picked it up and bound it on the camel, not doubting that I was in it. Then they took the camel by the head and went off with it. I returned to the place [where

the caravan had been] and there was not a soul there. The men had gone. So I wrapped myself in my smock and then lay down where I was, knowing that if I were missed they would come back for me, and by God I had but just lain down when Safwan b. al-Mu'attal al-Sulami passed me ... . He saw my form and came and stood over me ... . He asked me what had kept me behind but I did not speak to him. Then he brought up his camel and told me to ride it while he kept behind. [29]

At this point Safwan seats her on his camel and walks deferentially behind her. Knowing that she had done nothing wrong, Aisha does not give the matter further thought, but soon the gossip reaches her ears.

Then we came to Medina and immediately I became very ill and so heard nothing of the matter. The story had reached the apostle and my parents, yet they told me nothing of it though I missed the apostle's accustomed kindness to me. When I was ill he used to show compassion and kindness to me, but in this illness he did not and I missed his attentions ... . Now we were an Arab people: we did not have those privies which foreigners have in their houses; we loathe and detest them. Our practice was to go out into the open spaces of Medina. The women used to go out every night, and one night I went out with Umm Mistah ... . She [told me] 'Haven't you heard the news, O daughter of Abu Bakr?' and when I said that I had not heard she went on to tell me of what the liars had said, and when I showed my astonishment she told me that all this really had happened. By Allah, I was unable to do what I had to do and went back. I could not stop crying until I thought that the weeping would burst my liver. I said to my mother, 'God forgive you! Men have spoken ill of me and you have known of it and have not told me a thing about it.' [30]

Finally, the Prophet came to visit Aisha, and asked her to confess to the crime which others accused her of committing. She refused, knowing that she had done no wrong.

He sat down and after praising God he said, 'Aisha, you know what people say about you. Awe God and if you have done wrong as men say then repent towards God, for he accepts repentance from his servants.' As he said this, my tears ceased and I could not feel them. I waited for my parents to answer the apostle but they said nothing ... .When they remained silent my weeping broke out afresh and then I said: 'Never will I repent towards God of what you mention. By Allah, I know that if I were to confess what men say of me, God knowing that I am innocent of it, I should admit what did not happen; and if I denied what they said you would not believe me ... . I will say what the father

91

of Joseph said: 'My duty is to show becoming patience and God's aid is to be asked against what you describe."

And, by God, the apostle had not moved from where he was sitting when there came over him from God what used to come over him and he was wrapped in his garment and a leather cushion was put under his head ... . Then the apostle recovered and sat up and there fell from him as it were drops of water on a winter day, and he began to wipe the sweat from his brow, saying, 'Good news, Aisha! God has sent down word about your innocence.' I said, 'Praise be to God,' and he went out to the men and addressed them and recited to them what God had sent down concerning that. Then he gave orders about Mistah b. Uthatha and Hassan b. Thabit and Hamna b. Jahsh who were the most explicit in their slander and they were flogged with the prescribed number of stripes.[31]

In Islamic law, the accusation of adultery is taken as seriously as the adulterous act itself, and false accusation is punished only slightly less than a proven case of adultery. This equation makes sense since a false accusation of adultery brings nearly as much disorder into the world as fornication itself. In this case, Aisha is forced to remain secluded in her house while gossip destroyed her reputation and that of her husband.

The Qur'anic verse which was revealed on this occasion offers an explanation for the equation of accusation and adultery in a more theological manner.

The adulterer and the adulteress – lash each one of them one hundred lashes, and do not let tenderness for them take over you in God's religion, if you believe in God and the last day. A group of the believers should witness their punishment.

As for the adulterer, he only marries an adulteress or a polytheist, and as for the adulteress, she only marries an adulterer or a polytheist; such people are forbidden to the believers.

As for those who cast aspersions on sheltered women, but did not bring four witnesses, they are lashed with eighty lashes. Their testimony is never accepted again. Such people are an abomination.

Except those who repent afterwards and make amends, for God is forgiving and compassionate.

As for those who cast aspersions on their wives, having no witnesses except themselves, the testimony of one of them is to bear witness by God four times that he is telling the truth.

The fifth time he bears witness that the curse of God will be upon him if he should be lying.

If she bears witness by God four times that he is lying, then she avoids punishment.

She bears witness a fifth time, that God's anger will be upon her if he is telling the truth.

What if it were not for God's grace to you, his compassion, and that God is most forgiving, wise?

Those who brought the slander are related to you; do not reckon it as evil to you, but good. Every man of them will have the sin that he has acquired. And the one who took upon the greater portion of it, he will have a mighty punishment.

What if, when you heard it, the believing men and believing women had thought good thoughts saying: 'This is clearly a lie'?

What if they had brought four witnesses? But they did not bring witnesses, so they are liars before God.

What if it were not for God's grace to you, his compassion, in this world and the hereafter – a mighty punishment would have seized you for your mutterings.

When you met it with your tongues, and spoke with your mouths that of which you had no knowledge, you reckoned it insignificant, but before God it was mighty.

What if, when you heard it, you had said: 'It is not for us to speak about this; glory be to you! This is a mighty lie'?

God admonishes you to never repeat such words again, if you are believers.

God makes the signs clear to you; God is knowing, wise.

Those who love abomination to be spread about those who believe –

they will have a painful punishment in this world and the hereafter.
God knows; you know not.

(The Qur'an, 24:2–19)

In this substantial discussion of adultery, the Qur'an can be seen to address the institution of marriage in its negative form. Defined thus, marriage prevents wanton sexual behavior and limits disordered human contact. Put more positively, marriage is a contract between a man and a woman in which he gives her a gift and she leaves her parents' home to join that of her husband. Sexual intercourse is assumed and the consummation of the marriage contract has specific legal effects. Further, failure to provide for the sexual needs of either husband or wife is a cause for divorce.

6 INHERITANCE IN JUDAISM

The Torah's presentation of the laws of inheritance is set forth in the context of the conquest and division of the Land of Israel, which God has promised to Israel as a component of his covenant with the holy people formed at Sinai by the acceptance of the Torah. The Land, ideally, corresponds to Eden, and Israel to Adam and Eve, and the perfection of the Land, tended in accord with the rules of sanctification, matches that of Paradise. Thus, for example, just as the Sabbath marked the climax and perfection of creation, so the Land was to be given its Sabbath, its time of repose and rest, just as mankind, and then Israel, were to receive the sanctification of Sabbath rest. For the Land, that Sabbath took the form of the cessation of all work on the Land that signified ownership by the farmer; all the territory of the Land of Israel was to be left fallow in the Sabbatical or seventh year. That fact, among many, signals the importance of the Land in the social order of holy Israel for which the Torah legislated.

That brings us to the matter of inheritance, for principal among the issues involved is the division of the real estate of the deceased. Here the principal concern focused upon the preservation of the lines of the division of the Land among the original twelve tribes of Israel. The Rabbinic sages maintained for a time that the tribes could not even intermarry, lest the share in the Land of one tribe increase while that of another decrease, in consequence of the working of the natural laws of estates and inheritance. Tribal affiliation followed the male line: for example, the son of a priest (*kohen*) is a priest, but the son of the daughter of a priest who has married a non-priest is not. That explains why Scripture, continued by the halakhah of the Oral Torah, wants inheritances to remain in the male line. The right of the daughter to inherit, however, is also explicit, even though, when circumstances permit, inheritances pass through the male, not the female line. That matter is so anomalous, given the governing theory, that the Torah tells how Moses brought the question of the right of daughters to inherit land in the Land of Israel when no sons were present to claim the inheritance. It took a special revelation by God to Moses to secure that right to the daughters and so legitimate what the basic logic of the system found dubious:

> 'If a man dies and has no son, then you shall cause his inheritance to pass to his daughter. And if he has no daughter, then you shall give his inheritance to his brothers. And if he has no brothers, then you shall give his inheritance to his father's brothers. And if his father has no brothers, then you shall give his inheritance to his kinsman that is next to him of his family, and he shall possess it.'
>
> (Num. 27:8–11)

The halakhah spells out the prior claim of the sons over the daughters, and further works out the details of gifts as against inheritances, gifts in contemplation of death, and related matters.

Scripture contributes further facts. First comes the law that the firstborn receives two shares in the estate, the other heirs, one each. Thus if there are four heirs, the estate is divided into five parts, two to the firstborn, one to each of the others, and so throughout. The law further has to adjudicate the payment of the deceased's debts and other obligations: for example, the estate has to support those of his wives whose marriage contracts provide them with support after the husband's death. A person may dispose of his property in his lifetime as he wishes, which means, one may make gifts entirely outside of the law of inheritance. The law of inheritance then takes over only for the division of the estate.

Here are the principal texts of the Mishnah, Tosefta, and Talmuds:

> M.8:1 There are those who inherit and bequeath, there are those who inherit but do not bequeath, bequeath but do not inherit, do not inherit and do not bequeath. These inherit and bequeath: the father as to the sons, the sons as to the father; and brothers from the same father [but a different mother], [as to one another] inherit from and bequeath [to one another]. The man as to his mother, the man as to his wife, and the sons of sisters inherit from, but do not bequeath [to, one another]. The woman as to her sons, the woman as to her husband, and the brothers of the mother bequeath to, but do not inherit [from one another]. Brothers from the same mother do not inherit from, and do not bequeath [to one another].

> T.7:1 Whoever is closer [in relationship] than his fellow takes precedence over his fellow. And an inheritance goes on upward, even to Reuben [that is, the ultimate progenitor of the tribe]. And brothers so far as one another are concerned, sisters so far as one another are

concerned, brothers so far as the sisters are concerned, and sisters so far
as the brothers are concerned, both inherit and bequeath [M. B.B. 8:
1B–C]. A mamzer causes his relatives to inherit. A Gentile and a slave
who had intercourse with an Israelite girl, even though thereafter the
Gentile went and converted, the slave went and was emancipated – his
estate is in the status of the estate of a proselyte, or his estate is in the
status of a freed slave. So whoever acquired possession of them first
gains title to them.

Now comes the matter of the priority of the son but the possibility of the
daughter's sharing in the landed estate:

M.8:2 The order of [the passing of an] inheritance is thus: 'If a man
dies and had no son, then you shall cause his inheritance to pass to his
daughter' (Num. 27:8) – the son takes precedence over the daughter,
and all the offspring of the son take precedence over the daughter. The
daughter takes precedence over [surviving] brothers. The offspring of
the daughter take precedence over the brothers. The [decedent's]
brothers take precedence over the father's brothers. The offspring of the
brothers take precedence over the father's brothers. This is the
governing principle: Whoever takes precedence in inheritance – his
offspring [also] take precedence. The father takes precedence over all
[the father's] offspring [if none is a direct offspring of the deceased].

M.8:4 All the same are the son and the daughter as to matters of inheritance, except that the son takes a double portion in the estate of the
father [Deut. 21:17]. [The son] does not take a double portion in the
estate of the mother. The daughters are supported by the father's estate
and are not supported by the mother's estate.

T.7:10 And just as the son takes precedence over the daughter in the
estate of the father, so the son takes precedence over the daughter in the
estate of the mother.

As we saw, the firstborn gets a double portion. Here is how that matter is
spelled out in detail. From our perspective, the important point is is, can a
person stipulate a valid condition that contradicts the law of the Torah? Does
he, for example, have the power to stipulate that a son may be disinherited?
The answer is negative. The law of the Torah takes priority and dictates the
choices that face the individual. However, if the division of the estate is
through donation, that is, gifts, and not through inheritance (for example, if
the division takes place in the man's lifetime), then the free will of the actor
takes over and he may do as he likes:

M.8:5   He who says, 'So-and-so, my firstborn son, is not to receive a double portion,' 'So-and-so, my son, is not to inherit along with his brothers,' has said absolutely nothing. For he has made a stipulation contrary to what is written in the Torah. He who divides his estate among his sons by a verbal [donation], [and] gave a larger portion to one and a smaller portion to another, or treated the firstborn as equivalent to all the others – his statement is valid. But if he had said, 'By reason of an inheritance [the afore-stated arrangements are made],' he has said nothing whatsoever. [If] he had written, whether at the beginning, middle, or end, [that these things are handed over] as a gift, his statement is valid. He who says, 'Mr. So-and-so will inherit me,' in a case in which he has a daughter, 'My daughter will inherit me,' in a case in which he has a son, has said nothing whatsoever. For he has made a stipulation contrary to what is written in the Torah. He who writes over his property to others and left out his sons – what he has done is done. But [the] sages are not pleased with him.

T.7:4   The firstborn does not take a double portion in the increase which accrues to the estate after the death of the father.

T.7:6   How does the firstborn not take a double portion? [If] he inherited writs of indebtedness, he takes a double portion. [If] claims of collection went forth against him [as his father's heir], he pays out a double portion. But if he said, 'I don't want to take, and I don't want to pay out [a double portion],' he has every right to do so.

T.7 :7   How does [the firstborn] not take a double portion in what is going to accrue to the father's estate as he does in what is already possessed by the father's estate? [If] the father of his father dies in the lifetime of his father, he takes a double portion in the estate of his father, but he does not take a double portion in the estate of the father of his father. But if his father was firstborn, he takes a double portion in the estate of the father of his father.

T.7:11   He who says, 'Let my sons divide my estate equally,' and there was a firstborn there, if [the brothers] had acquired possession of the estate of their father while he was yet alive, [the firstborn] does not take a double portion. And if not, he takes a double portion.

T.7:12   He who says, 'Give two hundred dinars to So-and-so my firstborn son, with what is coming to him,' he takes the [money] and [also] takes a double portion as his right as a firstborn. And his hand is on top. [If] he wants, he takes [what the father has specified]. And [if] he wants, he takes the double portion [in the estate].

T.7:13 He who says, 'Give such-and-such a field to So-and-so my wife with what is coming to her' – she takes [the field] and also collects her marriage settlement. And her hand is on top. [If] she wants, she takes the field. [If] she wants, she collects her marriage settlement.

T.7:14 He who says, 'Give two hundred to Mr. So-and-so, my creditor' – he collects the money and [also] collects the debt owing to him. [If he had said,] 'For his debt,' he has a right only to collect the money owing to him.

T.7:15 [If] he had a field, and it had been made a surety for the wife for the settlement of her marriage contract and for a creditor for a settlement of what was owing to him, if he then said, 'Give such-and-such a field to my wife, So-and-so, in payment for her marriage contract, and to Mr. So-and-so, my creditor, in payment for what is owing to him,' what is owing to them has been received. And their hand is on top.

T.7:16 He who says, 'Give a portion to Mr. So-and-so in my estate – let him inherit with my sons in the position of the firstborn,' he does not take a double portion. He who says, 'Let Mr. So-and-so inherit me,' has said nothing whatsoever. If he said, 'Give my property to So-and-so,' his statement is carried out.

Since the donor disposes of his property, the issue is raised whether his statement of facts is accepted without further ado. The answer is, if he makes a statement to the advantage of the person concerning whom he speaks, his statement is validated; if it is to the disadvantage, it is not. If he says, 'So and so is my son,' all other things being equal, the man gets his share in the estate. If he says, 'He is my brother,' depriving the man of his share as heir, he is not believed, if the man was assumed to have been a son.

M.8:6 He who says, 'This is my son,' is believed. [If he said], 'This is my brother,' he is not believed, and [the latter] shares with him in his portion [of the father's estate] – [If the brother whose status is in doubt] died, the property is to go back to its original source. [If] he received property from some other source, his brothers are to inherit with him. He who died, and a will was found tied to his thigh – lo, this is nothing whatsoever. [If he had delivered it and] granted possession through it to another person, whether this is one of his heirs or not one of his heirs, his statement is confirmed.

The Tosefta takes the law and broadens the case into a principle by introducing a case deriving from another situation altogether. Now the midwife testifies to the status of twin males.

> T.7:2 A midwife is believed to say, 'This one came out first.' Under what circumstances? When there is no contesting opinion. But if there is a contesting opinion, she is not believed.

The testimony is accepted only if uncontested. Now we see how the Tosefta clarifies and refines the basic rule: the father deprives someone of the status of heir as son or as firstborn.

> T.7:3 [If] people took for granted concerning someone that he was a firstborn, and at the time of the gift, [the father] said, 'He is not the firstborn,' [the father] is not believed. [If] people took for granted concerning someone that he was not the firstborn, and at the time of the gift, [the father] said, 'He is the firstborn,' he is believed. [If] people took for granted concerning someone that he was his son, and at the time of his death, the [putative father] said, 'He is not my son,' he is not believed. [If] people took for granted concerning someone that he was not his son, and at the time of [the man's] death, he said, 'He is my son,' he is believed [M. B.B. 8:6A]. [If] people took for granted concerning someone that he was his son, and at the time of his death, he said, 'He is [my] brother,' he is believed [cf. M. B.B. 8:6B]. [If] people took for granted concerning someone that he was his brother, and at the time of his death, he said, 'He is my slave,' he is not believed. [If] people took for granted concerning someone that he was his slave, and at the time of his death, he said, 'He is my son,' he is believed. [If] he was standing among tax-collectors and said, 'He is my son,' and then he went and said, 'He is my slave,' he is believed. [If] he said, 'He is my slave,' and then he went and said, 'He is my son,' he is not believed.

> T.8:5 Two who were coming from overseas – even though their trading, eating and drinking were done in partnership, [if] one of them died, his fellow does not inherit him. But if he had conducted affairs in this way because of their being brothers, [the survivor] does inherit.

> T.8:6 He who went overseas with his son – and [the son] came home, and with him was a brother [born to the father, who had died overseas] – and [the son] said, 'This is my brother, who was born to me overseas' – and [the son who had come home] had five brothers, and before them was an estate of five kors of land – they do not give [to the other brother, born overseas] any portion whatsoever [M. B.B. 8:6B]. But the son [from overseas] gives him a sixth out of his share [M. B.B. 8:6C].

[If then the brother born abroad] died, [the brother who had given him a share] takes what [the decedent] had given to him [M. B.B. 8:6D], and the rest [of the decedent's estate] they bring and divide among [all surviving brothers] [M. B.B. 8:6E].

T.8:7 He who went overseas, he and his father – and the son died, or the father died – under all circumstances the property is assumed to belong to the elder [the father, and not the son, so that the father's other sons inherit].

T.8:8 He who was writing a will, and was afraid of the heirs – [the scribe and witnesses] go into visit him like ordinary visitors and hear what he has to say inside. Then they go out and write the will outside.

T.8:9 A healthy person who wrote a will – a dying man who wrote his property as a gift – even though he gave possession after the gift, he has done nothing at all. But he who writes over his property in the name of his fellow, and he gave him possession after the gift, his statement is confirmed [M. B.B. 8:6H–J].

T.8:10 He who writes a will can retract. He who writes a deed of gift cannot retract. What is a will? 'Let this be confirmed: If I die, let my estate be given to So-and-so.' And what is a deed of gift? 'As of this date let my property be given to So-and-so.'

T.8:11 He who writes a will, before he gives possession, whether it is he or another party – he can retract. Once he has given possession, whether it is he or another party – he cannot retract.

The laws of inheritance provide for the management of an estate by guardians if the heirs are too young to take care of their own affairs. Much concern therefore focuses upon the power and responsibilities of the guardians, who function as executors of the estate and managers of the property until the sons come of age.

T.8:12 Guardians [of the estate of minors] before they have made acquisition of the estate of minors, can retract. Once they have made acquisition of the estate of minors, they cannot retract.

T. 8:13A. A guardian whom the father of the orphans has appointed is to be subjected to an oath [that he has not misappropriated the property of the minor]. [If] a court appointed him, he is not required to take an oath.

Heirs owe their dues to the priests ('heave offering and tithes') and the guardians have the obligation to see to it that minor heirs' divine obligations are carried out.

> T.8:14 Guardians set aside heave offering and tithes out of the property of orphans. They sell houses, fields, vineyards, cattle, boy-slaves, girl-slaves, to provide maintenance for the orphans, [or] to build a *Sukkah,* acquire a *lulab,* show-fringes, and otherwise to make it possible to carry out any and all commandments stated in the Torah, to purchase a scroll of the Torah or prophets, [or] any matter which is written in the Torah. But they do not contribute to funds for the redemption of captives on their account, and they do not contribute to charity in the synagogue, [or provide for] any matter, the fixed amount of which is not set forth in the Torah. They have not got the right to emancipate slaves, but they may sell them to others, and the others emancipate them.

The guardians cannot engage in ordinary commerce and trade with an heir's property; they must hold it more or less intact. They may, however, take measures to increase the security of the estate. That means purchase real estate, which was regarded as the principal medium of long-term investment and the increase of solid wealth (the law of Judaism in its classical formulation had no understanding of market economics and liquid capital).

> T.8:1 [The guardians of estates of minors] do not sell land at a distance to buy land nearby, land of poor quality to buy land of good quality. They do not go to court to the disadvantage or to the advantage [of the trust], to collect or to disburse in behalf of the orphans, unless they get permission from the court.

> T.8:16 [The guardians of an estate of minors] sell slaves to buy real estate with the proceeds, but they do not sell real estate to buy slaves with the proceeds.

Women and slaves may serve as guardians (thus including the widow), if the deceased had chosen them; but the court cannot choose them.

> T.8:17 A court does not appoint women and slaves as guardians to begin with. But if their father had named them while he was alive, they do appoint them guardians.

> T.8:18A. [If] one has written in a document, 'I have money and utensils in the possession of Mr. So-and-so,' the witnesses have the right

to sign [the document]. But [the claimant] cannot collect until he brings proof [of his claim].

This brings us to the matter of gifts in contemplation of death. What happens if the father writes over his property to the son in what we would call an irrevocable trust, so that the son inherits when the father dies, but does not own the land in the father's lifetime? Both parties control the land in question.

> M.8:7 He who writes over his property to his son [to take effect] after his death – the father cannot sell the property, because it is written over to the son, and the son cannot sell the property, because it is [yet] in the domain of the father. [If] the father sold [it], the property is sold until he dies. [If] the son sold the property, the purchaser has no right whatever in the property until the father dies. The father harvests the crops and gives the usufruct to anyone whom he wants. And whatever he left already harvested – lo, it belongs to his heirs. [If] he left adult and minor sons, the adults may not take care of themselves [from the estate] at the expense of the minor sons, nor may the minor sons support themselves [out of the estate] at the expense of the adult sons. But they divide the estate equally. If the adult sons got married [at the expense of the estate], the minor sons [in due course] may marry [at the expense of the estate]. But if the minor sons said, 'Lo, we are going to get married just as you did [while father was still alive]' – they pay no heed to them. But what the father gave to them he has given.

When the deceased leaves both adults and minor children, how are the conflicting claims – the former to ownership of property, the latter to support – to be sorted out? The rights of all children are to be protected, no matter what their status, and equal shares (apart from the double portion owing to the first-born son) are assigned to all.

> M.8:8 [If] he left adult and minor daughters, the adults may not take care of themselves [from the estate] at the expense of the minor daughters, nor may the minors support themselves [from the estate] at the expense of the adult daughters. But they divide the estate equally. If the adult daughters got married [at the expense of the estate], the minor daughters may get married [at the expense of the estate] – And if the minor daughters said, 'Lo, we are going to get married just as you got married [while father was still alive],' they pay no heed to them. This rule is more strict in regard to daughters than to sons. For the daughters are supported at the disadvantage of the sons [M. 9:1], but they are not supported at the disadvantage of [other] daughters.

The minors may not lay excessive claims to support, but must show consideration for the assets of the estate, to which the adult heirs also have a claim.

> T.8:18 [If the decedent] had left adult and minor sons [M. B.B. 8:7J] and they continued to enjoy support without complaint, the minors should not say to the adults, 'Lo, we are going to be supported [at the expense of the estate] in the way in which you were supported when father was alive [and you were minors].' [If] the adults had been married during the lifetime of the father the minors should not say, 'Lo, we are going to be married [at the expense of the estate] in the way in which you were married.' And not only so, but even if the father [in his lifetime] had left [to the adults] slave-boys and slave-girls, silver and gold utensils, lo, they are theirs [cf. M. B.B. 8:7F].

> T.8:19 [If] he [the decedent] left adult and minor daughters, [M. B.B. 8:8A], and they continued to enjoy support without complaint, the minors should not say to the adults, 'Lo, we are going to be supported [at the expense of the estate] in the way in which you were supported [when father was alive, and you were minors].' [If] the adults had been married [during the lifetime of the father], the minors should not say, 'Lo, we are going to be married [at the expense of the estate] in the way in which you were married.' And not only so, but even if their father [in his lifetime] had left [to the adults] slave-boys and slave-girls, gold and silver utensils, lo, they are theirs [cf. M. B.B. 8:8].

What about the claims of sons and daughters? If the share of the sons can be paid while the estate supports the daughters, that happy arrangement governs. But what happens if there is insufficient money to provide an inheritance for the sons and support for the daughters? Then the daughters are supported, and the sons go begging.

> M.9:1 He who died and left sons and daughters – when the estate is large, the sons inherit, and the daughters are supported [by the estate]. [If] the estate is small, the daughters are supported, and sons go begging at [people's] doors.

As is the way of the halakhah, we now turn to interstitial problems. The case described below concerns a child whose sexual traits are not clearly defined: how is that heir classified between the sons and the daughters as to his or her claim?

> M.9:2 [If] he left sons and daughters and one whose sexual traits were not clearly defined, when the estate is large, the males push him over onto the females, [if] the estate is small, the females push him over onto

103

the males. He who says, 'If my wife bears a male, he will get a maneh,' – [if] she bore a male, he gets a maneh. [If he said, 'If she bears] a female, [she will get] two hundred [zuz],' [if] she bore a female, she gets two hundred [zuz]. [If he said, 'If she bears] a male, [he will get] a maneh, if [she bears] a female, [she will get] two hundred [zuz],' if she bore a male and a female, the male gets a maneh, and the female [gets] two hundred [zuz]. [If] she bore a child whose sexual traits were not clearly defined, he gets nothing. If he said, 'Whatever my wife bears will get [a maneh],' lo, this one gets [a maneh]. And if there is no heir but that [child lacking defined sexual traits], he inherits the entire estate.

Another mode of interstitiality involves those whose status is subject to doubt as to the facts of the matter. Here we deal with women who give birth in a cave lacking light (as happened in the war against Rome fought in 132–135 CE; in the repression that followed, people found themselves hiding out for long periods of time). They give birth to males and lose track of which baby belongs to which woman. Emerging from the cave after the war and the period of repression, the women revert to their husbands, who in the interim have survived with their lands intact. Who gets what?

> T.9:3 Two women who gave birth to two males in hiding, and [the women] went and gave birth to two males in hiding both of them go to the first [husband's estate] and take a portion of a male. [Then they go] to the second [husband's estate] and take a portion of a male. [If the women produced] a male and a female, [then another] male and female, both of them go to the first [husband's estate] and take the portion owing to a male. [Then they go] to the second [husband's estate] and take the portion owing to a female.

> 9:5 He who says, 'He who informs me that my wife has given birth to a male gets two hundred, [or if she gave birth] to a female, he gets a maneh' – [if] she gave birth to a male, [the messenger] gets two hundred. [If she gave birth to] a female, he gets a maneh. [If she gave birth to] a male and a female, the messenger gets only a maneh.

The laws of estates and inheritances encompass a great many more issues, forming the vehicle for the halakhah's presentation of its basic principles about such large and encompassing problems as the resolution of matters of doubt, the disposition of property subject to multiple claims (a present-day example might be a chain-crash on the highway), the conflict of claims among heirs and creditors, sons and daughters, and the like. What the law means to accomplish is to impose upon the innumerable cases of conflicting property claims the applied reason and practical logic of justice that the Torah intends to realize in the everyday and the here and now.

7 INHERITANCE IN ISLAM

In the section on betrothal, the family was defined by those women a man may not marry: his mother, sister, aunt, and so on. Comparison with the laws of Judaism highlights the fact that Islamic law includes two categories not normally associated with the family, those persons connected by the bond of milk, and those connected by slavery. That is to say, there are clear prohibitions against a man marrying his 'milk-sister' (a woman who was suckled at the same breast) or a female slave belonging to his wife. So in the law of marriage, negative commands define the family as those persons too close to marry. The law of inheritance also defines the Islamic family, but this time through positive commands that establish those persons who must receive a share of inheritance from the deceased. These commands see blood as that which connects the family and not milk; similarly, slaves do not inherit. Freed slaves are, however, connected to the family unit of their former masters: they both inherit from the former master's family and in the case of their death, that family inherits from them.

The Islamic law of inheritance is based on the idea of fixed shares that must be allocated to certain members of the family. These laws prevent a person from leaving his or her entire estate to a single individual, as any such bequests are limited to one-third of the value of the estate. They also ensure that certain members of the family who may not have access to income – widows, mothers, and daughters – receive a substantial share of the estate. The foundation for these rules is found in the Qur'an, which prefaces the specific laws with an important theological statement.

> Men have a share of what parents and family leave, and women have a share of what parents and family leave – an apportioned share, whether it is little or much.

> If they attend the division of the estate, put family, orphans and the poor first. Give them some of the wealth, and speak honorable words to them.

> Certainly those who leave weak seed behind should worry and fear for them; they should be in awe of God and speak pertinent words.

> Those who consume the wealth of orphans unjustly, will consume fire in their bellies, and will roast in a blaze.

God charges you, concerning your children: to the male the portion of
two females. If there are more than two women, then they will have
two-thirds of what he leaves. But if she is only one, then she will have
one-half. Each one of his parents will have one-sixth of what he leaves,
if he has children. If he has no children, and his heirs are his parents, his
mother will have one-third; but if he has brothers, his mother will have
one-sixth, after any bequest he bequeaths, or any debt. As for your
fathers and your sons, you do not know which of them is more benefi-
cial to you. Division of shares is from God; God is knowing, wise.

You will have one-half of what your wives leave, if they have no
children; but if they have children then you will have one-fourth of
what they leave, after any bequest they bequeath, or any debt. They will
have one-fourth of what you leave, if you have no children; but if you
have children, then they will have one-eighth of what you leave, after
any bequest you bequeath, or any debt. If a man, or a woman, has no
heir, but he has a brother or a sister, each of them will have one-sixth.
If there are more than two, they share in one-third, after any bequest he
bequeaths, or any debt that takes precedence. This is a bequest from
God; God is knowing, discerning.

These are God's boundaries. The one who obeys God and his
messenger, God will cause him to enter gardens underneath which
rivers flow, abiding there. This is the mighty triumph.

But the one who disobeys God and his messenger, and oversteps his
boundaries, God will cause him to enter a fire, abiding there. He will
have a humbling punishment.

(The Qur'an, 4:7–14)

These very specific injunctions are enframed by exhortations that establish the
theological context of inheritance; for inheritance in Islamic law is not about
conserving one's wealth, but rather caring for the weaker members of the
family and establishing justice by obeying 'God's boundaries.' Particularly
important here are two sets of rules. First, as in the laws of marriage, women
are not the same as men but have a separate set of rights. Second, the Qur'an
establishes that debts and bequests are to be taken care of in advance of division of the estate.

As for women's rights, it would be a mistake to overemphasize the
Qur'anic statement: 'to the male the like of the portion of two females' and
suggest that women are valued exactly half of men, since one must take both
proportion and order into account. That is to say, the Qur'an specifically
provides for shares to mothers, wives, daughters and sisters, but does not give a
specific share to sons, and only gives a specific share to the father in one case.

In practical application, those with shares mentioned in the Qur'an receive their inheritance first, and only then do other relatives inherit. Depending on the specific situation, these rules can lead to the lion's share of the estate going to the women of the family. Shi'i law takes this set of rules even farther, asserting that no one who is not specifically mentioned in the Qur'an receives any inheritance, leaving the possibility for a female heir to receive the entire estate, not merely her ordained share.

The second set of rules also concerns the question of order: before any apportioning of the estate, debts are paid; then bequests are honored; and finally the heirs split what remains. It is possible, therefore, that a debt could efface the entire estate, leaving the heirs nothing. Bequests are a special category within the Islamic law of inheritance and will be addressed below; they can be made to any person or institution, including those who would already receive a share according to the Qur'an.

The classical handbooks of the Sunni tradition follow these Qur'anic rules explicitly, but treat the law of inheritance as a modification of a world in which men are the primary heirs. In this world, certain classes have priority over others: descendants (such as children) over ascendants (such as parents), and ascendants over collaterals (such as siblings). Therefore, those persons who have specific shares mentioned in the Qur'an are limited to that amount, and the remainder devolves on the nearest male relative. Al-Qayrawani's chapter on inheritance (entitled '"allocation" of shares') begins with the establishment of this male order, followed by some sample cases that clarify the role of ascendants and descendants.

> Only ten men inherit: son, a son's son or lower descendants, father, paternal grandfather or higher ascendants, brother, brother's son or collaterals further removed, paternal uncle, paternal uncle's son or collaterals further removed, husband, and men granted the status of clientage. Only seven women inherit: daughter, a son's daughter, mother, grandmother, sister, wife, and women granted the status of clientage.
>
> The inheritance share for a husband from his wife is one-half if she is survived by no child, nor a child of her son, but if she is survived by a child or a child of her son – whether born of the surviving husband or someone else – the husband receives one-quarter. If the husband dies, the wife receives one-quarter if he is survived by neither child nor child of a son, but if he has a child or child of a son, then she receives one-eighth.
>
> The inheritance of a mother from her deceased son is a third if no descendant inherits, or as long as two siblings do not survive. These take precedence, except in shares allotted to the wife and to the parents.

In this case the wife gets a fourth and the mother a third of what remains, with the remainder going to the father.

In the case of a woman who dies leaving only a husband and parents, the husband receives one-half, the mother one-third of what remains, and the remainder belongs to her father, except for that which may reduce the mother's share. If the deceased had a child, child of a son or two siblings, the mother receives one-sixth in this case.

The share of a father from his child who dies without children or siblings is the complete inheritance. If his child is survived by a male child or a child of this male child, the father receives a sixth. If there is no male child or child of this male child, the father first receives a sixth, then other family members are given their shares; what remains belongs to the father.

The male child who is the only heir receives the entire inheritance from his deceased parent. Or if there are other survivors, such as wife, parents, grandparents, he takes what remains after their shares are divided. The grandson is in the position of the son as long as there is no son. If there is both a son and a daughter, then 'to the male the portion of two females' (The Qu'ran, 4:11); the same rule applies whether there are many sons and daughters or only a few of them: they inherit the entire inheritance in this way or they share what is left over after the division among the other legal heirs. The grandson is just like the son, assuming the son is absent, in what he inherits and in taking precedence over others.

The daughter who is the sole heir inherits one-half, and if there are two they inherit two-thirds. If there are more than two, they do not exceed this two-thirds. The daughter of a son inherits just like a daughter if there is no daughter. Similarly, his daughters inherit just like multiple daughters, assuming daughters are absent. If there is both a daughter and the daughter of a son, then the daughter receives half while the granddaughter receives one-sixth, the completion of the two-thirds. Even if there were more granddaughters, they do not exceed this sixth.[32]

In this way al-Qayrawani lays out the rules which combine the old Arab system of inheritance through the male line with the Qur'anic rules. Whereas the Qur'an defines specific shares, and all legal heirs who survive the deceased receive a share, the old system gives all the estate to the nearest male relative. No other male relative receives anything. So if a man is survived by only his grandson and his father, the grandson (a descendant) receives the entire estate, taking precedence over the father (an ascendant).

It is possible that all of those persons mentioned in the Qur'an survive. For instance, a man dies, leaving two daughters (one-third to each) both parents (one-sixth to each), and a wife (one-eighth), making one and one-eighth shares. For such a case, al-Qayrawani states: 'If all of the known recipients of shares as mentioned in God's book are gathered together and these shares exceed the total inheritance, then each of them must bear some loss; their shares are divided according to the ratio of their shares in total.' (121) In such a case, any brother or male cousin is fully excluded, and women receive almost the entire inheritance.

As mentioned earlier, emancipated slaves can inherit from their former masters, but only when all Qur'anic shares have been given out and when there are no other male relatives. This relationship between former master and freed slave is known as clientage (*wala'*) and forms a major category in Islamic law. Such a relationship was also known is Roman law, but the key Roman aspects of clientage (such as an expectation of continued service) are not found in Islamic law. In a case where a client might receive part of the estate, only the most senior of the emancipated slaves inherits; any others receive nothing. Al-Qayrawani writes:

> The senior client, whether male or female, inherits everything if there are no other heirs. If there are other legal heirs, the client inherits what remains after the shares are divided. The client does not inherit if there are other male relatives, but he has more of a right to the inheritance than female relatives who have no share provided for them in God's book – he is mighty and great! No female relatives inherit unless they have a share provided for them in God's book, nor do women inherit from clients unless they are slaves emancipated by the women or persons related to such emancipated slaves and then freed by birth or emancipation.[33]

Once again, the jurists are primarily concerned with proper organization of categories. Men, women and clients may all inherit, but under specific conditions. The combination of two interstitial categories, pregnant women and emancipated slaves, provides an opportunity for Muslim jurists to demonstrate the sophistication of inheritance law by addressing a peculiar situation: a female slave who was pregnant at the time of her emancipation and whose husband was a slave at that time.

> Malik told us on the authority of Rabia b. Abd al-Rahman that Zubayr b. al-Awwam bought a slave and freed him. That slave had some sons by a freed woman, and when Zubayr freed him Zubayr said: 'These children are also my clients.' But the clients of the mother said: 'No, they are our clients!' So they brought the case to Uthman b. Affan, and Uthman ruled that the right of clientage belonged to Zubayr.

Malik said: In the case of a female slave who is emancipated while she is pregnant, and while her husband is still a slave, and then her husband is emancipated either before or after her pregnancy, the clientage of that which is in her womb belongs to the party which emancipated the mother. This is because this child was already connected to that party in slavery before its mother was freed.[34]

The client relationship is not a commodity and cannot be bought, sold or given away; rather, it is a family connection by choice instead of blood. Muslim jurists demonstrate this connection by addressing the question of whether slave status blocks an inheritance line. In some cases it does; for instance, if the child of a free mother and a slave father dies, the inheritance of that child goes to the mother and her male relatives. But if the slave father has a free grandfather, then that grandfather attracts the remainder of the inheritance that would otherwise go to the mother's male relatives.

Of particular importance in the law of inheritance is the emancipation of slaves as a bequest. This type of bequest is strongly supported by the Qur'an, which urges believers to free slaves as a pious act and as expiation for certain sins. As noted above, however, bequests are limited to one-third of the estate, and this rule is sometimes predicated upon a story in which a man had no property other than six slaves and he wished to emancipate them all at his death. The Prophet, however, only allowed two of the slaves to be emancipated, and the other four were inherited by his heirs.

In addition to a simple bequest, a person may also make a vow that a certain slave will be freed upon the master's death. Most works of jurisprudence have a separate chapter for this type of slave, known as a *mudabbar*, and though there is no mention of this type of slave either in the Qur'an or among the early Muslims, it was a practice compatible with Muslim values. In most schools of law, declaration of the slave as a mudabbar is different from a simple bequest. First, while a bequest may be changed, a vow of emancipation may not. Second, the mudabbar's owner may not sell him, nor may he be exchanged for another slave. These rules are clearly set forth in the handbook of Ibn Abd al-Hekam (died 829).

I said: What is your opinion concerning the mudabbar, can his owner sell him? He said: As for the mudabbar, his owner may not sell him, nor may he be exchanged, while his master lives – neither for a debt, nor for anything else, as long as he lives. If the master dies, the slave is freed from the third of his estate which may be used for bequests, whether all of him goes forth from the third or not. For if the deceased had no assets from which the slave could be taken, not even some of him, then he remains a slave.[35]

Like the slave who is bequeathed emancipation, the mudabbar is freed from the master's discretionary third, and this rule can cause problems for the division of the estate. Further, just as in Jewish law, there is a general rule that bequests, like vows and declarations of divorce, are not accepted if a person is deathly ill. In the case of emancipation, however, deathbed bequests may be honored, though given second rank.

It is permitted for the man to withdraw from his estate whatever he wishes, except for the vow of making a slave a mudabbar. This may not be withdrawn.

As for someone who made his slaves mudabbars, but did not have any other assets besides them, one begins to free first one and then the other until one-third of the estate is reached. But if he makes them mudabbars altogether, but also says 'so-and-so is free and so-and-so is free if I am told that my illness is terminal' [lit.: it is told to me about my illness this which is told], then this is a bequest [and these specifically named slaves should be freed first].

As for someone who makes a slave of his a mudabbar, then he frees half of another while on his deathbed, one begins dividing the estate by freeing the mudabbar. As for someone who makes one slave a mudabbar while he is healthy and another when he is near death, one begins with the first of them. Similarly, if he makes one after another mudabbar while he is on his deathbed, one begins with the first, even if he did not intend these words to define the order of emancipation.

As for someone who dies and leaves no assets except for a mudabbar, but the mudabbar has assets, then one-third of the mudabbar is freed and his assets remain in his possession. But if the man dies, having no assets except the mudabbar [but he does have an outstanding debt], his debt is first reckoned against him, subsequently a third of what remains is freed.

Now if the master dies and leaves both a mudabbar as well as assets, which are not sufficient for the mudabbar to be taken from his third, and then more assets appear which were not previously known, the following is said. Either that the mudabbar is freed only from that which was known at the time and place of the bequest, or that he is emancipated from the two sets of assets together. But we say that if the mudabbar comes forth and the third did not exceed his emancipation, the assets must be gathered together. Something is removed from the newly discovered assets, taking into consideration that which remained of the assets on the day he should have been emancipated, and this is put towards the emancipation of the mudabbar.

As for one who makes a slave a mudabbar while he is healthy, then bequeaths his goods to alms in while he is on his deathbed, the mudabbar takes precedence.[36]

The special provisions for promises made from the deathbed also apply to the question of whether a woman inherits from a husband who divorces her (or marries her) while he is deathly ill. In this case, there is not only the standard length of a deathly illness to consider (three days), but also the 'waiting period' after a woman is divorced but before she may marry another.

The woman divorced three times while her husband is ill inherits from her husband if he dies from this illness, but he does not inherit from her. The same applies if only one pronouncement of divorce is made and he had died from his illness after her waiting period was completed, even if he truly divorced his wife with a single pronouncement the two of them inherit from one another as long as she is in her waiting period when he dies. If she completed the waiting period, then there is no inheritance between the two of them after the waiting period. As for someone who marries a wife on his deathbed, she neither inherits from him nor he from her.[37]

The Islamic law of inheritance is organized to ensure that specific members of the family, particularly women, receive a fair share of the deceased's estate. In Shi'i law, these Qur'anic rules are understood to have established an entirely new system of inheritance, while in Sunni law, the old system is still in force, merely modified by these new rules. In either case, inheritance rules enforce family connections and responsibilities. Included in these responsibilities is a strong emphasis on making charitable bequests, either for freeing slaves, giving of alms or establishment of an endowment. The limitation of such bequests to one-third of the total estate, however, prevents such pious intentions from impoverishing the family.

8 DIVORCE IN JUDAISM

The Written Torah at Deut. 24:1ff. dismisses the law of divorce in a few sentences, and its focus is then elsewhere. It makes the point that serial marriage, first to one man, then to another, then reversion to the first, is not permitted. The halakhah in the Oral Torah vastly increases the scope and intensifies attention to detail. On the one hand, the woman is treated as a passive onlooker to the process; on the other the woman is a most responsible party in many details, who has every right to know what is going on, to set conditions in the conduct of the transaction, and who has at the same time responsibility for the consequences if the transaction is not correctly performed.

In normative law, grounds for divorce know no bounds: the husband may issue a writ of divorce for any reason whatsoever. It is he who commissions the scribe to prepare the document and the witnesses to sign and the court or its agents to hand it over to the wife. She has the right only to receive the document properly, that is, in full awareness. And the wife may not initiate the process in any way, though under certain conditions the court of Judaism may intervene and compel the husband to agree on his own volition to issue such a writ. Grounds for divorce are debated between the Houses of Shammai and Hillel, referred to earlier. As may be seen, the wife takes an important role in the transaction and bears responsibility for the proper conduct of the proceedings.

On what constitutes proper grounds for divorce, the pertinent verse of Scripture, Deut. 24:1 – 'Because he has found in her indecency in anything' – is read differently. The House of Shammai finds a clear reference to 'indecency,' understood to mean adultery, and the House of Hillel stresses 'in any thing.' Aqiba then broadens the matter to yield no-fault divorce:

9:10 A. The House of Shammai say, 'A man should divorce his wife only because he has found grounds for it in unchastity,

B. since it is said, "Because he has found in her indecency in anything" (Deut. 24:1).'

C. And the House of Hillel say, 'Even if she spoiled his dish,

D. since it is said, "Because he has found in her indecency in anything."'

E. R. Aqiba says, 'Even if he found someone else prettier than she,

F. since it is said, "And it shall be if she find no favor in his eyes" (Deut. 24:1).'

(Mishnah-tractate Gittin, 9:10)

In any event, the husband is in nearly full control of the matter, so the latitudinarian position accommodates the facts of the relationship. But the husband can be persuaded by the court, even through legitimate violence such as a flogging, to declare that he wants to divorce the wife, and so to appoint a scribe and witnesses for the project. Here is a case in which the man is forced to divorce his wife:

113

7:10 A. And these are the ones whom they force to put her away: (1) he who is afflicted with boils, or (2) who has a polypus, or (3) who collects [dog excrement], or (4) a coppersmith, or (5) a tanner —

B. whether these [blemishes] were present before they were married or whether after they were married they made their appearance.

C. And concerning all of them did R. Meir say, 'Even though he made a condition with her [that the marriage is valid despite these blemishes], she still can claim, "I thought that I could take it. But now I find I cannot take it."'

(Mishnah-tractate Ketubot, 7:10)

The act of divorce depends upon the husband's specifying that the writ serves his purpose, with his and his wife's name therein, and instructing that the document be handed over. So a woman may write her own writ, since in any event it is the husband who activates it.

2:5 A. All are valid for the writing of a writ of divorce,

B. even a deaf-mute, an idiot, or a minor.

C. A woman may write her own writ of divorce, and a man may write his quittance [a receipt for the payment of the marriage contract],

D. for the confirmation of the writ of divorce is solely through its signatures [of the witnesses].

E. All are valid for delivering a writ of divorce,

F. except for a deaf-mute, an idiot, and a minor,

G. a blind man, and a Gentile.

(Mishnah-tractate Gittin, 2:5)

At the same time the husband must give explicit instructions in the matter, participating in the rite start to finish.

7:2 A. [If] they said to him, 'Shall we write a writ of divorce for your wife?' and he said to them, 'Write,'

B . [if] they then instructed a scribe and he wrote it, and witnesses and they signed it,

114

C. even though they wrote it and signed it and delivered it to him, and he handed it over to her,

D. lo, this writ of divorce is null,

E. unless he himself says to the scribe, 'Write,' and to the witnesses, 'Sign.'

(Ibid., 7:2)

The writ may not impose conditions upon the rights of the woman to remarry.

9:2 A. [If the husband said,] 'Lo, you are permitted to any man, except for my father, and your father, my brother, your brother, a slave, or a Gentile,'

B. or any man to whom she cannot become betrothed —

C. it is valid.

(Ibid., 9:2)

9:3 A. The text of the writ of divorce [is as follows]:

B. 'Lo, you are permitted to any man.'

(Ibid., 9:3)

The limitation that is stated at M. Gittin 9:2 is null in any event, the Torah having forbidden the woman to enter into such a union. The document then must specify the woman's new freedom; but from that point forward, the couple cannot be alone together.

7:4 A. She should not afterward continue together with him except in the presence of witnesses,

B. even a servant, even a girl servant,

C. except for her own servant girl, because she is shameless before her servant girl.

(Ibid., 7:4)

The law thus pays most attention to woman (and family) at those points at which the status of a woman shifts, the interstitial moments at which a woman is neither wholly the property of one man nor entirely of another (or, in unusual circumstances, in her own domain). These points of danger – betrothal, marriage, divorce – attract the concern of the legal system and require secure legal provision for the change in a woman's position within the social order, the whole resting upon the conviction that a woman's sexuality forms a principal source of social disruption.

What role is given to the wife? Even though only the husband may initiate the writ of divorce and have it written and handed over, the Oral Torah provides the wife with important points of participation in the process of ordinary divorce, even when the man initiates that process. And the woman's stake in the process correspondingly gains enormous consequence. She has the right to dictate the conditions of delivery. She has the right to be correctly informed, to participate in the transaction as an active player, determining how her half of the matter will be conducted by dictating the circumstances under which she will receive the document. And, above all, because the Oral Torah also imposes the most severe and long-lasting penalties upon a woman whose writ of divorce turns out to be impaired and so invalid, and who on the strength of such a document remarries, the woman must thoughtfully exercise her power within the transaction. So the woman is not only given a role in the process but also a very heavy responsibility in the correct implementation of the transaction. For that reason, she takes anything but a passive role in the matter.

The document must not only be particular to that woman, but it must also accommodate her preferences as to its delivery. Since the document must conform to the law (or it yields no effect and leaves her sanctified to that particular man), she has to make sure it is validly prepared at its critical points. That is why she dictates the conditions of the writ's delivery. While she cannot initiate the procedure – Scripture has accorded her no role in the transaction but the passive one of receiving the document – her will governs where and how the writ will be handed over to her. That is how the halakhah assigns to her a part by allowing her to dictate the conditions under which she receives the document; she may appoint an agent, specify the circumstance of delivery to her agent, and otherwise take an active role in severing the marital bond. Not only so, but the husband must explicitly identify the document as a writ of divorce, and the wife must receive it as such. Thus if he puts it into her hand while she is sleeping, then she wakes up, reads it, and sees that it is her writ of divorce, it is not a valid writ– until he says to her, 'Here is your writ of divorce.' Here again, the transaction requires the wife's full participation, and an explicit exchange, understood by both parties, for the marital bond to be severed.

What is at stake in these requirements? They serve to make certain the writ is valid and takes effect, so that all parties to the transaction know that the woman's status has changed irrevocably. That means that even an imperfection with no bearing on the substance of the transaction, such as mis-dating or mis-identifying the writ (using the wrong date, or mis-identifying the locale of the husband) suffices to invalidate it. Equally, if the scribe erred and gave the writ of divorce to the woman and the quittance to the man, rather than giving the writ to the man to give to his wife and vice versa, it is a complete disaster. Both these examples, and other comparable ones, bring to bear the most severe penalties. If the woman should then remarry on the strength of the impaired writ of divorce, her entire situation is ruined. She has to get a new writ of divorce from the first husband and from the second; she loses her alimony; and she loses many of the benefits and guarantees of the marriage settlement. Furthermore, the offspring from the marriage fall into the category of those whose parents are legally unable to wed, for example, the offspring of a married woman by a man other than her husband. Everything is lost by reason of the innocent actions of the wife in remarrying on the strength of an impaired writ; and that means the wife has an acute interest in, and bears full responsibility for, its validity. The husband's only unique power is to direct the writing and delivery of the writ; otherwise, the wife bears equal responsibility for the accurate preparation of the document, its valid delivery (hence insistence that she be alert to the transaction), and the fully correct details inscribed therein. So in the aggregate, the Rabbinic sages have not only guaranteed alimony but also erected protections for the wife and treated her as a fully sentient, intelligent being, possessed of freedom of will and endowed with responsibility.

9 DIVORCE IN ISLAM

Divorce in Islam has no stamp of sin, as in Christianity, and it is deceptively easy for the man to achieve. All that is required is for him to make three pronouncements of divorce to his wife, and unlike Jewish law, these may be spoken. Divorce, however, has specific legal effects which can make the matter more difficult, and in regulating divorce, Islamic law seeks to ensure that women and children are not left without support.

> A statement of divorce [*talaq*, lit. setting free] said three times in a single sentence goes against tradition, but if it occurs, it has legal effect. The traditional form of divorce is an indifferent act [neither recommended nor reprehensible] and it is as follows. The man issues a single statement of divorce to his wife while she is in a state of purity [between menstrual periods], during which he has not come near her. The final statement of divorce does not follow until she has completed the waiting period; during this period he has the right to retract his statement of divorce: as for free women who menstruate, this is as long as the third menstrual cycle after divorce does not begin; for slaves it is the second period. If she is one of those who do not menstruate, or one who has already gone into menopause, he divorces her whenever he wants. The same applies to the pregnant woman. The pregnant woman he may ask to return to him as long as she has not given birth; the woman undergoing a waiting period may be asked to return during the months in which her waiting period has not yet been completed.[38]

Although the pronouncement of divorce may be oral, it must be spoken three times. Preferably the husband makes one or two pronouncements, the wife undergoes her waiting period, and then he completes the remaining pronouncements. The waiting period is defined in the Qur'an as three menstrual cycles and is established for the purposes of ensuring that a divorced woman is not with child, and that if she is pregnant, the paternity of that child is known and mother and child are properly cared for. These and other rules are covered extensively in the Qur'an.

> Those who take an oath to stay away from their women have a wait of four months. If they revert, God is forgiving, compassionate.

> If they decide to divorce, God is hearing, knowing.

> Divorcées shall wait by themselves for three menstrual cycles. They are not allowed to hide that which God has created in their wombs, if they believe in God and the last day. In this their husbands have the right to make them return, if they wish restoration. Women have rights placed upon them by honor, but men have a degree over them; God is almighty, wise.

> Divorce is two times; thereafter is either honorable retention or setting free respectfully. You are not allowed to take anything of what you have given your wives, unless the two are afraid that they will not stay within God's boundaries. If you are afraid that they will not stay within God's boundaries, there is no harm in her acquiring her freedom by it. These are God's boundaries; do not overstep them. Whoever oversteps the boundaries of God – they are grave sinners.

> If he divorces her, she is not lawful for him afterwards, until she marries another husband; if subsequently he divorces her, then there is no harm in the two of them returning to one another, if they believe that they will stay within God's boundaries. These are God's boundaries, which he makes clear to a knowledgeable people.

> When you divorce women and they reach their term, then retain them honorably or set them free honorably. Do not retain them by force, so that you overstep. Whoever does that has sinned against himself. Do not take God's signs in mockery, but remember God's blessing upon you and that of the Book and the wisdom which he has sent down to you for your admonishment. And be in awe of God, and know that God has knowledge of all things.

When you divorce women, and they reach their term, do not keep them from marrying their husbands when they have agreed honorably. This is an admonition for those of you who believe in God and the last day. This is cleaner and purer for you. God knows, and you know not.

(The Qur'an, 2:225–232)

The waiting period is also of particular concern to Muslim jurists, and some devote a separate chapter to the intricacies of this institution. In his handbook, al-Qayrawani extends the logic of the Qur'anic rules to several new situations.

The waiting period of a divorced free woman is three menstrual cycles, whether she is Muslim or of the People of the Book. As for a female slave or anyone who is partially a slave: two cycles. Whether the husband is slave or free makes no difference in all these cases. The cycles are marked by the periods of purification in between the flows of blood.

If she is one of those who has not yet menstruated, or of those who have already ceased menstruating, then the waiting period is three months for both free and slave. The waiting period of a free woman or slave who has been divorced and is about to begin menstruating is a year. The waiting period of a pregnant woman, whether at the death of her husband or divorce, is until the completion of her pregnancy, whether she is free, slave or of the People of the Book.

No waiting period is required of the divorcée who has not had sex with her husband. The waiting period of a free woman after the death of her husband is four months and ten days, whether she is old or young, whether she had had sex with her husband or not, whether Muslim or of the People of the Book. For the female slave or anyone who is partially a slave: two months and five nights. But a mature woman who menstruates and whose cycle is late does not follow this order; rather she sits and waits until all doubt has passed.

As for those who do not menstruate, whether because of youth or old age, but their husbands did have sexual intercourse with them, they must wait three months after the death of their husbands before marrying again.

The restrictions of mourning for a woman in her waiting period after the death of her husband include not approaching any kind of adornment, such as jewelry, eye makeup, etc. And to avoid all dyed clothing, except black, and all perfume. She should not apply henna, nor even come close to anointing oils, nor should she comb her hair.

Restrictions of mourning are incumbent upon free and slave, but there is a difference of opinion as to whether they are required of People of the Book. These restrictions are not required of divorced women.

The free woman of the People of the Book is required to undergo the waiting period in the case of both divorce and death. The waiting period of a concubine at the death of her master is one menstrual cycle; the same applies if he had freed her. But if she has ceased to menstruate, then three months.

Separation from a female slave due to transfer of her ownership entails a waiting period of one menstrual cycle. Ownership is transferred by commerce, gift, capture, etc. As for a female slave who had just menstruated while she was in his possession, and then he bought her, no waiting period of separation is incumbent upon her if she did not leave his house.[39]

To prevent a man from frivolously marrying and divorcing the same woman, Islamic law forbids a man from marrying the woman he just divorced, unless she had an intervening marriage to another man. Even so, that intervening marriage may not be merely for convenience.

It is not permitted for a man to marry a woman in order to make her permissible to a man who divorced her conclusively; this action does not make her permissible to him ... . As for someone who divorces his wife conclusively, she is not permissible to him, neither by right of ownership nor by right of marriage, until she marries another husband.[40]

As Aisha ruled in the hadith quoted above on page 88, the woman must both marry this intervening husband and consummate the marriage; further, he must divorce her legally before she may remarry.

There are numerous ways to effect a divorce, and most of these are at the discretion of the husband. These instruments vary among the schools of Islamic law, but usually women are allowed some method of divorce for women by returning the marriage gift. This type of divorce is known as *khul'*, literally the slipping off of a garment.

As for someone who says to his wife: 'you are divorced' this is one pronouncement, even if he intended it to be more than one.

Khul' is a type of divorce in which there is no right of return, even though it is not called divorce. It is when she gives him something (of her marriage gift) and he accepts it in order to separate himself from her.

As for a man who says to his wife: 'you are divorced from me completely!' this has the value of a conclusive divorce whether or not he has had intercourse with her. But if he calls her 'free,' 'released,' or 'forbidden,' or says to her 'your rein is on your withers' then this has the value of a conclusive divorce in the case of a woman with whom he has had intercourse. In the case of those with whom he has not had intercourse, it is as he intended.

As for the woman who is divorced before consummation of the marriage, she retains half of the marriage gift, unless she is a woman who has been previously married and she forgoes it. If she is a virgin, any decision to forego the marriage gift is up to her father. Similarly, if she is a female slave, the decision belongs to her master.

As for someone who divorces, he ought to grant his divorced wife some gift. He is not forced to give a gift to a woman with whom he has not had sex; he allocates a share of inheritance to her, but does not give her a gift, nor does he give a gift to the woman divorced by khul'.

If he dies and is survived by a woman to whom he had neither allocated a share of inheritance nor had intercourse, she receives an inheritance but not the marriage gift. If he had had intercourse with her, she also receives an appropriate marriage gift, unless she is satisfied with some other thing of value.[41]

The variety of possible formulas of divorce is a subject of interest in collections of hadith, such as this set from Malik's *al-Muwatta'*.

Yahya told me on Malik's authority that he had been told that someone wrote to Umar ibn al-Khattab from Iraq that a man said to his wife, 'Your rein is on your withers.' Umar ibn al-Khattab wrote to his governor: 'Order him to come see me in Mecca during the pilgrimage.' While Umar was circumambulating the Ka'ba, a man came up to him and greeted him. Umar asked, 'Who are you?' and he replied, 'I am the one you ordered to be brought before you.' Umar said to him, 'I ask you by the Lord of this building, what did you mean by your statement, 'Your rein is on your withers'?' The man replied, 'Had you made me swear by any other place than this, I would not have told you the truth. I intended separation by this.' Umar ibn al-Khattab said, 'It is as you intended.'

Yahya told me on Malik's authority that he had be told that Ali ibn Abi Talib used to say that if a man said to his wife, 'You are forbidden to me,' it was like three pronouncements of divorce.

Malik said, 'This is the best of what I have heard on the subject.'

Yahya told me on Malik's authority from Nafi that Abdullah ibn Umar used to say that statements like 'you are cut off' or 'you are abandoned' were each like three pronouncements of divorce.

Concerning a man who said to his wife 'you are cut off' or 'you are abandoned' or 'you are separated,' Malik said that these were like three pronouncements of divorce for the woman with whom he had already had intercourse. As for the one with whom he had not had intercourse he professes whether he had meant it to be one or three. If he says one, he swears to this, then he becomes like one of those who seek to be engaged. This is because a woman whose husband has had intercourse with her is not set free by being cut off, abandoned or separated, but only by three pronouncements of divorce, but the one whose husband had not had intercourse with her is cut off, abandoned and separated by one pronouncement.

Malik said, 'This is the best of what I have heard on the subject.'[42]

In addition to divorce, a marriage may also be terminated due to annulment. A marriage is annulled when husband or wife is found to have a physical defect which would prevent them from performing their conjugal duties. As in the law of Judaism, a regular sexual relationship is seen as a duty of marriage and not a favor, so that which stands in the way of sex may be cause for divorce. Further, a marriage may be annulled when one of the two undergoes a change in status, either from slave to free or from one religion to another.

If one spouse renounces Islam, the marriage is annulled by divorce – although some say it is annulled without divorce. If two unbelievers become Muslim, they are confirmed in their marriage, but if only one becomes a Muslim, then this is annulment without divorce. If she is the one who became a Muslim, then he has right of marriage should he become a Muslim within her waiting period, but if he is the one who became a Muslim and his wife is one of the People of the Book, the marriage is confirmed. If she is a Zoroastrian and she becomes a Muslim after he did, she is in the same position and the two are considered husband and wife. But if she becomes a Muslim much later, then she is already separated from him.

If an unbeliever becomes a Muslim and he has more than four wives, he chooses four and separates himself from the rest of them. As for someone who divorces his wife through mutual cursing, she is never allowed to him again as a wife. The same holds for a man who marries a woman during her waiting period and has sexual intercourse with her during her waiting period.[43]

A woman may be returned to her family for reason of insanity, black leprosy, white leprosy, or a disease of the vagina. If he has intercourse with her and did not know of her condition, he takes her marriage gift and demands the return of his gift from her father; the same applies if she had been given away by her brother. But if she had been given in marriage by an agent who was not a close member of the family [and so would not have known of her illness], then nothing is incumbent upon him. She gets nothing but a quarter dinar. The time limit for objecting is one year when he has sex with her, but if he does not, the two are separated if she wishes.

The husband who is missing has a time period of four years from the day she mentions it [to the authorities]. The search for him ends and she undergoes a waiting period just like the waiting period at the death of a husband. She marries again if she wishes, but no one inherits from him until such time passes beyond which he could not be expected to live.[44]

Islamic law requires that a divorced woman receive alimony for herself and child support as long as she cares for the children. These rules are largely based on the sura from the Qur'an entitled 'Divorce,' and which is addressed directly to the Prophet Muhammad and his wives. Here many of the injunctions found in the second sura are repeated, along with the reiteration that these are limits set by God himself.

O Prophet, when you divorce women, divorce them at their waiting period. Keep track of the waiting period, and be in awe of God your Lord. Do not expel them from their apartments, nor will they go out, except if they have brought forth a clear abomination. These are God's boundaries. Whoever oversteps the boundaries of God has sinned against himself. You do not know; perhaps God will bring something entirely new to pass.

Then, when they have reached their term, retain them honorably or part with them honorably. Ask two from among yourselves who possess justice to testify, and bring the testimony before God. This is for you an admonishment for those who believe in God and the last day. And the one who is in awe of God, God will make a way for him.

And he will enrich him from a place he had never considered. And the one who puts his trust in God, he will account for him. God reaches his affair. God has appointed a measure for everything.

As for your women who have despaired of menstruating and those who have not yet menstruated, if you are in doubt then their waiting period will be three months. Those who are with child, their term is the completion of their pregnancy. The one who is in awe of God, God will appoint an easy path for him by his command.

This is God's command, which he has sent down to you. And whoever is in awe of God, he will acquit him of his evil deeds, and he will grant him a wage.

Let them live where you are living, in your place. Do not make difficulty for them in order to restrict them. If they are carrying, give to them until they complete their pregnancy. If they suckle for you, give them their wages, and confer with each other honorably. If you treat each other harshly, another woman will suckle for him.

Let the wealthy man expend out of his wealth. As for him whose provision is limited, let him expend that which God has given him. God charges no soul save with what he has given him. After harshness, God will make things easier.

(The Qur'an, 65:1–7)

The rules on suckling, which came to the fore in our discussion of the Islamic law of betrothal, again demonstrate concern for ties of milk. These rules are, in fact, repeated in the Qur'an.

Mothers suckle their children two full years, for such as desire to fulfil the suckling. It is for the father to provide for the mothers and clothe them honorably. No soul is charged save to its capacity; a mother shall not be pressed for her child, neither a father for his child.

(Ibid., 2:235)

Al-Qayrawani's version of the laws of alimony and child support begins on a negative note, listing those women who do not qualify for maintenance. While no direct references are made to the Qur'an, the dependence on the logic of the Qur'anic argument is obvious.

There is no maintenance except for the woman who is divorced without the third and final divorce, but there is for the pregnant woman, whether divorced three times or only once. There is no maintenance for the woman divorced by khul', except if she is pregnant. There is no maintenance for the woman divorced by mutual cursing, even if she is pregnant. There is no maintenance for all women in a waiting period due to the death of their husbands, but such a woman does have the right of abiding [in the house of her husband] if the house belonged to him or he had already paid the rent. She is not to be expelled from her house at divorce or death of the husband until the waiting period is completed, unless the landlord expels her because he had not received the rent or its equivalent. In this case he expels her and she stays in the place of residence to which she has moved until the waiting period is completed.

A woman suckles the child in her custody except when the child is like those who are not suckled. A divorcée has the right of suckling her child over her husband, and she has the right of taking a wage for suckling the child if she wishes. After a divorce, the woman has the right of custody until the male child reaches puberty or the female child marries and consummates her marriage. In case the mother dies or marries again, the grandmother and then the aunt have custody.[45]

In general, the Islamic laws of divorce are rather simple, allowing for easy divorce on the part of the man and some right of divorce for women. Although divorce ends the family relationship, it does not mean an end to mutual responsibilities, particularly if there are children. The specific rules on the waiting period are designed to ensure knowledge of paternity, maintaining the order of the Islamic family. During this period, men support their former wives, including providing for their living arrangements. Equally, men are expected to support their children who are being raised by women whom they have divorced.

10 CONCLUSIONS

In both Judaism and Islam, laws of marriage, divorce and inheritance help to mark out the ideal pattern of family relations, resulting in a theology of family life. The relative place of women and men is paramount, both in explicit and implicit terms. Explicitly, men instigate marriage and divorce, and in Judaism they are the usual heirs. Implicitly, laws are directed toward men who are seen as the guardians of women. Similarly, both traditions include specific rules protecting women, with the courts providing women a measure of power they would not otherwise have in society.

The rites of betrothal, marriage and divorce also serve to mark important changes in the woman's status, as she moves from the custody of father to husband. Men have no such equivalent status-shift, and whether a man has engaged in sexual intercourse previous to a marriage or not is not a subject for legal discussion. Importantly, however, a woman's role is more a receptive role than a passive one. The role she plays is determined by men – he offers to marry and she accepts, she receives his marriage gift and his seed during intercourse, and in Judaism she receives the writ of divorce – but whether she actively engages this role or passively accepts it is up to her.

Betrothal in both sets of law is a precursor to marriage, and no one may be betrothed who could not marry. But while in the laws of Judaism betrothal has the legal force of marriage, in Islamic law it has little legal effect. The distinction may be seen in the method by which a betrothal may be broken. For Islam, either party may unilaterally end the betrothal with no consequence, unless a gift had been exchanged. For Judaism, an actual writ of divorce is required. Islamic law makes a further distinction between marriage by contract alone and consummation of the marriage, since in the first case, the marriage is broken by only one pronouncement of divorce.

Importantly, marriage is as much a joining of families as a joining of two individuals. The laws of Judaism and Islam emphasize this by forbidding marital relations with a specific set of close family relatives. Islam, however, extends this shared set to include relations established by milk and ownership as well as blood. This extension of the family has no counterpart in Judaism, but it plays a significant role in the Islamic use of family ties to extend God's just society. The institution of *wala'* (the patron–client relationship) was used to attach converts to Muslim families, giving them rights of protection and inheritance.

Judaism and Islam share the ideal of marriage as a contract, not a sacrament. But whereas in Judaism both marriage contract and writ of divorce must be written documents, in Islam oral formulations are preferred. This dependence on orality seems anomalous, given what we know of the great literary wealth of the Islamic empires. In fact, however, Islam understands the spoken word to have a particular value, which ultimately goes back to the understanding of God as final guarantor of all contracts.

God's active role is exemplified in the differences with which the two religions treat an accusation of adultery, which is seen as a perverse inversion of marital order. While Judaism enacts God's perfect justice upon the accused woman, matching punishment to crime, Islam gives her the right of swearing, by God, that she is innocent. The understanding, of course, is that if she is lying, she will have to endure far worse punishments than the drinking of bitter water for all eternity. Both religions use rules of evidence to ensure that proving an accusation is difficult, but in the case of a woman who is inexplicably pregnant, punishment is severe.

Beyond the obvious difference between the form of statements of divorce, Judaism and Islam share many aspects of divorce law. First, the right of divorce is almost entirely with the man; since he instigated the relationship, he may end it. Further, the man need offer no explanation for his desire to divorce. However, both traditions are concerned with the treatment of the divorced woman, who is assumed to be the weaker partner in such an arrangement. The husband is also expected to care for any minor children from the marriage.

The Jewish law of inheritance, however, is markedly divergent from that of

Islam. Since in Jewish law a double portion of the entire estate is inherited by the firstborn male, that law is naturally concerned with the process of establishing who, among twins, was the firstborn. This question is of little interest to the Muslim jurists, since shares are fixed and a firstborn son only inherits after all other shares have been distributed. Both aim for justice, but in Judaism, a just system of inheritance is not the sole consideration; the disposition of the Land of Israel among the tribes, the maintenance of family property through generations – these form considerations as well. So the claim of the individual is weighed against the interest of the community in the condition of the Holy Land. Of course, there is also a greater responsibility placed on the heir to care for other members of the extended family. In Islam, God's rules take over this responsibility of distributive justice, outlining just who in the family is to receive a portion of the estate.

Finally, the order of the household is of key interest to both traditions, since it is the basic building block of a well-ordered society. Judaism and Islam are not primarily personal religions, satisfied with individual worship: rather, God is worshipped through submission to his divinely ordained order for the whole of society, the entirety of humankind, and that order includes family and politics. The theological foundation for this interest is, not surprisingly, quite different in each religion. For while Judaism sees the well-ordered family of all Israel in the Land of Israel as the replication of the paradisiacal state of Eden, Islam sees the family as the establishment of justice and a bulwark against ignorance. Here, we see in this one detail how the generative myth of humankind's history takes over. The age of ignorance and injustice in Islam corresponds to the generations from Adam to Noah and from Noah to Abraham. That is to say, God created man, who rebelled and lost Eden. Man entered a decline, committing ever more horrendous acts of rebellion against God, in the ten generations from Adam to Noah. God then wiped out all of humankind except Noah and his family from the flood, ten generations passed, leading from Noah to Abraham, whom God called and to whom God entrusted the Land – that is, the Land of Israel – as the setting for the restoration of Eden.

In line with the narrative of Scripture, Judaism divides history into the ten generations from Eden and man in God's image, after God's likeness, followed by rebellion and the fall, to the ten generations from Noah to Abraham. From Abraham comes holy Israel, his descendants and heirs, and Israel takes the path to restoration of paradise, now through the Land of Israel. But Israel recapitulates the story of Adam, for the giving of the Torah is followed by rebellion and ultimately the loss of the Land. Then for Judaism the restoration of the human condition to God's plan for man – life eternal in paradise – is the task of Israel through obedience to the Torah. The Torah then marks humanity's hope for regeneration and renewal, for the recovery of Eden and eternal life.

This supernatural narrative finds its counterpart in Islam's view of the division of history into the time of ignorance and injustice, and the time of justice brought about through Islam. The one tells the story of the human condition through the narrative of that sector of humanity that has received and accepted God's will in the Torah, which is called 'Israel,' and the other of the human condition through the narrative of the age of injustice and the age of justice. God's intervention in human history forms the shared and generative conviction, and his purpose in both narratives is the same: the realization of God's will of justice (always requiring, therefore, mercy as well), through the social order on earth.

If, then, the Judaic paradigm flows from Eden to the Flood, then from Noah to Abraham to Sinai, the Islamic paradigm takes its own course. The Islamic paradigm is one of establishing God's justice on earth. The key term for this process is a negative one, *jahiliyya*. Often misunderstood as merely the 'age of ignorance' before the coming of Islam, this term also refers to both the disordered and unjust world of the unbelievers and the deviations which Muslims may make from God's path. The Islamic laws on marriage are designed specifically to prevent fornication, a form of jahiliyya. Likewise, they seek to establish justice, by urging the care of orphans, widows and slaves, all of whom need to be brought within the boundaries of a just society. Further, Islamic laws of inheritance explicitly modify the old system of transferring wealth to the nearest male relative by identifying specific shares for female members of the family. Thus the paradigmatic movement, from jahiliyya to justice, is set forth in these laws. Islam and Judaism intersect on the principle of God's provision of the just world order through revealed law. But each tells its own story of the meeting point.

3

AMONG THE FAITHFUL [II]

ALMSGIVING AND CHARITY

1 INTRODUCTION

Eleemosynary actions in the West generally are deemed optional, not obligatory, in the way that taxes are not votive. An act of 'charity' comes about by reason of the goodwill of the donor. 'Almsgiving' lays stress on 'the gift,' an act of individual intentionality – whim, caprice. That conception is alien to both Judaism and Islam, which regard almsgiving and charity as both obligatory and voluntary. Both make provision for the gratuitous and selfless act of love that, in the secular West, charity is supposed to entail. The difference is, what is voluntary is also obligatory, and how the two religions sort out the obvious complications of such contradictory terms forms the problem of this chapter. What we shall see is that the legal systems of both Islam and Judaism make provision for both obligatory and voluntary charity, and each highly values giving beyond the measure of the law.

To begin with, in both Islam and Judaism laws that express both theology and public policy govern activities usually classed as 'almsgiving' or as 'charity.' These are not merely encouraged, they represent an absolute obligation. And that means, in both instances, that 'beggars' are not treated disdainfully but with respect, fully part of the social order and legitimately so. Both Islam and Judaism place a high value on almsgiving in particular, acts of charity in general. Both religious legal systems lay heavy stress on support for the poor. But, like the secular West, neither is prepared to leave the matter to individuals and their goodwill or to rely wholly upon private persons' sense of responsibility and obligation. The character of the laws governing action that must come from the heart embodies how the two traditions both provide for a just social order and also leave open the opportunity for the individual to act out of love for God, not only the good of society and its interest in maintaining the poor and the weak.

What is striking is how profound a theological message is conveyed through practical laws on almsgiving. The Hebrew word for philanthropy or almsgiving, *sedaqah*, bears the double meaning of 'righteousness' and 'charity,' and that fact conveys the centrality, in the halakhah, of support for the poor. But almsgiving vastly transcends the act of donating funds to a beggar. Indeed, it is not a merely votive action but obligatory, and, moreover, what one gives belongs to God and goes to those whom God has designated to receive his share. The term is virtually the same in Islam – *sadaqah* – from a root with the same range of meanings. That fact signals the broader concurrence of the two religions on the fundamental obligation of those that possess wealth to realize justice with what they hold. Islam builds its entire system on the imperative to do justice, to create a just social and world order, and Judaism agrees. Moses and Muhammad set forth a common goal for humanity. At no point in the comparison and contrast of the two religious traditions do we find such a close correspondence of doctrine and law, in principle and in detail, than here.

2 CHARITY IN ISLAM

There are two kinds of charity in Islam – required and voluntary. Required charity or almsgiving is called *zakat* and voluntary charity is called *sadaqah*, although the two terms are often used interchangeably in the classical sources, because in some ways they are both necessary for salvation. However, distinctions between the two are discernible in discussions of the results of failure to contribute and of the appropriate recipients.

Required charity or almsgiving (*zakat*) in the Qur'an

The requirement to contribute to the support of the community, especially the poor and needy, is one of the most frequently mentioned prescriptions for piety in the Qur'an. For example, among the most often quoted verses is the following:

> It is not piety that you turn your faces to the East or the West, but
> pious is one who believes in God and the Last Day and the angels and
> the Book and the prophets, and spends money despite his love for it, on
> relatives and orphans and the needy and travelers and those who ask
> and for captives, and who performs prayer and gives zakat and those
> who keep their promises when they make them and who are patient in
> poverty and strife and in time of war; those who do so are truthful and
> the ones who take protection in God.
>
> (Qur'an, 2:178)

In this verse, it is clear that zakat refers to required charitable contributions, while other 'spending' refers to supererogatory charity. In either case, it is noteworthy that of the five principles of piety given, two concern charity.

Zakat is mentioned in the Qur'an most often in connection with prayer, one of the other essential components of Islamic practice.

> These are verses of the Book of Wisdom, guidance and mercy for those who do good deeds, who perform prayer and give zakat and who believe firmly in the afterlife. They [act] upon guidance from their Lord and will prosper.
>
> (Ibid., 31:3–6)

> Believe in what I have sent down, confirming what is [already] with you, and do not be the first to disbelieve in it, and do not trade my signs for a small price, and take protection in me; and do not mix the truth with deception nor hide the truth purposely. And perform prayer and pay zakat and bow in prayer with those who bow.
>
> (Ibid., 2:42–44; cf:2:111; 4:78; 22:78; 24:38; 58:14–15)

> God has promised to those among you who believe and do good works that he will make them stewards on earth as he made those before them stewards, and to establish for them their religion which he chose for them, and to exchange their fear for security. They serve me, associating nothing with me and whoever is ungrateful after that is sinful. So perform prayer and give zakat and obey the Messenger, and you will be shown mercy.
>
> (Ibid., 24:56–57)

In fact, so important is charity in Islam that it is often listed, along with the true belief and prayer which are assumed to inspire it and all other good works, as sufficient for salvation.

> Indeed those who believe and do good deeds and perform prayer and give zakat will have their reward from their Lord, and have nothing to fear nor shall they grieve.
>
> (Ibid., 2:278)

The Qur'an even assures those who make the effort but cannot quite manage to recite the Qur'an, that prayer and charity will suffice.

> Indeed your Lord knows that you, and a group with you, stand almost two thirds of the night or a half or a third of it. And God determines the night and the day, knowing that you cannot keep track so he has turned toward you (in mercy). So recite from the Qur'an as much as is feasible. He knows that there will be among you the sick and others travelling the land seeking God's favor, and others fighting in the way of

God. So recite what is feasible and perform prayer and give zakat and lend to God a good loan. Whatever good you put forth for yourselves you will find it improved with God and a[n even] greater reward. And ask God's forgiveness. Indeed God is forgiving and merciful.

(Ibid., 73:21)

The chapter entitled 'Repentance' *(al-Tauba)* reinforces this notion by instructing believers to fight idolaters (except during a truce or those with whom treaties have been made) 'wherever you find them and seize them and hold them and wait for them in every lookout post, but if they repent and perform prayer and pay zakat, then let them go their way. Indeed, God is forgiving, merciful.' (9:5; cf. 9:11)

Indeed, true belief combined with prayer and charity are sufficient for salvation even for Jews and Christians –'People of the Book'– according to the Qur'an.

But those of [the People of the Book] who are firmly rooted in knowledge, and the believers, believe in what was sent down to you and what was sent down before you and performing prayer and giving zakat and believing in God and the Last Day. To them we will give a great reward.
(Ibid., 4:160–163)

That is because all previous prophets are described as having prescribed the same essentials – belief, prayer, and charity.

And we made them leaders, guiding by our command, and we sent revelation to them: do good works, establish prayer, and give zakat. And they served us alone.

(Ibid., 21:74)

They were ordered only to serve God, being sincere to him in religion, true believers and performing prayer and giving zakat; that is the established religion.
(Ibid., 98:5–6; cf.: 19:31–32; 19:55–56)

As these verses indicate, in the Qur'anic view, proper orientation toward charity is impossible without belief. For true belief gives proper motivation or intention, a prerequisite for merit in the Qur'an. The non-believers who controlled the sacred mosque in Mecca, for example, were severely criticized for thinking that their provision of water for the pilgrims was equivalent to belief in God and the Last Judgment, and the struggle to do God's will. Only 'those who believe and emigrate [in order to do the will of God] and exert every effort *(jahadu)* in the way of God with their wealth and their person' receive the highest rank with God (9:20). Therefore, the Qur'an stresses that giving wealth just for show is of no merit.

> Have you seen the one who makes a mockery of religion? That is the one who rejects the orphan and does not work to feed the poor. Woe to those who pray but make nothing of their prayer. They like to be seen but do not give charity.
>
> (Ibid., 107:2–8)

> Indeed, God does not love those who are proud and braggers, who are selfish and encourage people to be selfish and hide what God has given them in favor. We have prepared a humiliating punishment for the ingrates [or unbelievers] and for those who spend their wealth to be seen by people and do not believe in God or the Last Day.
>
> (Ibid., 4:37–39)

> It is not your responsibility to make them follow the right path, but God guides whomever he pleases. And whatever wealth you spend, it is for yourselves, if you spend only to seek the favor of God. And whatever wealth you spend [for charity], it shall be paid back to you in full and you shall not be wronged.
>
> (Ibid., 2:273)

Similarly, failure to give charity is equated with non-belief. In a well-known passage in the Qur'an, Muhammad is instructed to remind his followers that he is only a human being, like them, so they should turn directly to God and ask forgiveness. Listeners are then warned: 'Woe to the idolaters, who do not give zakat and deny the afterlife.' (41:7–8) Accordingly, the giving of charity is presented in the Qur'an as an integral component of righteous behavior, indeed, as an essential response to true belief, to recognition of the one god. True belief and charity are two sides of the same coin. There are no guarantees offered that charity will make up for lack of belief or for evil behavior, however. As we saw, charity that is motivated by pride rather than compassion is not meritorious. Nor is charity that is not part of an integrated pattern of virtuous behavior: 'Those who spend their wealth in the way of God, then do not follow what they have spent with insult or harm, their reward is with their Lord and they have nothing to fear nor will they grieve. Honorable speech and forgiveness are better than charity that is followed by injury.' (2:26–64)

The term zakat actually comes from a root meaning 'to be pure', and the term can also mean 'purity', 'integrity', 'honesty' or even 'justification'. The idea is that the wealth one receives is effectively sanctified – or made righteous – by being shared with those in need, by being contributed to society for its well-being. This sense of the term zakat as a means of purifying something is used in the Qur'an in a number of verses. One involves the death of a child and the hope that God will provide his parents with one 'better than him in zakat [purity] and closer in compassion.' (18: 82) In another, John, son of Zechariah, is described as having been endowed from childhood with wisdom and tenderness and zakat (purity). (19:13–14) Believers are told elsewhere that they are to 'purify' their souls, and not to be corrupt and ruin them (91: 8–11). The sense of zakat as a means of purifying wealth is also evident in the Qur'an: 'Take charity (sadaqah) from their wealth and cleanse them and purify them (from the same root as zakat) thereby.' (9:103) The Qur'an says that the pious, those who will be saved from damnation, are those who give their wealth, thus purifying it (again, using the verbal root of the term zakat; 92:18–19).

Wealth that has been thus purified is considered lawful. That is because the Qur'an teaches that wealth is not something earned by people and to which they are therefore entitled to do with as they will. Wealth comes to people as a result of God's favor; it could not be otherwise, since all power ultimately belongs to God. Yet wealth is not to 'circulate only among the wealthy': 'Whatever God has given to his Messenger...is for God and the Messenger and for relatives and orphans and the needy and the travelers, so it may not circulate [only] among the wealthy.' (59:8) Lawful wealth, therefore, is that which is spent on the well-being of the family and community, for the very purpose of wealth is to provide for the needs of the community. The Qur'an therefore stipulates the uses to which required charity is to be put. It is to be spent 'in way of God,' a phrase used repeatedly in scripture to refer to the workings of the overall divine plan (although sometimes interpreted in the more restricted sense of spreading Islam or fighting non-believers). Specifically, the Qur'an says that charity is to be spent 'for the needy and the poor, those who work with them, those whose hearts are to be won over, for captives, for debtors, for the cause of God, and for travelers, a ruling from God.' (9:60) In this verse, the term used is sadaqah, rather than zakat, but the import is the same. In another verse, the uses of charitable contributions are spelled out, referring simply to the 'wealth [believers] spend' in the way of God.

> [This charity] is for the poor who are detained in the way of God and are unable to move about in the land. The ignorant think of them as free from want because of [their] abstaining [from begging]. You will know them by their appearance; they do not beg openly. And whatever wealth you spend, surely God has perfect knowledge of it.

> (Ibid., 2:274)

The verse quoted above (9:60) is generally taken as designating the specific uses for all varieties of charitable contributions, but it is repeated with slight variations elsewhere. For example:

[T]he pious one is one who believes in God and the Last Day, the angels, the Book and the prophets; and gives of her/his wealth for [God's] love, to relatives and orphans, the needy, the wayfarers and beggars, and for captives; and performs the prayer and gives zakat.

(Ibid., 2:178)

Thus, wealth does not belong to those to whom it is given alone. The poor and needy have a rightful claim to it. Speaking of the righteous people, those who 'have taken protection with God,' the Qur'an says, 'And in their wealth was a share for those who asked for help and the needy.' (51:20) Nor is wealth any benefit in and of itself with regard to spiritual well-being.

Woe to every fault-finder, slanderer, who collects wealth and counts it repeatedly. He thinks his wealth will bring him eternal life. No, he will certainly be thrown into *hutama* and you know what hutama is? It is God's fire that he lights and that descends upon the heart.

(Ibid., 104:2–6)

Wealth is a gift from God and those who earn the wealth are to receive a portion of it: 'Men have a share of what they have earned and women a share of what they have earned.' (4: 33) But a portion also belongs to those for whom we are responsible: 'And to everyone we have appointed heirs to what the parents and relatives leave and those with whom your oaths have sealed a contract. So give them their portion. Indeed, God watches over all things.' (4:34) Interestingly, expenditure of wealth for others is how the Qur'an explains men's responsibility for women. We are told that men are responsible for women because God has favored 'some of them over others,' presumably in terms of wealth, since the verse continues: 'and for what they have expended of their property.' (4:35) That is, males are not preferred in general over women, but those who have received greater wealth are responsible for those who have received less.

So charity, or spending wealth for the support of the community, is a basic virtue in Islam, a source of great spiritual merit.

Those who spend their wealth in the way of God are like a grain of corn that grows seven ears, in every ear one hundred grains. And God increases further for whomever he pleases. God is bountiful, omniscient.

(Ibid., 2:262)

In fact, giving of one's wealth in charity is a commonly mentioned way of *jihad,* or 'strenuous effort'.

Those believers who [are inactive], except the disabled ones, and those who exert effort [or those who engage in jihad] in the way of God with their wealth and their persons are not equal. God has raised in rank those who exert effort with their wealth and their persons over those [who are inactive]. And to each God has promised a good reward. But God has raised in rank those who struggle over those [who are inactive] by a great reward.'

(Ibid., 4:96; cf. 9:20)

Go forth, light and heavy, and strive with your wealth and your persons in the way of God. That is better for you if you only knew.

(Ibid., 9:41; cf. 9:44)

And when a chapter is sent down: Believe in God and exert every effort with his Messenger, the elites among them ask of you saying, 'Leave us to be with those [who are inactive].' They are satisfied being with those left behind and their hearts are sealed so they do not understand. But the Messenger and those who believe with him exert every effort with their wealth and their persons and they will have rewards and will prosper.

(Ibid., 9:86–88)

The believers are those who believe in God and his Messenger and then do not doubt, but exert every effort with their wealth and their persons in the cause of God. They are the truthful ones.

(Ibid., 49:16)

O you who believe, shall I show you a bargain that will save you from painful punishment? That you believe in God and his Messenger and exert every effort in the cause of God with your wealth and your persons.'

(Ibid., 61:1–12)

The importance of charity in Islam reflects the Qur'an's overall concern for justice. The purpose of human life is to act as God's agents or stewards, *khulafa'* or 'caliphs', in Qur'anic language. Human beings were created to carry out the divine will, which is to recreate in society the equality all share in the eyes of their Creator. The Qur'an, therefore, calls upon us to 'establish justice,' to 'enjoin good and prevent evil,' common refrains taken to encompass the overall Qur'anic worldview. Working for social justice, therefore, is *islam*, submitting to the divine will. In that context, wealth is seen as a trial or test of human resolve. Poverty is an evil. It, too, is a trial of human fortitude.

136

And we will test you with some fear and hunger and loss of property and lives and produce. But good news for the patient, those who when disaster comes to them say, 'Indeed, we are God's and to him we return.' It is those upon whom are blessings from their Lord and mercy, and it is those who are correctly guided.

(Ibid., 2:156–158)

You will be tested in your wealth and your selves and you will hear much abuse from those who were given the Book before you and from those who are idolaters. But if you are patient and righteous, indeed that is true fortitude.

(Ibid., 3:187)

O you who believe, do not betray God and the Messenger nor betray your trusts knowingly. And know that your wealth and your children are a trial and that with God is a great reward.

(Ibid., 8:28–29; cf. 64:15)

In the face of such tribulations, perseverance is a virtue: 'It is not piety that you turn your faces to the East or the West, but pious ... [are those] who are patient in poverty and strife and in time of war; those who do so are truthful and take protection in God.' (2:178) However, poverty is also an evil to be overcome through charity. Wealth, on the other hand, is not an evil; in the Qur'anic context it is a challenge. Those in poverty are understandably eager to change their situation. Persons of wealth, by contrast, may well be disinclined to interfere with their fortune by relinquishing a part of it. The Qur'an, therefore, shows considerable concern with wealth. It is mentioned over eighty times, most often in verses encouraging charity (expenditures 'in the way of God,' as we have seen) and warning of the dangers of greed. For example:

Indeed, those who are ungrateful [or disbelieve], their wealth and their children will not protect them at all from God['s punishment].

(Ibid., 3:11)

As for those who are ungrateful [or disbelieve], their wealth and their children will not help them a bit against God. These will be the inhabitants of the fire, and in it they will remain.

(Ibid., 3:117)

In the Qur'anic worldview, therefore, if charity is required as a means of achieving the goal of human existence – doing the will of God by working for social justice – then wealth is not properly our own. It is a gift from God and a trial of our virtue, in addition to being necessary to fulfil the divine command to establish justice. In this light, we may understand the human role of stewardship (*khilafat* or 'caliphate'), and the Qur'an's insistence that God alone is the true master of all creation.

> Do you not know that to God belongs the kingship of the heavens and the earth?
>
> (Ibid., 2:108)

> And God owns the heavens and the earth and what is between them. He created what he wants; and God has power over everything.
>
> (Ibid., 5:18; cf. among others: 5:121; 6:74; 7:159; 9:116; 24:42; 25:3; 35:14; 39:7; 57:5)

In fact, the Arabic terms for kingship or sovereignty and ownership are the same (*mulk;* from *malaka,* to possess or to rule). Thus, another way to understand the many verses referring to God as the only true sovereign is that God is the only true owner of wealth: 'His is the ownership [or kingship or sovereignty]' (39:7) of the heavens and earth and all that is in between them. 'Say, "To God belongs all intercession; he is the owner of the heavens and earth, so to him you will return."' (39:45) 'To God belongs ownership of the heavens and earth; he creates what he pleases.' (42:50; cf.: 45:8; 48:15; 64:2; 67:2)

Whether sovereign or owner, the Qur'an insists that God is the only one truly deserving of complete obedience, the only true King: 'Indeed, I am God; there is no god except me, so serve me and perform prayer to remember me.' (20:15) 'So exalted is God, the true sovereign/owner.' (20:115) 'So exalted is God, the true sovereign/owner; there is not God but he, Lord of the sacred throne.' (23:117; cf. among others: 59:24; 62:2.) And we human beings were created to be the stewards of God's domain. The wealth, therefore, that we are given, is truly ours only to the extent that we use it 'in the way of God,' that is, to further the divine will. And we do that by giving our wealth for the well-being of others; the spiritual reward for such charity is ours to keep.

Required charity or almsgiving (*zakat*) in hadith literature

Hadith literature bears out the importance of charity in Islam. It confirms that almsgiving is required and that it is something to which the poor are entitled, reflecting the recognition that wealth is not earned, but rather is a gift given by God as a test, over which we as human beings only bear stewardship: 'Almsgiving is a duty unto you. Alms should be taken from the rich and returned to the poor.'[46] Hadith literature also discusses the requirement of charity even for those without financial or material means.

Muhammad said, 'It is indispensable for every Muslim to give alms.'
The companions asked, 'But if he hath not anything to give?' He said,
'If he hath nothing, he must do a work with his hand, by which to
obtain something, and benefit himself; and give alms with the
remainder.' They said, 'But if he is not able to do that work, to benefit
himself and give alms to others?' The Rasul [Muhammad] said, 'Then
he should assist the needy and oppressed.' They asked, 'What if he is
not able to assist the oppressed?' He said, 'Then he should exhort
people to do good.' They asked, 'And if he cannot?' He said, 'Then let
him withhold himself from doing harm to people; for verily that is alms
and charity for him.'[47]

Because zakat is legally obligatory, hadith literature also establishes the principle of minimum amount (*nisab*) of wealth necessary before one is required to
give a portion of it in charity. This amount varies with the kind of wealth
under consideration. Numerous reports confirm that charity is not payable
unless one has at least five measures (*wasq*) of dates or grains. (The measure
used is generous; although interpretations of what a *wasq* weighs vary, it was
clearly sufficient to support a household for a year.) Similarly, one was not
expected to contribute charity if one owned fewer than five camels, or five
weights (*uqiyas,* or forty dirhams) of silver: 'Abu Sa'id al-Khudri reported
Allah's Messenger (may peace be upon him) as saying: No sadaqah (zakat) is
payable on less than five wasqs of (dates or grains), on less than five
camel-heads and on less than five uqiyas (of silver).'[48]
    Hadith literature also specifies those kinds of wealth upon which the tax
must be paid. Slaves and horses, for example, are not subject to the tax by
agreement of virtually all reports. 'Abu Hurarira reported Allah's Messenger
(may peace be upon him) as saying: No sadaqah [zakat] is due from a Muslim
on his slave or his horse.'[49] These exemptions effectively remove these two –
slaves and horses – from the category of wealth. Regarding slaves, the exemption reflects the Islamic view that human beings are not property as such, even
when they are slaves. Based on Qur'anic injunctions, Islamic law stipulates
that slaves have rights. Some of those rights are of the order of the rights of a
minor within the family, as Joseph Schacht notes: '[T]he Islamic law of slavery
is patriarchal and belongs more to the law of family than to the law of property.'[50] Slaves may own property, must not be mistreated or overworked, and
must be maintained properly. They may sue for failure to abide by those rules
and the court may free the slave if the owner is in flagrant violation of the law.[51]
The exemption of horses from the wealth on which an owner is required to
give a portion in charity results from their being considered essential in doing
the work of God: supporting oneself and one's dependants, defending the
community against attack, and spreading true belief. If, however, horses are
being raised for show or trade – that is, to make a profit, then they are subject
to zakat.

The horses are of three kinds. They are a source of reward to a person, they are a covering to a person, and they are a burden to a person. [In the first case] a person would get reward who rears them for the sake of Allah and trains them for him and nothing disappears in their stomachs but Allah would record for him a good deed. And if they were to graze in the meadow, they would eat nothing but Allah would record for him a reward. And if they were to drink water from the canal, with every drop that would disappear in their stomachs there would be reward [for the owner]. He went on describing till a reward was mentioned for their urine and dung. And if they pranced a course or two, there would be recorded a reward for every pace that they covered. As for one for whom they are a covering, he is the man who rears them for honor and dignity but does not forget the right of their backs and their stomachs, in plenty and adversity. As regards one for whom they are a burden, he is that who rears them for vainglory and showing off to the people; for him they are a burden.[52]

Hadith literature also specifies another kind of zakat, that which must be paid at the end of the month of Ramadan (the month of fasting). The traditionist (hadith-compiler) Muslim lists a number of reports claiming that all Muslims – male and female, slave and free – must pay the *zakat al-fitr* (zakat for breaking of the Ramadan fast) in dates and barley or wheat: ' 'Abdullah b. 'Umar reported that the Messenger of Allah (may peace be upon him) ordered the (payment of) zakat al-fitr one [portion] of dates, or one [portion] of barley.'[53] There follows some discussion about the possibility of substituting a portion of quality wheat for the barley, as well as the possibility of including raisins or cheese in the offering. Reports are also included specifying that the offering should be made before going to the Fitr prayer, in order to allow the poor – who would receive the offerings – to participate in the celebrations.

More substantial discussion in hadith literature concerns the offense of failure to pay zakat. According to one telling of an account authenticated by multiple authorities:

Abu Huraira reported Allah's Messenger (may peace be upon him) as saying: No owner of the treasure who does not pay zakat [would be spared] but [his hoards] would be heated in the fire of hell and these would be made into plates and with these his sides, his forehead would be cauterized till Allah would pronounce judgment among his servants during a day, the extent of which would be fifty thousand years. He would then see his path, leading either to paradise or to hell. And no owner of the camels who does not pay zakat [would be spared] but a soft sandy plain would be set for him and they [the camels] would be made to pass over him till the last of them would be made to return, till Allah would pronounce judgment among his servants during a day the extent of which would be fifty thousand years. He would then see his path leading him to paradise or leading him to hell. And no owner of the [cattle] and goats who does not pay zakat [would be spared] but a soft sandy plain would be set for him, he would find none of them missing with twisted horns, without horns, or with broken horns, and they will gore him with their horns and trample him with their hoofs and they would be made to pass over him till the last of them would be made to return till Allah would pronounce judgment among his servants, during a day the extent of which would be fifty thousand years, and he would see the paths leading to paradise or to hell. Suhail said: I do not know whether he made mention of the cows. They said: Messenger of Allah, what about the horses? He said: The horses have goodness in their foreheads [or he said] or goodness is ingrained in the foreheads of the horses [Suhail said: I am in doubt as to what was actually said] up till the Day of Judgment.[54]

The report then concludes with a disclaimer concerning kinds of wealth not specified as subject to zakat payments, and a reiteration of the merit of good works:

They said: Messenger of Allah, what about asses? He said: Allah has not revealed to me anything in regard to it except his one comprehensive verse: 'He who does an atom's weight of good will see it [rewarded], and he who does an atom's weight of evil will see it [punished]' ([99:]7).[55]

This report not only allows for the kind of discretionary or voluntary (supererogatory) charity on items not covered in specific legislation, but encourages it. This issue will be discussed below.

The responsibility to return a share of one's wealth to the community is further stressed in hadith reports listed under categories detailing the punishments due those who fail to contribute zakat. These reports are virtually identical with those in the categories dealing with the seriousness of the responsibility to give charity. For example:

Abu Huraira reported Allah's Messenger (may peace be upon him) as saying: If any owner of gold or silver does not pay what is due [from] him, when the Day of Resurrection would come, plates of fire would be beaten out for him; these would then be heated in the fire of hell and his sides, his forehead and his back would be cauterized with them. Whenever these cool down, [the process is] repeated during the day the extent of which would be fifty thousand years, until judgment is pronounced among servants, and he sees whether his path is to take him to paradise or to hell. It was said: Messenger of Allah, what about the camel? He [the Holy Prophet] said: If any owner of the camel does not pay what is due [from] him, and of his due in that [camel] is [also] to milk it on the day when it comes down to water, when the Day of Resurrection comes a soft sandy plan would be set for him, an extensive as possible, [he will find] that not a single young one is missing, and they will trample him with their hoofs and bite him with their mouths. As often as the first of them passes him, the last of them would be made to return during a day the extent of which would be fifty thousand years, until judgment is pronounced among servants and he sees whether his path is to take him to Paradise or to Hell. It was [again] said: Messenger of Allah, what about cows [cattle] and sheep? He said: If any owner of the cattle and sheep does not pay what is due on them, when the Day of Resurrection comes a soft sandy plain would be spread for them, he will find none of them missing, with twisted horns, without horns or with a broken horn, and they will gore him with their horns and trample him with their hoofs. As often as the first of them passes him the last of them would be made to return to him during a day the extent of which would be fifty thousand years, until judgment would be pronounced among his servants. And he would be shown his path – leading him to paradise or to hell.[56]

The language used in this hadith is clearly meant to impress even the simplest listener with the seriousness of the offense of not contributing to community support. Some of the imagery is drawn from the Qur'an, especially that describing cauterization with heated metal plates. Among the Qur'an's descriptions of the painful punishment earned by selfish people is the following:

> And those who hoard gold and silver and do not spend it in the way of God, give them the news of painful punishment, the day they will be heated in the fire of hell, then their foreheads and sides will be branded. This is what you hoarded for yourselves, so now taste what you were hoarding.
>
> (Qur'an, 9: 34–35)

The mention of milking camels on the day when it comes to water is a reference to the custom of sharing milk with the poor when Bedouin (nomadic desert herders) bring their animals from the desert to an oasis; this generosity is also described as a duty, avoidance of which is punishable. Again, the seriousness of the offense of greed – the opposite of contributing zakat – is stressed.

> Abu Dharr reported: I went to the Apostle of Allah (may peace be upon him) and he was sitting under the shade of the Ka'ba. As he saw me he said: By the Lord of the Ka'ba, they are the losers … .I said: Messenger

142

of Allah, let my father be ransom for you, who are they [the losers]? He said: They are those having a huge amount of wealth except so and so and [those who spend their wealth generously on them whom they find in front of them, behind them and on their right side and on their left side] and they are a few. And no owner of camels, or cattle or goat and sheep, who does not pay zakat [would be spared punishment] but these [camels, cattle, goats and sheep] would come on the Day of Resurrection wearing more flesh and would gore him with their horns and trample them with their hooves. And when the last one would pass away, the first one would return [to trample him] till judgment would be pronounced among people.[57]

In yet another series of reports, the punishment for those who hoard wealth is described in even more highly picturesque language:

Ahnaf b. Qaid reported: While I was in the company of the [elites] of [the leading tribe of Mecca], Abu Dharr came there and he was saying: Give glad tidings to the hoarders of riches that their backs would be branded [so deeply] that [the hot iron] would come out of their sides, and when the backs of their necks would be branded, it would come out of their foreheads. He [Abu Dharr] then went away and sat down. I asked who he was. They said: he is Abu Dharr. I went to him and said to him: What is this that I heard from you which you were saying before? He said: I said nothing but only that which I heard from their Prophet (may peace be upon him). I again said: What do you say about this gift [given to me by a rich person]? He said: Take it, for today it is a help. But when it becomes a price for your religion, then abandon it.[58]

The horrific punishments described for failure to share one's wealth, reported in great detail in numerous collections, bear witness to the importance of charity in Islamic practice.

Required charity or almsgiving (zakat) in legal codes

The general principle, established by the Qur'an and sound hadith literature, is that Muslims are responsible for the well-being of those who cannot support themselves for whatever reason. This principle was expressed succinctly by the eleventh-century Andalusian (Spanish) jurist Ibn Hazm:

It is the obligation of the rich in every society to fulfil the needs of the poor. The government has to compel them to undertake this if zakat is insufficient for their needs. The poor must be insured for their necessary food, for their winter and summer clothing, and for a shelter

143

which is capable of warding off harm from them due to rains, cold and heat and which gives them privacy from the public eye.[59]

In order to realize this principle on a practical level, zakat was treated as a tax within the early Muslim community. Collectors of the tax were sent out and hadith literature includes reports calling upon Muslims to treat the collectors well and to satisfy them. Failure to pay zakat was considered a grievous offense, as indicated by the dire punishments described. The most serious punishments were described as taking place in the eternal world of the afterlife in this formative era before society ever conceived of a distinction between spiritual or religious and civil crimes. Yet collection had to take place in the secular world. Therefore, based on the principles articulated in the Qur'an and the precedents established in hadith literature, Islamic law carefully articulated details concerning minimum amounts of wealth and the types of wealth upon which zakat was due, and in what proportion.

The specification of details concerning the collection of zakat are a perfect example of analogical reasoning in Islamic jurisprudence. The Qur'an says, for example, that zakat on specific agricultural produce is to be paid on the day of harvesting.

> And he is the one who produces gardens, trellised and untrellised, and the date-palm and all the diverse crops, and olives and pomegranates, alike and unlike. Eat of their fruit when they produce, and pay its due on the day of harvest and do not be wasteful. Indeed, God does not love those who are wasteful.
>
> (Qur'an, 6:142)

From this it was determined that zakat is to be paid annually. But what about the types of wealth upon which zakat is due? We have seen above that the Prophet exempted horses from taxation, although camels, sheep, goats and cows are subject to the zakat. Al-Shafi'i inferred from this distinction the principle that zakat must be paid on some goods, but not all. He then went on to reason concerning zakat taxation on agricultural products, incorporating hadith material as he did so.

> As to men who possess sown and planted products such as palm-dates and grapes, [Prophet Muhammad] ordered payment of alms on both on [the basis of] a rough estimate [of the value of each tree]. The rate of payment was one-tenth [of the total value] if [the land] were watered by rain or from a spring and half of the one-tenth if it were watered by wells.
>
> Some of the scholars held by analogy to palm-trees and grapes that [zakat] on olive trees [should be one-tenth as well].

Since men possess crops of varied produce other than palm-dates, grapes and olives, such as walnuts, almonds, figs, and others, which the [Prophet] has exempted from payment, we concluded that God imposed the payment of alms on some crops, but not on all.

Shafi'i said: Men have produced wheat, barley, millet and similar products, on which, we are told, the [Prophet] ordered the payment [of zakat]. By analogy of wheat and barley, alms have been paid on grain, *sult* [a kind of barley], '*alas* [a kind of wheat], rice, and all other products which men have produced and eaten, such as bread, [various kinds of flour], chick-peas and [lentils] which may be made into flour or bread, etc., in the same way as the Prophet ordered the payment of the alms on similar products which men produced for food.[60]

Al-Shafi'i concludes his discussion by noting that various kinds of spices are excluded from zakat taxation, even though people grow them, since neither the Prophet nor his successors said that they should be taxed. This follows the precedent established above in the hadith report concerning asses; since nothing authoritative had been revealed about them, no charity tax would be levied on them. But the Prophet did order that silver be subject to zakat. Based either on analogical reasoning or on a hadith report that has not survived, al-Shafi'i says that Muslims agree that zakat is also due on gold. But the analogy does not apply, he claims, to other metals, 'such as brass, iron and lead,' because these are not 'used as standards for prices in all countries, and all other metals [nor may] all other metals ... be purchased by them on the basis of a specific weight at a certain time.'[61] He also reports that precious jewels like rubies and chryso-lite are exempt, even though they are more valuable than precious metals, because 'they are possessed by a special [class] and are not used as a medium of exchange – because they are not measures of price ... .'[62]

Regarding the amounts to be paid on precious minerals, al-Shafi'i relates a hadith report in which the Prophet specified one-fifth of their value, paid at the time they are brought forth from the earth. He concludes, confirming that he is reasoning analogically based on precedents established in sound hadith reports: 'If it were not for the evidence of the [hadith reports], all goods would have been treated on an equal footing on [the basis of] the literal meaning of the Qur'an, and the alms would have been imposed on all, not on some only.'[63]

As the legal schools developed, further gradations were incorporated, although not uniformly. There was general agreement on the kinds of live-stock, agricultural products, and minerals upon which zakat was due, as expressed by al-Shafi'i, and the obligation to pay zakat on gold and silver was also extended to currency and property acquired through trade conducted for profit. The schools disagree, however, on whether or not and to what extent debtors are required to pay zakat, and on the percentage of each kind of wealth that constitutes proper zakat. There are also differences of opinion on such details as the rates of taxation for crops watered by various means. However, the schools agree that those entitled to benefit from zakat are those specified in the Qur'an: 'the poor and the needy, and those who work for them, and for those whose hearts are to be reconciled, and for slaves, and debtors, and in the path of God, and for travelers.' (9:60) Again, there are slight variations among the schools concerning the specific applications of these categories. But there is general agreement that 'the poor and the needy' are those who do not have enough to be eligible to pay the zakat, and 'those who work for them' are the zakat collectors. Giving from zakat funds to 'those whose hearts are to be reconciled' is generally believed to have applied in the early days of Islam, but to have fallen out of usefulness once the community achieved great strength, although the verse has not been abrogated. The use of zakat funds for slaves is universally agreed to mean that it is to be used for the freeing of slaves, and there is also agreement that zakat funds may be used to help people get out of debt, and help stranded travelers return to their homes. Expenditure 'in the path of God' is universally agreed in the legal texts to mean primarily the support of jihad.

Voluntary charity (*sadaqah*) in the Qur'an

Much of the Qur'anic guidance concerning required charity applies in general terms as well to voluntary charity. In fact, the key verse specifying the recipients of zakat ('the poor and the needy and those who work for them, and for those whose hearts are to be reconciled and for slaves and those in debt, and in the way of God, and for travelers;' 9:60) actually uses the term sadaqah. Nevertheless, there is a distinction between required and supererogatory charity. As we saw, required charity (zakat) is meritorious, and failure to pay it incurs dire punishments in the afterlife. The texts' treatment of voluntary charity (sadaqah), by contrast, stresses the reward to be earned by those who give. For example: 'Those who spend their wealth by night and by day, secretly and openly, their reward is with their Lord; they have nothing to fear, nor shall they grieve.' (2:275) By definition, there is no specific punishment for failure to perform a voluntary act.

Voluntary charity not only earns reward in the afterlife, but it is described in the Qur'an – along with fasting – as effective in expiation for sins. For example, the *Hajj* (pilgrimage to Mecca) is required for those who are able, at least once in a lifetime. But there is great merit associated with performing the Hajj; missing it as a result of physical or financial disability means that one misses a chance to earn that merit. The Qur'an therefore guides those who cannot perform the pilgrimage that they may gain merit also through fasting or charity or offering a sacrifice.

And complete the Hajj [required pilgrimage] and the 'Umrah [voluntary pilgrimage] for God but if you are detained, then [offer] whatever gift you can, and do not shave your heads [part of the pilgrimage ritual] until the gift reaches its place. And whoever among you is sick or has a head injury, then make up for it by fast or charity or a sacrifice.

(Qu'ran, 2:197)

Similarly, in the chapter entitled 'Repentance', when the Qur'an discusses the failings of those who claim to follow the teachings of Prophet Muhammad but then 'mix a good work with another evil,' charity is recommended as a way to bring the offenders back into a proper relationship with God: 'Take from their wealth some charity to cleanse and purify them and pray for them.' (9:103)

In this sense sadaqah, like the zakat, is associated with the notion of purifying or sanctifying wealth. As we saw above, in the Qur'anic worldview wealth is given to individuals to test their virtue. Those who have been tested with poverty have a share in the wealth, and until those with wealth share it with the less fortunate, wealth is not divinely sanctioned. However, the root meaning of the term sadaqah is different from that of zakat, 'to be pure'. Sadaqah comes from a term meaning 'to be honest, true, or sincere,' and this meaning is evident in some of its Qur'anic uses. For example, 'So God knows those who are truthful and he knows those who are liars.' (29:4; cf. 9:43) Indeed, the term is used in this way when referring to God and the Prophet Muhammad: 'This is what God and his Messenger promised us and God and his Messenger were truthful.' (33:23) 'Say, "God was truthful so follow the religion of Abraham, the rightly-guided and he was not among the idolaters." ' (3:96) 'This is what the Merciful promised and the messengers were truthful.' (36:53) Interestingly, sadaqah is from the same root as some of the words used for dower (*sadaq* or *saduqah*), or bridal gift, as well as the terms for friend and friendship. So the word seems to carry the sense of demonstrating sincerity in actions that are not forced.

Still, as with zakat, the merit for sadaqah is not guaranteed: charity in and of itself is not sufficient to please God. The Qur'an chastises those who give charity but who are also cruel or commit other offenses:

Those who spend their wealth in the way of God and then do not follow what they have spent with insult or injury, for them their reward is with their Lord. They have nothing to fear nor shall their grieve.

Honorable speech and forgiveness are better than charity followed by injury.

O you who believe, do not invalidate your charity by insult and injury like the one who spends his wealth to be seen by people and does not believe in God and the last day. He is like a smooth rock with soil, and a flood hits it, leaving it lifeless. They have no power over what they earn and God does not guide ungrateful people.

And those who spend their wealth seeking to please God and to strengthen themselves are like a garden on a hill, and a flood comes and it produces double, and if no rain falls on it, then dew, and God sees what you do.

(Ibid., 2:263–66)

Thus, as with all prescribed actions in Islam, proper intention is essential in order for the performance of the action to be meritorious.

Voluntary charity (*sadaqah*) in hadith literature

It is in hadith literature that the distinction between obligatory and voluntary charity becomes clear. For one thing, sadaqah is described as including all good or kindly acts; it need not be a gift of a material or financial nature:

> Aa'id b. Abu Burda reported on the authority of his grandfather that the Apostle of Allah (may peace be upon him) said: Giving sadaqa is essential for every Muslim. It was said [to him]: What do you say of him who does not find [the means] to do so? He said: Then let him assist the needy, the aggrieved. It was said: What do you say of one who cannot even do this? He said: Then he should enjoin what is reputable or good. He said: What about him if he cannot do that? He [the Holy Prophet] said: He should then abstain from evil, for verily that is sadaqa on his behalf.[64]

Secondly, hadith literature distinguishes voluntary from obligatory alms in its description of the ideal recipients of this charity. We have seen that the recipients of zakat were identified in the Qur'an (9:60), and codified in Islamic legal texts (the poor and those who work for them, for instance). But hadith literature stresses the family as the most deserving recipients of sadaqah. For example:

> Thauban reported Allah's Messenger (may peace be upon him) as saying: The most excellent dinar is one that a person spends on his family, and the dinar which he spends on his animal in Allah's path, and the dinar he spends on his companions in Allah's path. Abu Qilaba [one of the narrators] said: He [the narrator] started with family, and then Abu Qilaba said: Who is the person with greater reward than a person who spends on young members of his family [and thus] preserves [saves them from want] [and by virtue of which] Allah brings profit for them and makes them rich.

148

Abu Huraira reported Allah's Messenger (may peace be upon him) as saying: Of the dinar you spend as a contribution in Allah's path, or to set free a slave, or as a sadaqa given to a needy [person], or to support your family, the one yielding the greatest reward is that which you spend on your family.

Khaithama reported: While we were sitting in the company of 'Abdullah b. 'Umar there came in his steward. He [Ibn 'Umar] said: Have you supplied the provision to the slaves? He said: No. Upon this he said: Go and give [the provision] to them, for the Messenger of Allah (may peace be upon him) has said: This sin is enough for a man that he withholds the subsistence from one whose master he is.[65]

Anas b. Malik is reported as saying: Abu Talha was the one among the [supporters of Prophet Muhammad at] Medina who possessed the largest property and among his property he valued most was his garden known as Bairaha' which was opposite the mosque, and the Messenger of Allah (may peace be upon him) often visited it and he drank of its sweet water. When this verse was revealed: 'You will never attain righteousness till you give freely of what you love' [3:93], Abu Talha got up and, going to Allah's Messenger (may peace be upon him), said: Allah says in his Book: 'You will never attain righteousness till you give freely of what you love,' and the dearest of my property is Bairaha' so I give it as sadaqa to God from whom I hope for reward for it and the treasure with Allah; so spend it, Messenger of Allah, on whatever purpose you deem it proper. The messenger of Allah (may peace be upon him) said: Bravo! that is profit-earning property. I have heard what you have said, but I think you should spend it on your nearest relatives. So Abu Talha distributed it among the nearest relatives and his cousins on his father's side.[66]

Sadaqah, voluntary charity, therefore, is equivalent to simple generosity. As such, it cannot be regulated by earthly law as zakat can be, but it is highly meritorious. Believers are therefore encouraged to be generous now, lest they lose the chance:

Haritha b. Wahb reported Allah's Messenger (may peace be upon him) as saying: 'give sadaqah for a time is about to come when a person would walk with alms' and the one to whom it is to be given would say: 'had you brought it yesterday, I would have accepted it. For the present I do not need it.' [And the giver of sadaqah] would not find anyone to accept it.[67]

3 ALMSGIVING IN JUDAISM

For Judaism the Torah makes ample provision for support of the poor. Almsgiving is framed in two distinct ways, particular and general. First, support for the poor to begin with, in the laws of the Pentateuchal book of Leviticus, forms a chapter in the story of the relationship of the holy people, Israel, to the Land of Israel. The law of the Torah presupposes that support for the poor (the widow, the orphan) proceeds in an orderly and regular manner, and the provisions of Scripture are fully articulated in the Oral Torah's rules on the subject. The poor claim a share in the produce of the Land of Israel, and God has assigned that share to them; it is part of what Israel owes to God in response to its possession of the Land of Israel. Indeed, the poor form a scheduled caste, along with the priests and the Levites, for the support of whom God has a special interest. That explains how, in line with what was stated at the outset of this chapter, the poor are supported not as a votive act but an obligatory one, a portion of the crops of the Land being reserved for them.

But a second conception of almsgiving – a more abstract one – registers as well, laying stress on the supererogatory, not only the obligatory, act of philanthropy. That is expressed in a peculiar usage, in which the word for 'acquire merit' is used for an act of philanthropy, so that a poor person – as in the stories we shall consider in a moment – addresses a donor in the language, 'acquire merit through me' which bears the exact meaning, 'give me alms.' A study of this second, more abstract concept of almsgiving is more readily accessible than the concept particular to Judaism of the poor as God's surrogates on the Land in particular.

The theology of almsgiving comes to expression in the larger concept expressed in the language the needy use when they approach donors. They say (in the Talmudic stories), '*zakhé bi*,' which uses the root for the word, *zekhut*, roughly translated as 'merit,' and the expression thus yields something like, 'acquire merit through me [by giving me alms].' Exactly how 'merit' is acquired in the philanthropic transaction then defines the terms of the specific transaction of almsgiving: what is it that God notes and to which God responds in the transaction of philanthropy? The answer introduces us to the votive, not obligatory, dimension of almsgiving in Judaism. In the framework of this answer, philanthropy transcends almsgiving in a narrow sense and encompasses all actions of self-sacrifice for the other, deeds of placing the needs of the other above one's own interests. These acts of self-abnegation, whether giving a poor person scarce resources, which one needs for one's own use, or giving up as an act of self-surrender one's own advantage in some other-than-material relationship, attract God's interest; uncoerced acts of love, transcending the narrow requirements of the law, win his respect and response.

Here is how the Talmud of the Land of Israel represents the act of philanthropy. In all three instances that follow, defining what the individual must do to gain zekhut, the point is that the deeds of the heroes of the story make them worthy of having their prayers answered, which is a mark of the working of zekhut. It is deeds beyond the strict requirements of the Torah, and even the limits of the law altogether, that transform the hero into a holy man, whose holiness served just like that of a sage marked as a holy man by knowledge of the Torah. The following stories should not be understood as expressions of the mere sentimentality of the clerks concerning the lower orders, for they deny in favor of a single action of surpassing power the sages' lifelong devotion to what they held to be the highest value: knowledge of the Torah.

> F. A certain man came before one of the relatives of R. Yannai. He said to him, 'Rabbi, attain zekhut through me [by giving me charity].'
>
> G. He said to him, 'And didn't your father leave you money?'
>
> H. He said to him, 'No.'
>
> I. He said to him, 'Go and collect what your father left in deposit with others.'
>
> J. He said to him, 'I have heard concerning property my father deposited with others that it was gained by violence [so I don't want it].'
>
> K. He said to him, 'You are worthy of praying and having your prayers answered.'
>
> (Y. Taanit, 1:4.I)

The point of K, of course, is self-evidently a reference to the possession of entitlement to supernatural favor, and it is gained through deeds that the law of the Torah cannot require but must favor: what one does on one's own volition, beyond the measure of the law. Here I see the opposite of sin. A sin is what one has done by one's own volition beyond all limits of the law. An act that generates zekhut for the individual is the counterpart and opposite: what one does by one's own volition that also is beyond all requirements of the law.

> L. A certain ass-driver appeared before the rabbis [the context requires: in a dream] and prayed, and rain came. The rabbis sent and brought him and said to him, 'What is your trade?'
>
> M. He said to them, 'I am an ass-driver.'
>
> N. They said to him, 'And how do you conduct your business?'

O. He said to them, 'One time I rented my ass to a certain woman, and she was weeping on the way, and I said to her, "What's with you?" and she said to me, "The husband of that woman [me] is in prison [for debt], and I wanted to see what I can do to free him." So I sold my ass and I gave her the proceeds, and I said to her, "Here is your money, free your husband, but do not sin [by becoming a prostitute to raise the necessary funds].'"

P. They said to him, 'You are worthy of praying and having your prayers answered.'

(Ibid.)

The ass-driver clearly has a powerful lien on Heaven, so that his prayers are answered, even while those of others are not. What he did to get that entitlement? He did what no law could demand: impoverished himself to save the woman from a 'fate worse than death'.

Q. In a dream of R. Abbahu, Mr. Pentakaka ['Five sins'] appeared, who prayed that rain would come, and it rained. R. Abbahu sent and summoned him. He said to him, 'What is your trade?'

R. He said to him, 'Five sins does that man [I] do every day, [for I am a pimp:] hiring whores, cleaning up the theater, bringing home their garments for washing, dancing, and performing before them.'

S. He said to him, 'And what sort of decent thing have you ever done?'

T. He said to him, 'One day that man [I] was cleaning the theater, and a woman came and stood behind a pillar and cried. I said to her, "What's with you?" And she said to me, "That woman's [my] husband is in prison, and I wanted to see what I can do to free him," so I sold my bed and cover, and I gave the proceeds to her. I said to her, "Here is your money, free your husband, but do not sin."'

U. He said to him, 'You are worthy of praying and having your prayers answered.'

(Ibid.)

Q moves us still further, since the named man has done everything sinful that one can do, and, more to the point, he does it every day. So the singularity of the act of zekhut, which suffices if done only once, encompasses its power to outweigh a life of sin – again, an act of zekhut as the mirror-image and opposite of sin. Here again, the single act of saving a woman from a 'fate worse than death' has sufficed.

152

V. A pious man from Kefar Imi appeared [in a dream] to the rabbis. He prayed for rain and it rained. The rabbis went up to him. His householders told them that he was sitting on a hill. They went out to him, saying to him, 'Greetings,' but he did not answer them.

W. He was sitting and eating, and he did not say to them, 'You break bread too.'

X. When he went back home, he made a bundle of faggots and put his cloak on top of the bundle [instead of on his shoulder].

Y. When he came home, he said to his household [wife], 'These rabbis are here [because] they want me to pray for rain. If I pray and it rains, it is a disgrace for them, and if not, it is a profanation of the Name of Heaven. But come, you and I will go up [to the roof] and pray. If it rains, we shall tell them, "We are not worthy to pray and have our prayers answered."'

Z. They went up and prayed and it rained.

AA. They came down to them [and asked], 'Why have the rabbis troubled themselves to come here today?'

BB. They said to him, 'We wanted you to pray so that it would rain.'

CC. He said to them, 'Now do you really need my prayers? Heaven already has done its miracle.'

DD. They said to him, 'Why, when you were on the hill, did we say hello to you, and you did not reply?'

EE. He said to them, 'I was then doing my job. Should I then interrupt my concentration [on my work]?'

FF. They said to him, 'And why, when you sat down to eat, did you not say to us "You break bread too"?'

GG. He said to them, 'Because I had only my small ration of bread. Why would I have invited you to eat by way of mere flattery [when I knew I could not give you anything at all]?'

HH. They said to him, 'And why when you came to go down, did you put your cloak on top of the bundle?'

II. He said to them, 'Because the cloak was not mine. It was borrowed for use at prayer. I did not want to tear it.'

JJ. They said to him, 'And why, when you were on the hill, did your wife wear dirty clothes, but when you came down from the mountain, did she put on clean clothes?'

KK. He said to them, 'When I was on the hill, she put on dirty clothes, so that no one would gaze at her. But when I came home from the hill, she put on clean clothes, so that I would not gaze on any other woman.'

LL. They said to him, 'It is well that you pray and have your prayers answered.'

(Ibid.)

The pious man of V, finally, enjoys the recognition of the sages by reason of his lien upon Heaven, able as he is to pray and bring rain. What has so endowed him with zekhut? Acts of punctiliousness of a moral order: concentrating on his work, avoiding an act of dissimulation, integrity in the disposition of a borrowed object, his wife's concern not to attract other men and her equal concern to make herself attractive to her husband. None of these stories refers explicitly to zekhut; all of them tell us about what it means to enjoy not an entitlement by inheritance but a lien accomplished by one's own supererogatory acts of restraint.

Now we grasp the context in which almsgiving finds its natural location. Almsgiving stands for those acts of will consisting of submission, on one's own, to the will of Heaven. What we cannot by will impose, we can by will evoke. What we cannot accomplish through coercion, we can achieve through submission. God will do for us what we cannot do for ourselves, when we do for God what God cannot make us do. When the sages wished to conceive of a reciprocal response between Heaven and Israel on earth, beyond the acts of devotion required by the Torah but all the same defined by it, they could find no better example than almsgiving. Heaven cannot force us to do those types of deeds that yield zekhut, and that, story after story suggests, is the definition of a deed that generates zekhut: doing what we ought to do but do not have to do. But then, we cannot coerce Heaven to do what we want done either, for example, by carrying out the commandments. These are obligatory, but do not obligate Heaven.

Whence then our lien on Heaven? It is through deeds of a supererogatory character – to which Heaven responds by deeds of a supererogatory character: supernatural favor to this one, who through deeds of ingratiation of the other or self-abnegation or restraint exhibits the attitude that in Heaven precipitates a counterpart attitude, hence generating zekhut, rather than to that one, who does not. The simple fact that rabbis cannot pray and bring rain, but a simple ass-driver can, tells the whole story. The relationship measured by zekhut – Heaven's response by an act of uncoerced favor to a person's uncoerced gift, for example, act of gentility, restraint, or self-abnegation – contains an element of unpredictability for which appeal to the zekhut inherited from ancestors accounts. So while I cannot coerce heaven, I can through zekhut gain acts of favor from Heaven, and that is by doing what Heaven cannot require of me. Heaven then responds to my attitude in carrying out my duties – and more than my duties. That act of pure disinterest – giving the woman my means of livelihood – is the one that gains for me Heaven's deepest interest.

Now we come to almsgiving in its more conventional framework and how, in Judaism, that abstraction comes to concrete expression in obligatory law. In line with the conception of zekhut attached to the giving of alms, which exemplifies the truly right relationship with God, we realize that philanthropy is not a personal or individual action, and it is not done merely out of the goodness of one's heart. Rather, support for the poor in the halakhah engages the entire community of holy Israel. It is not deemed a principally individual activity, though every person bears responsibility, but a public and collective duty. A tractate of the Mishnah (extending into the Tosefta and the Talmud of the Land of Israel)[68] systematically defines the public obligations to the poor that are incumbent on the society's units of production, assumed to be the farmers. This is part of a still larger exposition of how society must support other scheduled castes besides the poor, specifically, the priests, the Levites, and, in its context, Jerusalem as well (in that instance, by making sure that a steady flow of food reached the holy place).

In the halakhah the poor constitute legitimate recipients of the produce of the Land of Israel. The main rules express a theory of what it means for Israelite householders to possess the Land in particular. Support for the poor, like support for the priesthood and Levites, underscores God's ownership and reinforces the provisional character of the householder's possession. For the landless – the priesthood, the Levites, and the poor – God sets aside what is coming to him from the produce of the Land. That equalizes Israel in relationship to the Land. Some possess, others do not, portions of the Land, but all gain what they need from its produce; the householders then hold what they have on sufferance, covenantally. In that way those either not 'enlandised' with Israel to begin with or dispossessed of their portion of the Land later on gain a position within that holy community that is nourished – and given definition – by the Land.

God accords to all three components of the social order part of his portion of the crop, giving them a stake in the Land and making up for their not possessing the Land as (by definition of the halakhah) do the householders. The poor in this context represent a legitimate, important component of the social order, not a social burden. Like the priests, they represent a way in which Israel relates to God; but it is a different way from that of the priests'. At the end of this chapter, I shall specify what as a religious classification the poor embody, as distinct from the householders and the priests – and I shall show that the sages themselves defined matters in just this way. So the halakhah, once again, emerges as a statement in the language of social norms of a well-crafted theological system of surpassing simplicity and purity: an entire community living with God.

That theological statement should not obscure the quotidian structure set in place actually to care for the poor in their own circumstances, and not as a medium of sociotheological conviction. When we deal with support for the poor in its own, this-worldly terms, the halakhah makes provision in practical ways. That is through the soup-kitchen and the dole, such as the concluding unit of the halakhah takes up. The soup-kitchen provides food, the dole, emergency support for transients, and long-term support for local residents.

It follows that the issue of economic entitlement takes a subordinate position. The food given out in the dole and the soup kitchen serves a practical purpose and does not exhibit marks of God's intervention, as selection of produce for the gifts to the poor does. Merely to support the priesthood and the poor, the elaborate provisions of sanctification of the Land's produce are hardly required, as the halakhah of the dole and the soup-kitchen for the poor makes abundantly clear. That food is not subject to divine selection nor removed from human ownership and even the significations of personal possession, as is the case with the food for the poor that is provided by the halakhah out of the householder's crops.

The presence of the poor, rather, forms the occasion for the householder giving a powerful signal of his relinquishing possession (not merely ownership) of the Land and subordinating his possession of it to God's ownership. The householder tastes landlessness by being dis-enlandised, on the one hand, or by relinquishing what he has harvested but lost on the other. In both classes of gifts to the poor, the upshot is the same: the householder no longer subjects to his will the produce of his own labor on his own land. Ownership is compromised, possession replaced by dispossession.

But in so defining almsgiving as a matter of public policy, the halakhah of the Oral Torah built upon the commandments of the Written Torah. Scripture forms the starting point: the pe'ah-portion – a part of a field left unharvested, specified at Lev. 19:9, gleanings at the same verse, forgotten produce at Deut. 24:19–20, the separated grapes at Lev. 19:10, defective clusters at Lev. 19:10, poorman's tithe at Deut. 26:12–13, and the definition of the poor at Lev. 19:10, Deut. 24:19, 21. Moses made provision for the poor in an interesting way, specifically involving two distinct but related principles: first, through Moses God insisted that the farmers do not thoroughly reap their harvest, picking every last olive from the tree and grape from the vine; rather, they are to leave over part of the crop for the poor, just as they were to designate part of the crop for the support of the priests, the Levites, and Jerusalem. So the first principle is that philanthropy (and not merely 'almsgiving') represents sharing abundance that is owed in the end to God.

The halakhah knows four classes of produce reserved by God for the support of the poor, and, as usual, the Tosefta provides a convenient handbook. Matters are systematized by reference to the taxonomic traits of what is given and why. Thus the construction – a two-dimensional grid – is divided by the classification of the source: vineyard, grain-field, fruit-tree at the vertical lines, the classification of the character of the produce – neglected, imperfect – at the horizontals:

T.2:13 There are four gifts that must be designated for the poor from the produce of a vineyard:

(1) separated grapes,

(2) forgotten sheaves,

(3) pe'ah,

(4) and defective clusters.

There are three gifts that must be designated for the poor from a field of grain:

(1) gleanings,

(2) forgotten sheaves,

(3) and pe'ah.

There are two gifts that must be designated for the poor from the fruit of a tree:

(1) forgotten sheaves,

(2) and pe'ah.

None of these gifts to the poor may be given to a specific poor person as a favor. Even a poor Israelite – they take any produce given to him as a favor from his hand. But any other gifts, which are designated for the priesthood, such as the shoulder, the two cheeks, and the stomach of a sacrificial animal which are given to the Levites as simple gifts, may be given to a specific Levite or priest as a favor. And the householder may give them to whichever priest he wishes. They may not take a priestly gift from a priest to whom it has been given as a favor, nor a Levitical gift from a Levite to whom it has been given as a favor.

The Tosefta's formulation covers the topic of pe'ah, and points toward one dimension of the problematic that guides the sages' reading, with its emphasis that none of these gifts to the poor may be given to a specific poor person as a favor.

The difference between gifts to the poor and those to the priesthood then emerges: the former must be treated as ownerless, assigned to the entire class of the poor, not to a specific person. The halakhah then treats the gifts to the poor in the category of produce in the Sabbatical year, which must be treated as ownerless. Part of the produce distinguished through the passage of the Sabbatical cycle, moreover, poorman's tithe, like second tithe, is subject to God's very particular regulations. Second tithe is preserved and eaten in the holy city; poorman's tithe is selected for the poor by God's intervention into the harvesting process. The disposition of both kinds of tithe then is subject to God's will in very particular ways, and in both cases, God dictates the rules that govern possession of what none in Israel rightly owns at all.

Second, what is assigned to the scheduled castes is not deliberately designated at all but comes about as a matter of chance. If, for instance, a farmer forgets to collect a sheaf of grain, he may not go back for it; the act of forgetting is deemed the result of someone else's intention, namely, God's. The parallel is how grain is designated as the priests' and Levites' share. That is not to be weighed or measured but to represent an act of casual disposition. At the altar of the Temple, when the priests receive their share of the beast, the blood of which has been offered, the sacrificial parts of which have been burned up, the division is to take place through tossing, not through a deliberate act of donation. So the element of chance is preserved. That unpredictable component of the transaction represents God's point of entry. So what goes to the poor represents God's share of what is given to the farmer. That means the farmer gives what is not his to begin with, but what he owes to God as God's share in the fruits of the land that God possesses and that the farmer works as a sharecropper in partnership with God.

Scripture's provision for the poor is defined at several points. At all points, the share of the crop reserved by God for the poor is particular, that is, it is not confused with what is reserved by God for the priests and Levites and Jerusalem, even though the same basic theology and governing principles come to expression in all cases in which God's share of the crop is designated. What is specifically set aside for the poor? First, Lev.19:9–10 specifies that the corner of the field (pe'ah) is to be left for the poor, so too gleanings and separated grapes of the vineyard: 'When you reap the harvest of your land, you shall not reap your field to its very border, neither shall you gather the gleanings after your harvest. And you shall not strip your vineyard bare, neither shall you gather the fallen grapes of your vineyard; you shall leave them for the poor and for the sojourners: I am the Lord your God.' Lev. 23:22 goes over the same ground: 'And when you reap the harvest of your land, you shall not reap your field to its very border, nor shall you gather the gleanings after your harvest;

you shall leave them for the poor and for the stranger, I am the Lord your God.' Deut. 24:21 goes over the ground of the defective cluster: 'When you gather the grapes of your vineyard, you shall not glean it afterward; it shall be for the sojourner, the fatherless, and the widow. You shall remember that you were a slave in the land of Egypt, therefore I command you to do it.' The forgotten sheaf is specified at Deut. 24:19: 'When you reap your harvest in your field and have forgotten a sheaf in the field, you shall not go back to get it; it shall be for the sojourner, the fatherless, and the widow, that the Lord your God may bless you in all the work of your hands. When you beat your olive trees, you shall not go over the boughs again; it shall be for the sojourner, the fatherless, and the widow.' Finally, in the third and sixth years of the seven-year cycle ('Sabbatical') a tithe of the crop is regularly set apart for the poor, so Deut. 26:12: 'When you have finished paying all the tithe of your produce in the third year, which is the year of tithing, giving it to the Levite, the sojourner, the fatherless, and the widow, that they may eat within your towns and be filled, then you shall say before the Lord your God, "I have removed the sacred portion out of my house, and, moreover, I have given it to the Levite, the sojourner, the fatherless, and the widow, according to all thy commandment that thou hast commanded me." '

What has been said leaves no doubt that provision for the poor represents a principal communal responsibility. The basic principle is that the poor have to go out and put their hands on that part of the crop left for their gleaning or recovery. The priesthood and Levites, by contrast, receive what the farmer deliberately designates for them, that is, a portion of the crop that the farmer declares is the priestly ration therein, and so throughout. True, the priest has to make the rounds of the threshing floors to collect his share of the grain, but that is not the same thing as going out into the fields and finding what has been left behind, or going into the vineyards and olive groves and collecting the remnant of the fruit.

The difference between sharing one's crops with the poor and paying obligatory taxes should, however, be noted. What the farmer assigns to the poor, when it comes to the corner of the field, is without limit; he can give nearly the entire field. That crop is then exempt from the other agricultural dues, such as those owing to the priests, Levites, and the support of Jerusalem, that God exacts. Not only so, but support for the poor is deemed an act of such surpassing virtue that it is treated in the same context as the performance of acts of righteousness and the consequent response of Heaven to such an action is carried over into the world to come and the last judgment:

1:1 A. These are things which have no [specified] measure:

B. (1) [the quantity of produce designated as] pe'ah, (2) [the quantity of produce given as] first fruits, (3) [the value of] the appearance offering, (4) [the performance of] righteous deeds, (5) and [time spent in] study of Torah.

C. These are things the benefit of which a person enjoys in this world, while the principal remains for him in the world to come:

D. (1) [deeds in] honor of father and mother, (2) [performance of] righteous deeds, (3) and [acts which] bring peace between a man and his fellow.

E. But the study of Torah is as important as all of them together.

(Mishnah-tractate Pe'ah, 1:1)

To understand the setting in which we speak of reward in the world to come, we take account of the opposite, acts in this world that affect the actors' fate in the last judgment and in the world to come:

1:2 A. For these things they punish a person in this world, while the principal [i.e. eternal punishment] remains for the world-to-come:

B. (1) for [acts of] idolatrous worship, (2) for incest, (3) for murder, (4) and for gossip, [which is] worse than all of them together.

C. Doing good creates a principal [for the world-to-come] and bears interest [in this world].

1:3 A. A transgression creates a principal [i.e. eternal punishment, in the world-to-come] but bears no interest [in this world].

(Tosefta-tractate Pe'ah, 1:2–3)

Now the full importance assigned to supporting the poor emerges clearly. It is an action as weighty as Torah-study. Its counterpart and opposite is represented by idolatry, incest, and murder, the trilogy of cardinal sins of the halakhah.

Clearly, defining the several classes of crops, subject to diverse expressions of 'fate' or 'chance' but in fact divine intentionality forms the focus of the halakhah. The first principle is, what someone wants, must be shared with God, a partner, and thus with God's designated agents, the poor or the priests. That principle is most lucidly expressed in connection with the produce that is subject to being left for the poor at the corner of the field. That is not going to be produce that the farmer neglects because of disdain. It must be produce that is edible, privately owned, produced by the holy land, harvested systematically as a crop (not treated casually), and thereafter stored away as valuable:

> 1:4 A. They stated a general principle concerning [the designation of produce as] pe'ah:
>
> B. Whatever is: (1) edible, (2) privately owned, (3) grown from the ground, (4) harvested as a crop, (5) and can be preserved in storage, is subject to [designation as] pe'ah,
>
> C. Grain and legumes are included in this general principle.
>
> (Mishnah-tractate Pe'ah, 1:4)

The same definition pertains to crops that are subject to the designation of tithes and priestly rations, and the same principle pertains. That fact indicates the classification of alms, once again represented as not a matter of whim or personal will but as a matter of unavoidable obligation: God's share.

That same point emerges in the consideration of how the poor are to collect what is owing to them. In general, the poor must come and take what belongs to them by right; it is not by an act of wilful generosity of the farmer. It is not even his choice. But that principle is modified by another: the farmer is not to suffer damage to his property when the poor come to glean. Therefore the farmer may harvest and divide among the poor what grows on a trellis or a palm tree and the like, to protect his property. But the basic right of the poor to take what is theirs on land owned by the farmer cannot be compromised:

> 4:1 A. Pe'ah is designated from [produce which as yet is] unharvested [Lev. 23:22].
>
> B. [As regards produce which grows] on a trellis, or [the produce of] a palm tree [either of which might be damaged if the poor attempted to collect pe'ah] —
>
> C. the householder cuts down [the produce] and distributes it among the poor.
>
> D. R. Simeon says, '[The preceding rule applies] also to [nuts which grow on] smooth nut trees, [since the poor cannot easily climb these trees to pick the produce].'
>
> E. Even if ninety-nine [poor people] say that [the householder should] distribute [the produce] and [only] one [poor person] says that [the

poor should] take [the produce by themselves, leaving the householder out of the distribution process completely],

F. they listen to the latter, [who said that the poor should take the produce themselves],

G. for he has spoken according to the law.

(Ibid., 4:1)

The law once more underscores that the poor take what is theirs by right, not on sufferance. Philanthropy is not a choice one makes but a duty one carries out by reason of obligation, as much as one performs acts of righteousness because one has to, not merely because one wants to.

The role of chance in the specification of that portion of the crop that belongs to God and therefore to the poor comes to the fore when we deal with the forgotten sheaf. There, in particular, intentional designation is excluded, chance happening emphasized. All parties must bear responsibility for the neglect of the sheaf. The poor cannot hide it so that the householder and his workers will miss it. The householder cannot exercise deception either. All parties must share in the general act of neglect; that oblivion, as we have noted, represents God's role in the process:

5:7 A. A sheaf which (1) workers forgot, but which the householder did not forget, (2) which the householder forgot, but which the workers did not forget, (3) [or if] poor people stood in front [of a sheaf] or covered it with straw [in order to hide it so that the workers would forget it],

B. lo, this [sheaf] is not [subject to the restrictions of the] forgotten sheaf, [for either the poor received it by deception, or it was never forgotten by both the worker and the householder] [cf. Deut. 24:19–22].

(Ibid., 5:7)

Not only so, but the process by which a sheaf may be classified as 'forgotten' commences only when the work is complete. If the workers are still binding the sheaves, what is neglected does not qualify as forgotten; when their work is done, then it does. But the definition remains restrictive, for the occasion for forgetting the sheaf draws to a close when the threshing begins. So it is a brief interval at which authentic 'forgetting' takes place, and that underscores the importance accorded to chance in the process:

5:8 A. He who binds [sheaves] into stack covers, stack bases, temporary stacks, or [ordinary] sheaves —

B. [while the sheaves are being bound, they] are not [subject to the restrictions of the] forgotten sheaf.

C. [While the bound sheaves are brought] from [the binding area] to the threshing floor,

D. they are [subject to the restrictions of the] forgotten sheaf. [The point is that liability to the law of the forgotten sheaf begins only once the binding process is completed. Additionally, sheaves are no longer subject to the law of the forgotten sheaf after the threshing process begins.]

E. He who binds [sheaves which will be placed in] a grain heap —

F. [the bound sheaves in the grain heap] are [subject to the restrictions of the] forgotten sheaf.

G. [Once the sheaves are brought] from [the grain heap] to the threshing floor,

H. [they] are not [subject to the restrictions of the] forgotten sheaf.

I. This is the general [principle]:

J. All who bind sheaves at a place where binding will be completed —

K. [the sheaves] are [subject to the restrictions of the] forgotten sheaf.

L. [Once the sheaves are brought] from [such a place, where binding is completed] to the threshing floor,

M. [the sheaves] are not [subject to the restrictions of the] forgotten sheaf.

N. But if the sheaves are bound] at a place where binding will not be completed,

O. [they] are not [subject to the restrictions of the] forgotten sheaf.

P. [While the sheaves are gathered together, which marks the end of the binding process, [and are brought] from [the place where they were bound] to the threshing floor,

Q. [they] are [subject to the restrictions of the] forgotten sheaf.

(Ibid.)

The sheaf that falls, the one left behind, the one ignored at the place where the sheaves are bound – those are the ones that God designates for the poor.

The same basic principles that operate for the forgotten sheaf come to bear upon the other crops for which the Land is noted, grapes and olives, which, together with wheat, constitute the principal produce of the Land. (The equivalent for Babylonia, the other important locale where the halakhah took shape in the formative period, namely, beer for wine, sesame oil for olive oil, and barley for wheat, never comes within the purview of the Written Torah.) Here, once more, what decides the status of a grape is chance; intentional designation of a grape as 'separated' does not serve. The grape still belongs to the farmer. The farmer can cheat the poor by collecting every last grape; that violates the intent of the law.

> 7:3 A. What [produce is subject to the law of the] separated [grape] [Lev. 19:9]?
>
> B. [Individual grapes] which fall [to the ground] during the harvest,
>
> C. [If a worker] was harvesting, [and] cut an entire cluster,
>
> D. [and] it became entangled in the leaves [of the vine],
>
> E. [so that the cluster] fell from his hand to the ground, and separated [into individual grapes],
>
> F. lo, [the individual grapes and the remaining cluster] belong to the householder.
>
> G. One who places a basket under the vine while he harvests [in order to catch the grapes which fall, so that they will not be in the status of separated grapes],
>
> H. lo, that man steals from the poor.
>
> I. Concerning that man it is stated, 'Remove not the landmark of the poor,' [a play on words on Prov. 22:28, which reads Remove not the ancient landmark].
>
> (Ibid., 7:3)

Here then we discern the outer limits of the law. On the one side, the poor cannot steal what belongs to the farmer, that is, what is not forgotten, what is not tangential to the harvesting process (the corner of the field), and what does not fall to the ground on its own. On the other hand, the farmer cannot try to control the natural course of the harvest by preventing grapes from separating from the grape-cluster.

Like the separated grape, the defective cluster represents a chance abnormality in the crop, and the abnormality is affected by the act of cutting the grapes. A defective cluster is one that is unnatural in its shape, for example, lacking a shoulder and a pendant. If such a cluster is harvested with the normal ones, however, it remains the property of the householder. If it is not normally harvested, then it belongs to the poor:

7:4 A. What [produce is subject to the law of the] defective cluster, [such that it belongs to the poor]?

B. Any [cluster] which has neither a shoulder [a wide upper part] nor a pendant [a cone-shaped lower part] —

C. If [a cluster] has either a shoulder or a pendant,

D. it belongs to the householder.

E. If it is uncertain [if the cluster has either a shoulder or a pendant] ,

E. [it] belongs to the poor [cf. M. 4:111].

G. A defective cluster [which grows] on [the portion of the vine which] joins [a normal cluster to the vine], [such that it might be considered part of the normal cluster],

H. if it is harvested at the same time as the normal cluster,

I. lo, it belongs to the householder.

J. But if [the defective cluster] is not [harvested with the normal cluster to which it is attached],

K. lo, it belongs to the poor.

L. [As regards] a grape [which grows] singly,

M. R. Judah says, '[It is deemed] a [normal] cluster, [which belongs to the householder].'

(Ibid., 7:4)

What the Oral Torah has contributed to the elucidation of the halakhah is we see the introduction of considerations that Scripture has not taken up. The main point running through the definition of the several types of food left for the poor focuses upon a fair determination of matters. That means on the one hand that chance or accident govern, and on the other that the normal process of harvesting determines what falls into the category of chance: that is to say, the farmer goes about his business in the normal way. If by his act he designates as useful and desired a defective cluster, or if he indicates that a sheaf is not yet subject to 'being forgotten,' then the matter is settled in favor of the householder. Otherwise chance takes over, with the consequences we now anticipate.

So much for the poor at home, those who have the occasion to go out into the fields and share in the crops of their village. But the law also provides for transients, even while according priority to the locals. The community must provide food and lodging for travelers. It owes a loaf of bread per day and a night's lodging, and, for the Sabbath, food for the three statutory meals. The soup-kitchen that provides the food may turn away people who have enough food for two meals, and those who have enough for fourteen may not take money from the community fund. The entire transaction, then, rests upon mutual responsibility: the community to the poor, but the poor to the community as well. The poor are not to take advantage, and the principle that governs, expressed in later times, is: 'Give the poor not a fish but a fish-hook.' Here is the rule governing the transient poor:

> 8:7 A. They give to a poor man traveling from place to place no less than a loaf [of bread] worth a dupondion, [made from wheat which costs at least] one sela for four seahs.
>
> B. [If such a poor person] stayed overnight,
>
> C. they give him enough [to pay] for a night's lodging.
>
> D. [If such a poor person] spent the Sabbath,
>
> E. they give him food for three meals.
>
> F. Whoever has sufficient food for two meals may not take [food] from a soup-kitchen.
>
> G. [Whoever has sufficient] food for fourteen meals may not take [money] from the [communal] fund.

H. [Money for] the [communal] fund is collected by
distributed by three [people].

That the definition of who is poor requires amplification

To summarize: annually, the poor are given neglected or
crop that the householder has possessed but accidentally relinquished. ...,
receive, in addition, the tithe of the crop in the third and sixth years of the Sabbatical Cycle; in the first, second, fourth, and fifth it is that same portion of the
crop that the householder eats with his family at the pilgrimage to Jerusalem.
Both represent God's share of the crop for the other-than-sacerdotal classes.
Support for the poor, then, has to be divided into two categories: provision for
their ordinary needs through the year, and special support every third and
sixth year of the Sabbatical cycle, a tenth of the residuary crop, to which the
halakhah pays only cursory attention.

Unlike the priests but like Adam and Eve and humanity until Noah, the
poor are assigned a vegetarian diet. Grain and legumes alone are included in
this general principle. The farmer's herds and flocks, however, are not subject
to pe'ah-offering; meat is not at issue. When God lays claim to meat, it goes to
only the cult and the priesthood. In this regard, accordingly, the poor take up
the position of Adam and Eve, who had free choice of the fruit and vegetables
of Eden but did not eat meat.

4 SUPPORT FOR THE POOR IN JUDAISM

While the halakhah focuses upon the support for the poor in the Land of Israel
as part of God's claim to ownership of the Land in particular, the law of Judaism provides more generally for support for the poor, and that is without specific regard to the Land but situated wherever the holy community, Israel, is
located, whether in the Land or abroad. It is through provision of regular
meals for the poor as well as other necessary items.

The halakhah takes for granted that the community maintains a
soup-kitchen for the distribution of food and also a community fund that provides financial support in other ways. The former serves transients, the latter,
permanent residents. The halakhah that covers general support for the poor, as
distinct from the shares in the crop treated above, is set forth in the following
precis. It involves two emoluments. First, while all Israelites must tithe their
crops, food given to the poor, such as the agricultural donations described
above, does not have to be tithed. So the poor are tax exempt. Second, at certain points in the seven-year cycle of tithing, the tithe is reserved for the poor,
rather than used for a trip to Jerusalem to participate in the Temple rites. This
is over and above the portion of the crops reserved for the poor by God's claim

...essed through the chance leaving of gleanings and the like. The poor ...emselves administer their own tax exemption.

A The Poor man's Claims Regarding Poor Offerings and Poorman's Tithe

M. 8:2 [The poor] are believed [if they say that tithes need not be separated] on behalf of gleanings, forgotten sheaves, and pe'ah, [from produce that is] in season, and on behalf of poorman's tithe in its proper year, [for we assume that householders actually gave them this produce. And a Levite is always believed [if he says that first tithe in his possession is exempt from the separation of heave offering of the tithe]. But [the poor] are only believed with regard to that which men usually [give them, for we assume that any other produce they might possess has not been given to them by householders and so tithes have not been separated].

M. 8:3 [The poor] are believed [if they say that] wheat [in their possession is exempt from the separation of tithes, since the produce was designated for the poor]. But they are not believed with regard to flour or a loaf [of bread, for householders do not usually designate processed produce]. They are believed with regard to panicles of rice, but they are not believed [with regard to husked rice], whether raw or cooked. They are believed with regard to beans, but they are not believed with regard to bean meal, whether raw or cooked. They are believed with regard to oil, [if they] say that [the oil] is in the status of poorman's tithe. But they are not believed with regard to [oil], if they say that [the oil] derives from olives [left on the] crown [of a tree for the poor].

M. 8:4 They are believed with regard to raw vegetables, but they are not believed with regard to cooked [vegetables], unless [the poor person] has a small amount [of the cooked vegetable]. For it is the custom of householders to take [a small amount] out of their stew, [and to give it to the poor].

T.4:1 R. Judah says, '[In] a place where [householders] press [the grapes on] defective clusters, [and give the resulting wine to the poor], a poor person is believed if he claims (1) "This wine is in the status of defective clusters, [and so no tithes need be separated from it]." [A poor person also is believed if he claims], (2) "My brothers, relatives, and I gathered these gleanings." But he is not believed if he claims, (1) "I purchased [this food] from so-and-so, a Gentile [who claimed that the produce has the status of gleanings,]" or (2) "I purchased it from so-and-so, a

Samaritan [who made the same claim]." ' Poor Samaritans are deemed
equivalent to poor Israelites and so are deemed credible under all
circumstances in which Israelites are believed. But as regards poor
Gentiles, we do not believe anything they say about anything.

We turn, next, to the halakhah of tractate pe'ah on how much poorman's tithe
is required to be set aside at the threshing floor.

B Definition: The Proper Amount of Food to Give to Each Poor Person as Poorman's Tithe

M.8:5 [When dispensing poorman's tithe] they may give to the poor at
the threshing floor no less than (1) one-half qab of wheat, (2) one qab
of barley, (R. Meir says, 'one-half qab [of barley]'), (3) one and a half
qabs of spelt, (4) one qab of dried figs, (5) one maneh of fresh figs, (R.
Aqiba says, 'one-half [of a maneh of fresh figs]'), (6) one-half log of
wine, (R. Aqiba says, 'a quarter [of a log of wine]') (7) a quarter-[log] of
oil, (R. Aqiba says, 'an eighth [of a log of oil]'). And [as regards] all
other types of produce – said Abba Saul, '[They must give to the poor]
enough [produce] so that they may sell it [and use the revenue to] buy
sufficient food for two meals.'

M.8:6 This single measure [for each type of produce] applies when
distributing poorman's tithe to poor] priests, Levites, and Israelites. [If a
man wished to] save [some of the produce he designated as poorman's
tithe for his own poor relatives], he may take only half [for his relatives]
and must give half [of the poorman's tithe to other poor people]. If he
had [only] a small amount of any type [of produce, less than the
measure specified at M. 8:5], he places [the produce] before [the poor],
and they divide it among themselves.

T.2:18 [As regards] poor people who are making the rounds of
threshing floors – [if a householder wishes to distribute the poorman's
tithe from his home, he need not give the poor any poorman's tithe at
the threshing floor. [Rather he must] designate tithes [from some
common produce] and give them this grain [as a gift]. [And] decent
people bring out in their hand food [worth a small amount of] money,
and give [a poor person] this trifle, so that he will [have something to]
eat before he reaches the city. [And] the portion of the poor offerings
that [remains] in the fields, to which the poor pay no attention – lo,
this [produce] belongs to the householder.

T.4:2 During the proper year for dispensing poorman's tithe, they may give to the poor no less than one-half qab of wheat or a qab of barley [M. Pe'ah. 8:5] – under what circumstances does this apply? It applies of the householder distributes the produce at the threshing floor. But if he distributes produce from his own house, he may give to the poor any amount and need not scruple that he has given them less than the required amount. But as regards the remainder of gifts distributed at the threshing floor, namely those given to the priesthood and to the Levites, he may give any amount and need not scruple that he has not given enough.

T.4:2 If he wishes, he may retain half of the poorman's tithe for his own poor relatives' use and give half to other poor people [M. Pe'ah. 8:6]. Abba Yosé b. Dosetai says in the name of R. Eliezer, 'If he wishes, he may give to the other poor people a third of the poorman's tithe and give two-thirds to his own poor relatives.'

T.4:3 As regards priests and Levites who stand by the threshing floor waiting to be given the gifts due them, heave offering and first tithe, and other priests came and stood there for a short time only – the priests who came by later may not take the priestly gifts out of the hands of the priests who were there first. Said Rabban Simeon b. Gamaliel, 'Rich priests used to be generous, and in order not to send out their poor brothers empty-handed, they used to take a handful of the food they had collected as heave offering and give it to them.' R. Simeon b. Eleazar says, 'If some priests came to the threshing floor after the householder had given out one round of offerings, but before he had given out the second round, they must stand at the end of the line and take the offerings only in turn.'

T.4:4 As regards the wives and slaves or priests, they may not apportion them priestly offerings at the threshing floor. But dispensing this produce from the house, they may give them priestly or Levitical gifts as an act of favor.

T.4:5 Rabban Simeon b. Gamaliel says, 'Just as, [when produce is] distributed at the threshing floor, [a person's receiving] heave offering is prima facie evidence [that he is a member] of the priesthood, so too, [when produce is] distributed at the threshing floor, [a person's receiving] first tithe prima facie evidence [that he is one] of the Levites.' [But when] distributing through the agency of a court [an inheritance containing produce in the status of tithes that never was given to priests, a person's receiving a portion of the food] is not prima facie evidence [that he is a member of the] priesthood, [for this produce can be given, by the court, to anyone].

T.4:6 [There are] two [matters that constitute] prima facie evidence [that a person is a member of] the priesthood: within the Land of Israel – (1) raising one's hands [during the priestly benediction], and (2) receiving [heave offering] at the threshing floor. And in Syria, up to the place where the messenger [who tells of the new] moon reaches – (1) raising one's hands [during the priestly benediction], but (2) [they do] not receive [heave offering] at the threshing floor. And Babylonia [is in the same status] as Syria. R. Simeon b. Eleazar says, 'Also Alexandria [had the same status as Syria], during the early times, when there was a court there.'

T.4:7 A more stringent rule applies to holy things of the Temple than applies to holy things of the provinces. And a more stringent rule applies to holy things of the provinces than applies to holy things of the Temple. [As regards] the holy things of the provinces – (1) minor [priests] may partake of them, (2) unclean [priests] may partake of them, (3) they may divide them in conditions of uncleanness, (4) and they may measure out an equivalent amount [of common food to be used in place of the holy things]. [As regards] the holy things of the Temple – (1) [priests] are charged with the responsibility of caring for them, (2) and [with the responsibility] to bring them to the Temple building. [As regards] holy things of the provinces – they give them to any haber[-priest] [merely as a gift]. But [as regards] holy things of the Temple – priests are charged with the responsibility of caring for them and with the responsibility to bring them to the Temple building. As regards holy things of the provinces, they give them to any haber-[priest] merely as a gift. But as regards holy things of the Temple, they give them only to the members of the officiating priestly watch of that span of time.

What about the poor who do not reside in one's own village, travelers for example? They too are provided for in local soup-kitchens.

C Types of Charity Given throughout the Year from One Harvest to the Next

M.8:7 They give to a poor man traveling from place to place no less than a loaf [of bread] worth a dupondion, [made from wheat that costs at least] one sela for four seahs. [If such a poor person] stayed overnight, they give him enough [to pay] for a night's lodging. [If such a poor person] spent the Sabbath, they give him food for three meals. Whoever has sufficient food for two meals may not take [food] from a soup-kitchen. [Whoever has sufficient] food for fourteen meals may not take [money] from the [communal] fund. [Money for] the [communal] fund is collected by two [people] and distributed by three [people].

T.4:8 They give to a poor person travelling from place to place no less than a loaf of bread worth a dupondius, made from wheat that costs at least one sela for four seahs. If such a poor person stayed overnight, they must give him enough food for a night's lodging (M. Pe'ah. 8:7), namely, oil and beans. If such a poor person spends the Sabbath, they give him food for three meals, namely, oil, beans, fish, and a vegetable. Under what circumstances does this provision pertain? It applies so long as the townspeople do not recognize the poor person. But if they recognize him, they must even provide clothing for him. If a poor person went from door to door, begging for food from each family, they are not obligated to him in any way, because he should collect his needs from the communal fund.

T.4:9 The soup-kitchen provides enough food for a full day, but the communal fund gives sufficient food to last from one week to the next. The soup-kitchen provides food for anybody, but the communal fund gives support only to the poor of that locale. If a poor person dwelt there for thirty days, lo, he is considered in the status of resident of the locale for purposes of receiving assistance from the communal fund. But to receive shelter, he must have dwelt there for six months. And to be liable to pay the town-tax, he must have been a resident for twelve months.

T.4:10 As regards a poor person who, like anyone else, gave a penny to support the communal fund or a piece of bread to help out at the soup-kitchen, they do take the money or food from him. But if he did not contribute, they also do not force him to give. If they gave to a poor person new clothes from the communal fund and he exchanged his worn-out clothes in partial payment, they may take the clothes from him. But if he did not exchange his worn-out clothes, they do not force him to give. If he used to wear fine wool before he became poor, they supply him with clothes of fine wool. If he used to receive a coin as a salary, they give him a coin. If he used to eat dough before he became poor, they give him dough. If he used to eat bread before he became poor, they give him bread. If they used to spoon-feed him before he became poor, they spoon-feed him. These rules accord with what is written in Scripture, 'You shall open your hand to the poor person and provide him sufficient for his need, whatever it may be' (Deut. 15:8). This refers to providing even a slave or a horse if this is deemed his standard of living. 'For his need' (Deut. 15:8) – this refers to providing him with a wife, as it is written in Scripture, 'Then the Lord God said,

It is not good that the man should be alone. I will make a helper for his need' (Gen. 2:18).

T.4:11 [If a poor person] was used to using golden utensils he must sell them, and use silver ones. [If he was used to] silver utensils, he must sell them, and use brass ones. [If he was used to brass utensils, he must sell them and use glass ones. They told [the following story]: A family from Bet Nebaltah was [visiting] in Jerusalem. They were related to the family of Arnon, the Jebusite [that is, their family was among the original inhabitants of Jerusalem]. The sages sent them three hundred gold sheqels, for they did not want them to [be forced to] leave Jerusalem [because of a lack of money].

T.4:12 '[As regards] one who says, "I shall not be supported by others" – they act considerately toward him, and support him by giving [this convert] a gift,' the words of Rabbi. But the sages say, 'They give [the poor person money] as a gift, and [when he refuses to take the charity] they convert it to a loan.'

T. 4:13 [As regards] one who says, 'I cannot support myself' – they act considerately toward him, and support him by giving [this to him] [as a gift].

Finally, the halakhah defines who is poor, and specifies the minimum amount of capital that makes a householder ineligible for public support out of God's share of the crop.

M. 8:8 Whoever has two hundred zuz [in liquid assets] may not collect gleanings, forgotten sheaves, pe'ah, or poorman's tithe. If he had two hundred [zuz] less one dinar [he had one hundred and ninety-nine zuz], even if one thousand [householders each are about to] give him [one dinar], all at the same time, lo, this man may collect [produce designated for the poor, because at the moment he takes charity, he has less than two hundred zuz]. [If he had two hundred zuz that served as] collateral for a creditor, or for his wife's marriage contract, lo, this man may collect [produce designated for the poor, since this money is not available for his use]. They may not compel him to sell his house nor the tools [of his trade in order that he might have two hundred zuz].

M. 8:9 Whoever has [only] fifty zuz, yet conducts business with them, lo, this man may not collect [produce designated for the poor]. And anyone who does not need to collect [such produce] but [nevertheless] collects [it] will not depart from this world before he in fact depends on other people. And any man who is not lame, dumb, or handicapped, but pretends to be will not die of old age before he actually has such [an injury]. And anyone who needs to collect [such produce] but does not collect [it] will not die of old age before [he is able] to support others from that which belongs to him. And with regard to this man Scripture states, 'Blessed is the man who trusts in the Lord, whose trust is the Lord' (Jer. 17:7). And so a judge who judges for justice's sake [is blessed]. As it is stated in Scripture, 'Justice and only justice shall you follow' (Deut. 16:20). But any judge who accepts a bribe, and on its account changes his judgment, will not die from old age before his eyes grow weak. As it is stated [in Scripture], '[And you shall take no bribe], for a bribe blinds the officials [and subverts the case of those who are in the right' (Exod. 23:8).

T. 4:15 Charity collectors are not permitted to separate their own money from that which they collect for charity by placing their own money in a separate purse, lest it appear that they steal for themselves some of the money they gather as charity. Even if his friend paid him money that he owed him, even if he found money in the road, he may not take it for himself. For it is written in Scripture, 'You shall be free of obligation before the Lord and before Israel' (Num. 32:22). But they may separate their own money from that which they collect for charity if they are collecting in a private courtyard or within their own shop.

T.4:16 [As regards produce in the status of] second tithe – (1) they may not use it to repay loans or [other] debts, (2) they may not use it to repay favors received, (3) they may not use it to ransom prisoners, (4) they may not use it to purchase groomsmen's gifts, (5) and they may not give any part of it as charity, [lest the poor person eat it without observing the produce's special status]. But (1) they may send part of it [to another] as an act of loving kindness, but he must inform [the other person of the produce's status]. And (2) they may give it to a citizen who is known to scruple [regarding the proper dispensation of conse- crated produce] as a favor.

T.4:17 [If] one pledged to give [money to charity], and then gave [this money], they accord him merit both on account of pledging [to give] and on account of actually [giving]. [If] he pledged to give [money to charity], but then, [when the time came to pay his pledge, he] no [longer] had enough [cash] in hand to give [the amount that he had pledged] they accord him merit on account of pledging [to give] just as [they would have accorded him] merit on account of actually [giving]. If he did not pledge [to give money to charity] but said to other people, 'Give!' they accord him merit on account of this as it is stated [in Scripture], '… and for his word, the Lord will bless you' (Deut. 15:10).

[If] he did not say to other people, 'Give!' but placed [a poor person's mind] at ease with kind words, from what [verse may we derive] that he should be accorded merit? It is stated [in Scripture], '... and for this word [i.e., the kind words spoken to the poor man] the Lord will bless you' (Deut. 15.10).

T.4:19 Charity and righteous deeds outweigh all other commandments in the Torah. Nevertheless, charity [can be given only to the] living, but righteous deeds [can be performed for the] living and the dead. Charity [is given only] to the poor people, but righteous deeds [are done for both] poor and rich people. Charity [is given as an aid for a poor person's] finances, but righteous deeds [aid both a poor person's] finances and his physical needs.

T.4:20 Said R. Joshua b. Qorha, 'From which [verse] may we derive the fact that anyone who loses sight [of the importance of giving] charity [is viewed] as if he worshipped idolatry? It is stated [in Scripture], "Take heed lest there be a base thought in your heart, and you say, the seventh year, the year of release, is near, and your eye be hostile to your poor brother, and you give him nothing" Deut. 15:9). And elsewhere [Scripture] states, "If you hear ... that certain base men have gone out among you, ... saying, Let us go and serve other gods, ... you shall surely put the inhabitants of that city to the sword, destroying it utterly."(Deut. 13:12–15). Just as in the latter case "base" explicitly refers to idolatrous worship, so too in the former case "base" refers to [something deemed equivalent to] idolatrous worship.'

The halakhah distinguishes between liquid assets (cash, or 'capital') and material provisions. If at the moment at which he contemplates taking charity, someone has two hundred zuz – which is the sum a virgin at marriage receives for support should she be divorced later on and the amount assumed to provide minimal needs for a year – that person may not benefit from gleanings, forgotten sheaves, pe'ah, or poorman's tithe. That is a formal limit. As is the way of the law, subsidiary cases come up. What if someone has two hundred zuz, but the money is designated as collateral? Then he may take food reserved for the poor; the money is not available. And still more important, the poor may not be stripped of all their possessions in order to become eligible for food assistance. They are not required to sell their residence, their tools, or their clothing. These do not enter into the calculation of whether or not they are classified as worthy for food.

The dignity of the poor transcends provision of tools for work. The poor are to be supported in accord with the dignity that is owing to them. They are not to be treated with disdain but with honor. The Talmud of the Land of Israel sets forth an analysis of what is required in that connection:

[Y. Pe'ah 8:8 II.A] A family from Bet Nebaltah was [visiting] in Jerusalem. They were related to the family of Arnon, the Jebusite [that means, their family was among the original inhabitants of Jerusalem]. The sages sent them three hundred talents of gold, for they did not want them to [be forced to] leave Jerusalem [due to a lack of money] (T. Pe'ah 4:11). This was because they interpreted [Deut. 14:28–29's double use of 'within your settlements,' as follows]: '[Every third year you shall bring out the full tithe of your yield of that year, but leave it] within your settlements. [Then the Levite, who has no hereditary portion as you have, and the stranger, the fatherless, and the widow] in your settlements [shall come and eat their fill ...]' (Deut. 14:29). [These phrases imply that the family should be supported while still] in Jerusalem.

B. And has it not been stated on Tannaitic authority, 'Hillel the elder once gave to a certain poor person, a member of a good family, a horse for the man to ride for exercise, and a slave to be the man's servant' (T. Pe'ah 4:10a). Likewise, 'The people of Galilee each day would send to a certain old man a pound of meat [according to the weights used in] Sepphoris' (T. Pe'ah 4:10b).

C. Now is it possible [that poor people would be supported so lavishly]?

D. Yes, because this poor man never ate alone in his entire life, [so he required enough to share with his compatriots].

E. It has been taught [in the Tosefta]: [If a poor person] was accustomed to using golden utensils, he must sell them, and use silver ones. [If he was accustomed to] silver utensils, he must sell them, and use brass ones. [If he was accustomed to] brass utensils, he must sell them and use glass ones (T. Pe'ah 4:11).

F. Said R. Mana, '[This refers even to his selling his fancy stuff, and [purchasing] silver or glass personal utensils.'

G. But is it not stated on Tannaitic authority, [If] he used to wear fine wool [before he became poor], they supply him with [clothes of] fine wool. [If he used to receive] a coin [as a salary before he became poor], they give him a coin. [If he used to eat] dough [before he became poor], they give him dough. [If he used to eat] bread [before he became poor], they give him bread. [If they used] to spoon feed him [before he became poor], they spoon feed him] (T. Pe'ah 4:10)?

H. [The two passages do not contradict one another.] For the former passage, [directing the poor person to accustom himself to a lower standard of living], refers not to his personal possessions, [but to that which he needs for his work]. But the latter passage, [which states that the poor person must receive assistance at the level to which he is accustomed], refers to possessions that are of a personal nature, [such as his clothes and the like]. [R. Mana's position remains at variance with this solution.]

The passage underscores the way in which a dialectical argument illuminates the several possible positions and mediates among them. But there is no compromise when it comes to deception: the halakhah takes very seriously indeed any fraud in connection with the use of philanthropic funds. Just as the crops and money belong to God and are shared by him with those for whom he has special concern, so the deceiver steals from God and will ultimately be punished by him for his deceit.

Why does the halakhah assign so high a status to the poor? The poor are assumed to own no land and to be unable to take care of themselves. The un-enlandised, for example, the traveler, and the dis-enlandised – those who have had to sell their land to support themselves – then enter into their own framework of interaction with God: different from the householder's, and holier than that. That is because, unlike the householder, they own nothing and possess nothing in the Land. But among the sacerdotal castes, the poor reach the pinnacle: they not only do not possess a portion in the Land, but the very food that the Land yields to them itself bears no marks of individual ownership. They do not own even what they eat – and they also do not worry. They embody that purity, that autonomy from all possessions, that makes possible the highest form of faith, that signified by not worrying about what tomorrow will bring. As Eliezer b. Hyrcanus says: 'Whoever has a piece of bread in his wallet and says, "What shall I eat tomorrow?" is only one of those of little faith' (Bavli Sotah 48a); and as Hillel says:

A. *It is taught on Tannaite authority:*

B. They said concerning Shammai the elder that all of the days of his [life] he would eat with an eye to the honor of the Sabbath.

C. [If] he found a fine animal, he would say, 'This is for the Sabbath.'

D. [If] he found a different animal, finer than the first, he would put aside the second [finer one for the Sabbath] and would immediately] eat the first.

E. But Hillel the elder had a different trait.

F. For all of his actions were for the sake of Heaven.

G. as it is written [Ps. 68:19], 'Blessed be the Lord day by day.'

(Bavli Besah 2:1 I.6/16a)

None more than the landless poor finds more ample grounds to bless God day by day. Within the halakhic theory, theirs is the perfect faith that God provides, by reason of the obedient character of holy Israel, and what everyone needs. The poor place their hope in God, confident of their share in the scarce resources made available to the Israelite social order by reason of God's ownership of all things. So the poor embody in their lives that perfect trust in God that all Israel owes, just as the priesthood and the Levites realize in the conduct of their lives that entire sanctification that all Israel is meant to attain. In the halakhah of Pe'ah we see how the theological virtue of faith – the poor acknowledging God's reliability, the rich and enlandised God's ownership – finds articulation in the Land and the disposition of its benefits among those that possess and those that do not possess land.

5 CONCLUSIONS

The teachings on charity are a profound reflection of overall Islamic social attitudes. They effectively transform the poor from marginalized outcasts into people worthy of concern, and at the same time, opportunities to earn spiritual reward. In the process, those who take advantage of those opportunities are helping to create the kind of society Islam clearly envisions: one in which there will no longer be those in need of charitable donations. This view is emphasized in numerous reports, for example:

> Abu Huraira reported Allah's Messenger (may peace be upon him) as saying: The Last Hour will not come before wealth becomes abundant and overflowing, so much so that a man takes zakat out of his property and cannot find anyone to accept it from him, and till the land of Arabia becomes meadows and rivers.[69]

'The poor will never cease from the Land' (Deut. 15:4) is how Moses puts the same thought. Both Judaism and Islam, Moses and Muhammad, make provision for the poor as a critical component of their design for the social order God can accept.

Judaism concurs in the Islamic insistence that the poor have just claims on society, so that philanthropy is not votive but obligatory. Not only so, but society must so organize itself that the poor are provided for. Nor is the condition of poverty deemed a disgrace or explained by reference to the sins or failures of the poor person. 'A fish-hook, not a fish' would capture the social policy of Judaism. If there is a difference between Islam and Judaism in the matter of almsgiving and charity, it is not in the basic commitment to the poor. Both concur that a just society will make ample provision for the less successful, and neither would accord to those that possess wealth the right of unrestricted ownership and disposition of that wealth – God has a stake. In the language of Judaism, God and the householder form a partnership, and the householder is the steward and trustee; he possesses and controls, but he does not own outright, and therefore he is answerable. On this Islam concurs. So the comparison and contrast yield many comparisons, but few contrasts.

4

BETWEEN THE FAITHFUL AND THE OUTSIDER

DEFINING THE COMMUNITY AND THE OTHER

1 INTRODUCTION

Societies set their own bounds and dictate who is inside and who out. How a legal system legislates concerning the outsider – that other who falls beyond the social world that reaches expression within the system – reveals the system's deepest convictions about itself. The laws that embody those convictions actualize the story that the participants tell themselves about their group. Being religious communities, both Judaism and Islam (and Christianity) concur that 'the other' is defined by unbelief. The faithful – Judaism's 'Israel,' formed at Sinai by those who declare 'we shall do and we shall obey' and continued by their descendants – constitute holy Israel (not to be confused with the contemporary state of Israel or the Jewish ethnic group, both of which define themselves in secular categories). Islam is formed of those who submit to God's will. The outsider by that definition only is the infidel. 'Not-Israel' (the Gentiles, undifferentiated) then corresponds to 'the infidels' (also undifferentiated for most purposes). Other criteria of race or ethnicity, economic standing, cultural qualities, not to mention gender, geography, and politics, make no difference at all – and the theology will always make explicit that such matters are insignificant. What marks a religious system as religious and not political, then, are the criteria that the system selects to indicate who belongs and who does not. The law then realizes the theology – at this most critical point above all.

What, then, the law takes to require its attention – the topical program, the range of problems to be solved – tells us about the critical commitments that animate that law. Judaism calls the faithful 'Israel' as a group, and 'Israelites' as individuals, and endows the faithful with a genealogy beginning with Abraham and Sarah, whom God called to his service and identified as the first believers. Whoever accepts the Torah (also called 'Judaism') then becomes part

180

of a sacred story (the word 'history' does not apply) and is transformed into a participant in that story on a plane of eternity. What of the non-Israelite, the outsider? These are called 'Gentiles,' meaning simply, everyone who does not know the one true God and therefore belong to Israel, the people of the faithful to that one and only, revealed God.

And who might that outsider be? The outsider is so indicated by a single mark: rejection of God in favor of idols. The classical law of Judaism defines the other as an idolater, and it defines 'us' in relationship to 'the other' as 'Israel,' meaning, those who know, worship, and obey the one and only God who created heaven and earth.

In Islamic law, on the other hand, 'us' – if we understand by the term those who share the rights and responsibilities set out in our legal system – includes those who have declared themselves Muslim, but takes into consideration as well Jews and Christians, since they are also believers in the one God, and all those for whom we have pledged responsibility (*dhimmah*), regardless of faith. Islam comes at the end of a long history of God's self-manifestation: first to Moses and Israel, then to Jesus and Christianity – Islam represents itself as the final and perfect revelation. Hence it forms a theory of its predecessors, who possessed the truth in part but who erred as well. It takes an affirmative position toward Judaism and Christianity, recognizing that they stand in the chain of God's revelation to prophets, coming to its climax in the seal of prophecy. Its critique of Judaism recapitulates that of Christianity: what Moses brought to Israel, Jesus, then, brings to all humanity. The upshot is that Islam (like Christianity) forms a theory of holy Israel that differentiates its predecessor from the rest of humanity, a theology of the genealogy of monotheism, while Judaism, with nothing to account for beyond itself, has no reason to do so.

The sources set forth here focus on how Judaism and Islam define their respective communities of the faithful and how each of them deals with the outsider: the one who does not know God. That very formulation captures their common conviction that 'we' are a 'we'– a community – but 'they' are merely isolated individuals.

2 DEFINING THE COMMUNITY IN THE LAW OF JUDAISM

By Judaism, 'Israel' then is defined entirely in terms of religion: the holy people, whom God singled out for the redemption of mankind, variously represented in both the Written and the Oral Torah as an extended, holy family, a people or nation chosen by God for sanctification and service, God's community and venue on earth. One antonym for Israel is Gentile. Gentiles worship idols, Israel worships the one, unique God. Another is Adam: Israel is Adam's counterpart, the other model for man. Israel came into existence in the aftermath of the failure of Creation with the fall of man; in the restoration that followed the Flood, God identified Abraham to found a supernatural social entity to realize his will in creating the world. Called variously a family, a community, a nation and a people, Israel above all forms God's resting place on earth. This definition of Israel cannot be confused with any secular meanings attributed to the same word, for example, nation or ethnic entity, counterpart to other nations or ethnic groups. In its basic exposition of the theme of idolatry, the halakhah rests squarely on the foundations of Scripture, supplying rules and regulations that carry out the fundamental Scriptural commandments about destroying idols and everything that has to do with idolatry. But the halakhah so formulates matters as to transform the entire topic of idolatry into an essay on Israel's relationships with the Gentiles, who are idolaters by definition.

What marks Israel is the promise of a portion in the world to come, when the dead have been raised and judgment has taken place, and then eternal life takes place. Who is out has no share, and who is in, with stated exceptions, does. The best – and most telling – definition within the halakhah of who belongs to Israel is as follows:

> M.11:1 All Israelites have a share in the world to come, as it is said, 'your people also shall be all righteous, they shall inherit the land forever; the branch of my planting, the work of my hands, that I may be glorified' (Isa. 60:21). And these are the ones who have no portion in the world to come: He who says, the resurrection of the dead is a teaching which does not derive from the Torah, and the Torah does not come from Heaven; and an Epicurean.

> T.12:9 They added to the list of those [who have no portion in the world to come] [M. San. 11:1]: he who breaks the yoke, violates the covenant, misinterprets the Torah, pronounces the Divine Name as it is spelled out [M. San. 10:1G], who have no portion in the world to come.

> T.13:5 But heretics, apostates, traitors, Epicureans, those who deny the Torah, those who separate from the ways of the community, those who deny the resurrection of the dead, and whoever both sinned and caused the public to sin and those who sent their arrows against the land of the living and stretched out their hands against the 'lofty habitation' [the Temple], Gehenna is locked behind them, and they are judged therein for all generations, since it is said, 'And they shall go forth and look at the corpses of the men who were transgressors against me, for their worm dies not, and their fire is not quenched. And they shall be an abhorring unto all flesh' (Isa. 66:24). Sheol will waste away, but they will not waste away, for it is written, 'and their form shall cause Sheol to waste away' (Ps. 49:14). What made this happen to them? Because they

stretched out their hand against the 'lofty habitation,' as it is said, 'Because of his lofty habitation, and lofty habitation refers only to the Temple, as it is said, I have surely built you as a lofty habitation, a place for you to dwell in forever' (I Kgs. 8:13).

Besides the specified classes of person, individuals are singled out for exclusion, their sins having marked them indelibly:

M.11:2 Three kings and four ordinary folk have no portion in the world to come. Three kings: Jeroboam, Ahab, and Manasseh. Four ordinary folk: Balaam, Doeg, Ahitophel, and Gehazi.

So too, besides individuals and persons who do not affirm the critical components of the faith, participants in enormous, collective activities of rebellion against God do not rise from the dead and stand in judgment but are left in their graves.

M.11:3 The generation of the flood has no share in the world to come, and they shall not stand in the judgment, since it is written, 'My spirit shall not judge with man forever' (Gen. 6:3) neither judgment nor spirit. The generation of the dispersion has no share in the world to come, since it is said, 'So the Lord scattered them abroad from there upon the face of the whole earth' (Gen. 11:8). 'So the Lord scattered them abroad' – in this world, 'and the Lord scattered them from there' – in the world to come. The men of Sodom have no portion in the world to come, since it is said, 'Now the men of Sodom were wicked and sinners against the Lord exceedingly' (Gen. 13:13) 'Wicked' – in this world, 'And sinners' – in the world to come. But they will stand in judgment. The spies have no portion in the world to come, as it is said, 'Even those men who brought up an evil report of the land died by the plague before the Lord' (Num. 14:37). 'Died' – in this world, 'by the plague' – in the world to come.

M.11:4 The townsfolk of an apostate town have no portion in the world to come, as it is said, 'Certain base fellows [sons of Belial] have gone out from the midst of thee and have drawn away the inhabitants of their city' (Deut. 13:14). And they are not put to death unless those who misled the [town] come from that same town and from that same tribe, and unless the majority is misled, and unless men did the misleading. [If] women or children misled them, of if a minority of the town was misled, or if those who misled the town came from outside of it, lo, they are treated as individuals [and not as a whole town], and they [thus] require [testimony against them] by two witnesses, and a statement of warning, for each and every one of them. This rule is more strict for individuals than for the community: for individuals are put to death by stoning. Therefore their property is saved. But the community is put to death by the sword, therefore their property is lost.

T.14:1 They do not declare three towns to be apostate towns in the Land of Israel, so as not to wipe out settlement in the Land of Israel. But they declare one or two [to be apostate cities].

M.11:5 'And you shall surely smite the inhabitants of the city with the edge of the sword' (Deut. 13:15). Ass-drivers, camel-drivers, and people passing from place to place – lo these have the power to save it, as, it is said, 'Destroying it utterly and all that is therein and the cattle thereof, with the edge of the sword' (Deut. 13:17). On this basis they said, the property of righteous folk which happens to be located in it is lost. But that which is outside of it is saved. And as to that of evil folk, whether it is in the town or outside of it, lo, it is lost.

T.14:2 Ass-drivers, camel-drivers, and people passing from place to place [M. San. 10:5B] who spent the night in its midst and became apostate with [the others of the town], are put to death by the sword. Their property and the town are prohibited. And if they spent thirty days in the town, they are put to death by the sword, and their property and the town are prohibited. But if they did not spend thirty days in the town, while they are put to death by the sword, their property and the town are permitted. But under all circumstances those who have incited the town to apostatize are put to death by stoning, and their property and the town are prohibited. [If] women and children enticed the townsfolk to apostatize, they are put to death by the sword, but their property and the town are permitted. [If] women enticed the population to apostatize and not men, children and not adults – is it possible that the town should be declared an apostate town? Scripture says, the inhabitants of their town (Deut. 13:14) – the matter is deter-mined by the deeds of the residents of the town, and the matter is not determined by the deeds of all such sorts as these [cf. M. San. 10:4C–I].

T.14:3 The minor children of the residents of an apostate city who apostatized with it are not put to death.

T.14:4 The property of the righteous which is in the town is lost, but that which is outside of it is saved. And that of the wicked, whether in it or outside of it, is lost [M. San. 10:5D–E].

T.14:5 If there were holy things in it, things that have been consecrated for use on the altar are left to die; things which are consecrated for the upkeep of the Temple building are to be redeemed; heave offering left therein is allowed to rot; second tithe and sacred scrolls are hidden away.

M.11:6 [As it is said,] 'And you shall gather all the spoil of it into the midst of the wide place thereof' (Deut. 13:17). If it has no wide place, they make a wide place for it. [If] its wide place is outside of it, they bring it inside. 'And you will burn with fire the city and all the spoil thereof, (ever whit, unto the Lord your God)' (Deut. 13:17). 'The spoil thereof' – but not the spoil which belongs to Heaven. On this basis they have said: things which have been consecrated which are in it are to be redeemed; heave offering left therein is allowed to rot; second tithe and sacred scrolls are hidden away. 'And there shall cleave naught of the devoted things to your hand [that the Lord may turn from the fierceness of his anger and show you mercy and have compassion upon you and multiply you]' (Deut. 13:18) for so long as evil people are in the world, fierce anger is in the world. When the evil people have perished from the world, fierce anger departs from the world.

So much for the general theory of the matter of who belongs to that Israel that is constituted by those who, after death, will rise from the grave, stand in judgment, and enter into eternal life – and who belongs perpetually to the grave. The 'we' of Judaism is comprised by those who will live forever, the 'they' is made up of those who are destined to die.

But how to deal with Israelites who sin? Do they lose their 'portion in the world to come,' meaning, eternal life? This definition of Israel leaves open a critical issue: what is the status of those who, in this life, have sinned and been punished – the murderer, for instance? What is the fate of the Israelite sinner after death? The most profound question facing Israelite thinkers concerns the fate of the Israelite at the hands of the perfectly just and profoundly merciful God. Essential to their thought is the conviction that all creatures are answerable to their Creator, and absolutely critical to their system is the fact that at the end of days the dead are raised to eternal life; the criminal justice system thus encompasses deep thought on the interplay between God's justice and God's mercy: how are these reconciled in the case of the sinner or criminal?

Within Israel's social order the halakhah addresses from a theological perspective the profound question of social justice: what shall we make of the Israelite sinner or criminal? Specifically, does the sin or crime, which has estranged the individual from God, close the door to life eternal? If it does, then justice is implacable and perfect. If it does not, then God shows his mercy – but what of justice? We can understand the answer only if we keep in mind that the halakhah takes for granted the resurrection of the dead, the final judgment, and the life of the world to come beyond the grave. From that perspective, death becomes an event in life but not its end. And, it must follow, the death penalty too does not mark the utter annihilation of the person of the sinner or criminal. On the contrary, because he pays for his crime or sin in this life, he situates himself with all of the rest of supernatural Israel, ready for the final judgment. Having been judged, he will 'stand in judgment,' meaning, he will find his way to the life of the world to come along with everyone else. Within the dialectics formed by those two facts – punishment now, eternal life later on – we identify as critical the two passages in the halakhah of Sanhedrin-Makkot, M. Sanhedrin 6:2 and 10:1. Achan pays the supreme penalty but secures his place in the world to come, all Israel, with only a few exceptions, is going to stand in judgment and enter the world to come, explicitly including all manner of criminals and sinners.

That is what defines the stakes in this critical component of the sages' account of God's abode in Israel. What the halakhah wishes to explore is, how is the Israelite sinner or criminal rehabilitated, through the criminal justice system, so as to rejoin Israel in all its eternity? The answer is, the criminal or sinner remains Israelite, no matter what he does – even though he sins – and the death penalty is exacted by the earthly court. So the halakhah of Sanhedrin embodies these religious principles: (1) Israel endures for ever, encompassing (nearly) all Israelites; (2) sinners or criminals are able to retain their position within that eternal Israel by reason of the penalties that expiate the specific sins or crimes spelled out by the halakhah; (3) it is an act of merciful justice that is done when the sinner or criminal is put to death, for at that point, he is assured of eternity along with everyone else. God's justice comes to full expression in the penalty, which is instrumental and contingent; God's mercy endures forever in the forgiveness that follows expiation of guilt through the imposition of the penalty.

That explains why the governing religious principle of Sanhedrin-Makkot is the perfect, merciful justice of God, and it accounts for the detailed exposition of the correct form of the capital penalty for each capital sin or crime. The punishment must fit the crime within the context of the Torah in particular so that, at the resurrection and the judgment, the crime will have been correctly expiated. Because the halakhah rests on the premise that God is just and that God has created humanity in his image, after his likeness, the halakhah cannot deem sufficient that the punishment fit the crime. Rather, given its premises, the halakhah must pursue the issue, what of the sinner once he has been punished? And the entire construction of the continuous exposition of Sanhedrin-Makkot aims at making this simple statement: the criminal, in God's image, after God's likeness, pays the penalty for his crime in this world but like the rest of Israel will stand in justice and, rehabilitated, will enjoy the world to come.

Accordingly, given their conviction that all Israel possesses a share in the world to come, meaning, nearly everybody will rise from the grave, the sages took as their task the specification of how, in this world, criminals and sinners would receive appropriate punishment in a proper procedure, so that, in the world to come, they would take their place along with everyone else in the resurrection and eternal life. So the religious principle that comes to expression in Sanhedrin-Makkot concerns the meaning of man's being in God's image. That means, it is in man's nature to surpass the grave. And how, God being just, does the sinner or criminal survive his sin or crime? It is by paying with his life in the here and now, so that at the resurrection, he may regain life, along with all Israel. That is why the climactic moment in the halakhah comes at the end of the long catalogue of those sins and crimes penalized with capital punishment. It is with ample reason that the Bavli places at the conclusion and climax of its version the ringing declaration, 'all Israel has a portion in the world to come, except … .' And the exceptions, as we have seen in our precis of the halakhah, pointedly do not include any of those listed in the long catalogues of persons executed for sins or crimes.

That the two religious principles just now specified play a critical role in the formulation and presentation of the halakhah of Sanhedrin-Makkot is made explicit in the context of legal exposition itself. The rite of stoning involves an admonition that explicitly declares the death penalty the means of atoning for all crimes and sins, leaving the criminal blameless and welcome into the kingdom of Heaven:

A. [When] he was ten cubits from the place of stoning, they say to him, 'Confess,' for it is usual for those about to be put to death to confess.

B. For whoever confesses has a share in the world to come.

C. For so we find concerning Achan, to whom Joshua said, 'My son, I pray you, give glory to the Lord, the God of Israel, and confess to him, [and tell me now what you have done; hide it not from me.] And Achan answered Joshua and said, 'Truly have I sinned against the Lord, the God of Israel, and thus and thus I have done' (Josh. 7:19). And how do we know that his confession achieved atonement for him? For it is said, 'And Joshua said, Why have you troubled us? The Lord will trouble you this day' (Josh. 7:25) – This day you will be troubled, but you will not be troubled in the world to come.

D. And if he does not know how to confess, they say to him, 'Say as follows: "Let my death be atonement for all of my transgressions." '

(Mishnah-tractate Sanhedrin, 6:2)

So within the very center of the halakhic exposition comes the theological principle that the death penalty opens the way for life eternal. It follows that at stake in the tractate Sanhedrin-Makkot is a systematic demonstration of how

God mercifully imposes justice upon sinners and criminals, and also of where the limits to God's mercy are reached: rejection of the Torah, the constitution of a collectivity – an 'Israel' – that stands against God. God's merciful justice then pertains to private persons. But there can be only one Israel, and that Israel is made up of all those who look forward to a portion in the world to come: who will stand in justice and transcend death. In humanity, idolaters will not stand in judgment, and entire generations who sinned collectively as well as Israelites who broke off from the body of Israel and formed their own Israel do not enjoy that merciful justice that reaches full expression in the fate of Achan: he stole from God but shared the world to come. And so will all of those who have done the dreadful deeds catalogued here.

But there is more. What is God's stake in all this? The sages recognize that, in the setting of this life, the death penalty brings anguish, even though it assures the sinner or criminal expiation for what he has done. That matter is stated in so many words:

> A. Said R. Meir, 'When a person is distressed, what words does the Presence of God say? As it were: "My head is in pain, my arm is in pain." '
>
> B. 'If thus is the Omnipresent distressed on account of the blood of the wicked when it is shed, how much the more so on account of the blood of the righteous!'
>
> (Ibid., 6:5)

God is distressed at the blood of the wicked, shed in expiation for sin or crime; so too is humanity. So while the sages recognize the mercy and justice that are embodied in the sanctions they impose, they impute to God, and express in their own behalf, common sentiments and attitudes. They feel the same sentiments God does, as the exposition of the court process in Chapters 3 and 4 makes explicit.

That fact alerts us to the fundamental principle embodied in the halakhah: people are responsible for what they do, because they are like God. That is the basis for penalizing sins or crimes, but it also is the basis for the hope in eternal life for nearly all Israel. Like God, human beings are in command of, and responsible for, their own will and intentionality and consequent conduct. The very fact that God reveals himself through the Torah, which humanity is able to understand, there to be portrayed in terms and categories that can be grasped, shows how the characteristics of God and human beings prove comparable. The first difference between the two is that people sin, but the one and the just God, never; connecting 'God' and 'sin' yields an unintelligible result. And the second difference between creature and Creator, humanity and God, is that God is God.

It is not an accident that in the setting of the category formation of

Sanhedrin-Makkot, sages set forth how God's emotions correspond with those of humanity. Like a parent faced with a recalcitrant child, he takes no pleasure in man's fall but mourns. Not only so, but even while he protects those who love him – Israel – from his, and their, enemies, he takes to heart that he made all the human race; he does not rejoice at the Sea when Israel is saved, because, even then, his enemies are perishing. This is said in so many words in the context of a discussion on whether God rejoices when the wicked perish:

A. Therefore man was created alone [4:5J]:

B. 'And there went out a song throughout the host' (1 Kgs. 22:36) [at Ahab's death at Ramoth in Gilead].

C. Said R. Ahab b. Hanina, 'When the wicked perish, there is song' (Prov. 11:10).

D. 'When Ahab b. Omri perished, there was song.'

(Bavli-tractate Sanhedrin, 4:5 VI.1/39b)

Does God sing and rejoice when the wicked perish? Not at all:

E. But does the Holy One, blessed be he, rejoice at the downfall of the wicked?

F. Is it not written, 'That they should praise as they went out before the army and say, "Give thanks to the Lord, for his mercy endures forever" (2 Chr. 20:21).

G. And said R. Jonathan, 'On what account are the words in this psalm of praise omitted, "Because he is good"? Because the Holy One, blessed be he, does not rejoice at the downfall of the wicked.'

(Ibid.)

Now we revert to the conduct of God at the very moment of Israel's liberation, when Israel sings the Song at the Sea:

H. For R. Samuel bar Nahman said R. Jonathan said, 'What is the meaning of the verse of Scripture [that speaks of Egypt and Israel at the sea], "And one did not come near the other all night" (Exod. 14:20)?'

I. 'At that time, the ministering angels want to recite a song [of rejoicing] before the Holy One, blessed be he.'

'Said to them the Holy One, blessed be he, "The works of my hands [ar]e perishing in the sea, and do you want to sing a song before me?"'

Now the matter is resolved:

> K. Said R. Yosé bar Hanina, 'He does not rejoice, but others do rejoice. Note that it is written, "[And it shall come to pass, as the Lord rejoiced over you to do good, so the Lord] will cause rejoicing over you by destroying you" (Deut. 28:63) – and not "so will the Lord [himself] rejoice" '

> L. That proves the case.

(Ibid.)

God's emotions correspond, then, to those of a father or a mother, mourning at the downfall of their children, even though their children have rebelled against them. Even at the moment at which Israel first meets God, with God's act of liberation at the Sea, God cannot join them in their song. God and Israel then correspond, the eternal God in Heaven, Israel on earth, also destined for eternal life. Israel forms on earth a society that corresponds to the retinue and court of God in heaven. In its way, the halakhah in Sanhedrin-Makkot says no less. But it makes the statement, as we have seen, in all of the intimacy and privacy of Israel's interior existence: when (in theory at least) Israel takes responsibility for its own condition. Sanhedrin-Makkot, devoted to the exposition of crime and just punishment, turns out to form an encompassing exercise in showing God's mercy, even, or especially, for the sinner or criminal who expiates the sin or crime: that concludes the transaction, but a great deal will follow it – and from it.

3 HOW THE OUTSIDER IS TREATED IN THE LAW OF JUDAISM

Now that we know the insider – who belongs to 'Israel' – and that is, everyone who rejects idols and worships the one and only, the true God, what about the outsider, or, in the context of Judaism, the Gentiles, which is to say, everybody else? Judaism sets forth an eschatological monotheism; the hope that, at the end of days, all of humanity will acknowledge the one true God. But in the interim, Scripture is clear, Israel is to obliterate all mention of idols (Exod. 23: 13), not bow down to Gentiles' gods or serve them but overthrow them and break them into pieces (Exod. 23:24): 'You shall break down their altars and dash in pieces their pillars and hew down their Asherim and burn their graven images with fire' (Deut. 7:5). Israelites are commanded along these same lines:

190

The graven images of their gods you shall burn with fire; you shall not covet the silver or the gold that is on them or take it for yourselves, lest you be ensnared by it; for it is an abomination to the Lord your God. And you shall not bring an abominable thing into your house and become accused like it.

(Deut. 7:25–26)

You shall surely destroy all the places where the nations whom you shall dispossess served their gods, upon the high mountains and upon the hills and under every green tree; you shall tear down their altars and dash in pieces their pillars and burn their Asherim with fire; you shall hew down the graven images of their gods and destroy their name out of that place.

(Deut. 12:2–3)

Accordingly, so far as the Written Torah supplies the foundations for the treatment of the matter by the Oral Torah, the focus of discourse concerning the Gentiles is idolatry. Scripture's halakhah does not contemplate Israel's co-existence, in the Land, with Gentiles and their idolatry.

The halakhah of the Oral Torah commences its treatment of the same subject with the opposite premise: Gentiles live side by side (whether or not in the Land of Israel) with Israelites, and Israelites have to sort out the complex problems of co-existence with idolatry. It is simply taken for granted that, at this time, Israel the holy people cannot complete the obliteration of idolatry, though God will do just that in his own time. But the Oral Torah uses the occasion of idolatry to contemplate a condition entirely beyond the imagination of Scripture, which is the hegemony of idolatrous nations and the subjugation of holy Israel. The Oral Torah, fully considered, makes of the discussion of idolatry the occasion for the discussion of Israel's place among the nations of the world and of Israel's relationships with Gentiles. Not only so, but the Oral Torah's theory of who Israel is finds its context in the contrast with the Gentiles. The meeting point with the Written Torah is defined by the indicative trait of the Gentiles, which is their idolatry; that is all that matters about them. But, as we shall now see, while the halakhah of the Oral Torah expounds the local details of everyday relationships with Gentiles, the aggadah of the same Oral Torah vastly expands the range of thought and takes up the more profound issues of Gentile dominance in this age, Israel's subjugated position, the power of the idolaters, and the like. We observe that once more the aggadah deals with the world at large; the halakhah, the world at home.

Specifically, the halakhah of the Oral Torah deals first with commercial relationships; second, with matters pertaining to idols; and finally with the particular prohibition of wine once any part of it has served as a libation to an idol. The whole is regularized and ordered. There are relationships with Gentiles that are absolutely prohibited, particularly occasions of idol worship; as we shall see, the halakhah recognizes that these are major commercial events. When it comes to commerce with idolaters Israelites may not sell or in any way benefit from certain things, may sell but may not utilize certain others, and may sell and utilize yet others. Here, we see immediately that the complex and systematic mode of thought that governs the Oral Torah's treatment of the topic vastly transcends the rather simple conception that animates Scripture's discussion of the same matter. There are these unstated premises within the halakhah: (1) what a Gentile is not likely to use for the worship of an idol is not prohibited; (2) what may serve not as part of an idol but as an appurtenance thereto is prohibited for Israelite use but permitted for Israelite commerce; (3) what serves idolatry is prohibited for use and for benefit. In reflecting upon relationships with the Gentiles (meaning idolaters) the Oral Torah moreover takes a number of facts for granted. These turn out to yield a single generalization: Gentiles are assumed routinely to practice bestiality, murder, and fornication. Further negative stereotypes concerning idolaters occur. The picture of the halakhah finds its context in the larger theory of idolatry and its ephemeral hegemony.

I Commercial Relationships with Gentiles

A Festivals and Fairs

M.1:1 Before the festivals of Gentiles for three days it is forbidden to do business with them. (1) To lend anything to them or to borrow anything from them. (2) To lend money to them or to borrow money from them. (3) To repay them or to be repaid by them.

T.1:1 Under what circumstances [M. Abodah Zarah 1:1A]? In the case of recurrent festivals, but in the case of festivals which do not recur, prohibited is only that day alone. And even though they have said, it is forbidden to do business with them [M.A.Z. 1:1A] – under what circumstances? In the case of something which lasts. But in the case of something which does not last, it is permitted. And even in the case of something which lasts, [if] one bought or sold it, lo, this is permitted.

T.1:2 A person should not do business with a Gentile on the day of his festival, nor should one talk frivolously, nor should one ask after his welfare in a situation which is taken into account. But if one happened to come across him in a routine way, he asks after his welfare with all due respect.

M.1:2 Before their festivals it is prohibited, but after their festivals it is permitted.

M.1:3 (1) On the day on which [a Gentile] shaves off his beard and lock of hair, (2) on the day on which he came up safely from an ocean voyage, (3) on the day on which he got out of prison. And a Gentile who made a banquet for his son – it is prohibited for only that day, and in regard to only that individual alone [to enter into business relationships of any sort, as listed at M. 1:1].

M.1:4 A city in which there is an idol – [in the area] outside of it, it is permitted [to do business]. [If] an idol was outside of it, [in the area] inside it is permitted. What is the rule as to going to that place? When the road is set aside for going to that place only, it is prohibited. But if one is able to take that same road to some other place, it is permitted. A town in which there is an idol, and there were in it shops which were adorned and shops which were not adorned – those which are adorned are prohibited, but those which are not adorned are permitted.

B Objects Prohibited Even in Commerce

M.1:5 What are the things that are forbidden to sell to Gentiles? (1) fir cones, (2) white figs, (3) and their stalks, (4) frankincense, and (5) a white cock. And as to everything else, [if] they are left without specification [as to their proposed use], it is permitted, but [if] they are specified [for use for idolatry], it is prohibited.

M.1:7 They do not sell them (1) bears or (2) lions, or (3) anything which is a public danger. They do not build with them (1) a basilica, (2) scaffold, (3) stadium, or (4) judges' tribunal. But they build with them (5) public bathhouses or (6) private ones. [Once] they reach the vaulting on which they set up an idol, it is forbidden [to help build any longer].

M.1:8 And they do not make ornaments for an idol: (1) necklaces, (2) earrings, or (3) finger rings. They do not sell them produce as yet unplucked. But one may sell it once it has been harvested.

M.2:1 They do not leave cattle in Gentiles' inns, because they are suspect in regard to bestiality. And a woman should not be alone with them, because they are suspect in regard to fornication. And a man should not be alone with them, because they are suspect in regard to bloodshed. An Israelite girl should not serve as a midwife to a Gentile woman, because she serves to bring forth a child for the service of idolatry. But a Gentile woman may serve as a midwife to an Israelite girl. An Israelite girl should not give suck to the child of a Gentile woman. But a Gentile woman may give suck to the child of an Israelite girl, when it is by permission.

T.3:1 They leave cattle in Samaritans' inns, even male [cattle] with women, and female [cattle] with men, and female [cattle] with women. And they hand over cattle to their shepherds, and they hand over a child to him to teach him reading and to teach him a craft, and to be alone with him. An Israelite girl serves as a midwife and gives suck to the child of a Samaritan woman. And a Samaritan woman serves as midwife and gives suck to an Israelite child.

M.2:2 They accept from them healing for property, but not healing for the person.

T.3:4 They accept from them healing as to matters of property, but not healing as to matters of the person [M. A.Z. 2:2A–B]. A Gentile woman should not be called upon to cut out the fetus in the womb of an Israelite girl. And she should not give her a cup of bitters to drink, for they are suspect as to the taking of life. And an Israelite should not be alone with a Gentile either in a bathhouse or in a urinal. [When] an Israelite goes along with a Gentile, he puts him at his right hand, and he does not put him at his left hand.

M.2:3 These things belonging to Gentiles are prohibited, and the prohibition affecting them extends to deriving any benefit from them at all: (1) wine, (2) vinegar of Gentiles which to begin with was wine, (3) Hadrianic earthenware, and (4) hides pierced at the heart. With those who are going to an idolatrous pilgrimage – it is prohibited to do business. With those that are coming back it is permitted.

C Objects Prohibited For Use but Permitted in Commerce

M.2:4 Skins of Gentiles and their jars, with Israelite wine collected in them – the prohibition affecting them does not extend to deriving benefit from them. Grape pits and grape skins belonging to Gentiles if they are moist, they are forbidden. If they are dry, they are permitted. Fish brine and Bithynian cheese belonging to Gentiles – the prohibition of them does not extend to deriving benefit from them.

M.2:6 And what are things of Gentiles which are prohibited, but the prohibition of which does not extend to deriving benefit from them? (1) milk drawn by a Gentile without an Israelite's watching him; (2) their bread; and (3) their oil – (4) stewed and pickled [vegetables] into which it is customary to put wine and vinegar; (5) minced fish; (6) brine without kilkit fish floating in it; (7) hileq fish, (8) drops of asafoetida, and (9) sal-conditum – lo, these are prohibited, but the prohibition affecting them does not extend to deriving benefit from them.

M.2:7 These are things which [to begin with] are permitted for [Israelite] consumption. (1) milk which a Gentile drew, with an Israelite watching him; (2) honey; (3) grape clusters, (even though they drip with moisture, they are not subject to the rule of imparting suscepti-bility to uncleanness as liquid); (4) pickled vegetables into which it is not customary to put wine or vinegar; (5) unminced fish; (6) brine containing fish; (7) a [whole] leaf of asafoetida, and (8) pickled olive cakes. Locusts which come from [the shopkeeper's] basket are forbidden. Those which come from the stock [of his shop] are permitted. And so is the rule for heave offering.

II Idols

A General Principles

M.3:1 Images are prohibited that have in its hand a staff, bird, or sphere.

M.3:2 He who finds the shards of images – lo, these are permitted. [If] one found [a fragment] shaped like a hand or a foot, lo, these are prohibited, because objects similar to them are worshipped.

M.3:3 He who finds utensils upon which is the figure of the sun, moon, or dragon, should bring them to the Salt Sea. One breaks them into pieces and throws the powder to the wind or drops them into the sea. Also: they may be made into manure, as it is said, 'And there will cleave nothing of a devoted thing to your hand' (Deut. 13:18).

M.3:5 Gentiles who worship hills and valleys – these [hills or valleys] are permitted, but what is on them is forbidden [for Israelite use], as it is said, 'You shall not covet the silver or gold that is upon them not take it.' On what account is an asherah prohibited? Because it has been subject to manual labor, and whatever has been subject to manual labor is prohibited.

B The Asherah

M.3:7 There are three sorts of houses [so far as use as a shrine for idolatry is concerned]: (1) a house which was built to begin with for the purposes of idolatry – lo, this is prohibited. (2) [If] one stuccoed and decorated it for idolatry and renovated it, one removes the renovations. (3) [If] one brought an idol into it and took it out – lo, this is permitted. There are three sorts of stones: (1) a stone which one hewed to begin with for a pedestal – lo, this is forbidden. (2) [If] he set up an idol on [an existing] stone and then took it off, lo, this is permitted. There are three kinds of asherahs: (1) a tree which one planted to begin with for idolatry – lo, this is prohibited. (2) [If] he chopped it and trimmed it for idolatry, and it sprouted afresh, he may remove that which sprouted afresh. (3) [If] he set up an idol under it and then annulled it, lo, this is permitted.

C The Merkolis

M.4:1 Three stones, one beside the other, beside a merkolis statue, – those which appear to belong to it are forbidden, and those which do not appear to belong to it as permitted.

M.4:2 If] one found on its head coins, clothing, or utensils, lo, these are permitted. [If one found] bunches of grapes, garlands of corn, jugs of wine or oil, or fine flour or anything the like of which is offered on the altar – it is forbidden.

D Nullifying an Idol

M. 4:3 An idol which had a garden or a bathhouse – they derive benefit from them [when it is] not to the advantage [of the temple], but they do not derive benefit from them [when it is] to the advantage [of the temple]. If it belonged both to the idol and to outsiders, they derive benefit from them whether or not it is to the advantage [of the temple].

M.4:4 An idol belonging to a Gentile is prohibited forthwith [when it is made]. And one belonging to an Israelite is prohibited only after it will have been worshipped. A Gentile has the power to nullify an idol belonging either to himself or his fellow Gentile. But an Israelite has not got the power to nullify an idol belonging to a Gentile. He who nullifies an idol has nullified its appurtenances. [If] he nullified [only]

196

its appurtenances, its appurtenances are permitted, but the idol itself [remains] prohibited.

T.5:3 He who purchases metal filings from Gentiles and found an idol therein takes it and tosses it away, and the rest – lo, this is permitted. An Israelite who found an idol before it has come into his domain may tell a Gentile to nullify it. For a Gentile has the power to nullify an idol, whether it belongs to him or to his fellow [M.A.Z. 4:4C], whether it is an idol which has been worshipped or whether it is one which has not been worshipped, whether it is inadvertent or deliberate, whether it is under constraint or willingly. But an Israelite who made an idol – it is prohibited, even though he has not worshipped it [vs. M.A.Z. 4–4B]. Therefore he has not got the power to nullify it.

III Libation Wine

M.4:8 They purchase from Gentiles [the contents of] a wine press which has already been trodden out, even though [the Gentile] takes [the grapes] in hand and puts them on the heap ['apple'], for it is not made into wine used for libations until it drips down into the vat. [And if wine has] dripped into the vat, what is in the cistern is prohibited, while the rest is permitted.

M. 4:9 [Israelites] tread a wine press with a Gentile [in the Gentile's vat]. But they do not gather grapes with him. An Israelite who prepares [his wine] in a state of uncleanness – they do not trample or cut grapes with him. But they do take jars with him to the wine press, and they bring them with him from the wine press. A baker who prepares bread in a state of uncleanness – they do not knead or cut out dough with him. But they may take bread with him to the dealer.

M.4:10 A Gentile who is found standing beside a cistern of wine – if he had a lien on the vat, it is prohibited. [If] he had no lien on it, it is permitted. [If] he fell into the vat and climbed out, or (2) [if Gentiles] measured it with a reed – or (3) [if] he flicked out a hornet with a reed, or [if] (4) he patted down the froth on the mouth of a jar – in regard to each of these there was a case let it be sold. [If] (5) he took a jar and threw it in a fit of temper into the vat – this was a case, and they declared it valid.

M.5:1 A [Gentile] who hires an [Israelite] worker to work with him in the preparation of libation wine – [the Israelite's] salary is forbidden. [If] he hired him to do some other kind of work, even though he said to him, 'Move a jar of libation wine from one place to another,' his salary is permitted. He who hires an ass to bring libation wine on it – its fee is forbidden. [If] he hired it to ride on it, even though the Gentile [also] put a flagon [of libation wine] on it, its fee is permitted.

M.5:2 Libation wine which fell on grapes – one may rinse them off, and they are permitted. But if [the grapes] were split, they are prohibited. [If] it fell on figs or dates, if there is sufficient [libation wine absorbed] to impart a flavor [to them], they are forbidden. This is the governing principle: anything which bestows benefit through imparting a flavor is forbidden, and anything which does not bestow benefit through imparting a flavor is permitted – for example, vinegar [from libation wine] which falls on crushed beans.

This brief reprise of main points of the halakhah of the outsider yields a single point. The Oral Torah takes as the problematics of the halakhah the way in which the Israelite can interact with the idol-worshipping Gentile in such a way as to be uncorrupted by his idolatry. So the treatment of the halakhah of Abodah Zarah not only shifts the focus but vastly broadens the treatment of it, providing a handbook for the conduct of foreign relations between Israel and the Gentiles. How, exactly, is Israel supposed to live in a world dominated by idolatry?

The presentation of the halakhah accords the position of prominence to what must be deemed the most fundamental question it must address: may Israelites participate in the principal trading occasions of the commercial life, which are permeated with idolatrous celebrations? Since the festival defined a principal occasion for holding a market, and since it was celebrated with idolatrous rites, the mixture of festival and fair formed a considerable problem for the Israelite merchant: the sages so legislated as to close off a major channel of commerce. In connection with Gentile festivals, which were celebrated with fairs, Israelites – meaning, traders, commercial players of all kinds – could not enter into business relationships with Gentile counterparts (let alone themselves participate); cutting off all contractual ties, lending or borrowing in any form, meant the Israelite traders could in no way participate in a principal medium of trade.

But the sages differentiate between actual commercial relationships on the occasion of festivals and fairs, on the one side, and transactions of a normal, human character, on the other. They do not require Israelites to act out Scripture's commandments utterly to destroy idolatry; they permit them to maintain normal social amenities with their neighbors, within some broad limits. First, while the general prohibition covers all Gentiles on the occasion of fairs and festivals, it pertains to individual celebrations in a limited way. All Gentiles are not subjected to a prohibition for all purposes and at all times, and that is the main principle that the extension and the amplification of the law instantiates in many concrete cases. The effect is to re-shape Scripture's implacable and extreme rulings into a construction more fitting for an Israel that cannot complete the task of destroying idolatry but is not free to desist from trying.

The problematics of the halakhah also encompass relationships other than commercial ones. The basic theory of Gentiles – all of them assumed to be idolaters – is, first, that Gentiles always and everywhere and under any circumstance are going to perform an act of worship for one or another of their gods. Second, Gentiles are represented as thoroughly depraved (not being regenerated by the Torah), and so they will murder, fornicate, or steal at every opportunity; they routinely commit bestiality, incest, and various other forbidden acts of sexual congress. Within that datum, the halakhah will be worked out, and the problematics then precipitate thought on how Israel is to protect itself in a world populated by utterly immoral persons, wholly outside the framework of the Torah and its government.

The governing premise, so different from Islam's – that Israel cannot change the world but must negotiate with its repugnant reality – contradicts Scripture. Basically, the halakhah embodies the same principle of compromise where possible – but rigid conformity to the principles of the Torah under all circumstances, at whatever cost – that governed commercial transactions. Just as Israel must give up all possibility of normal trading relationships with Gentiles, depriving itself of the most lucrative transactions, those involving fairs, so Israel must avoid more than routine courtesies and necessary exchanges with idolaters.

That involves the principle that one must avoid entering into situations of danger: for example, in allowing opportunities to arise for Gentiles to carry out their natural instincts of murder and bestiality. Cattle are not to be left in their inns; a woman may not be left alone with them, nor a man – the former by reason of probable fornication, the latter, murder on the part of the Gentile. Their physicians are not to be trusted, though when it comes to using them for beasts, that is all right. One also must avoid appearing to conduct oneself as if one were an idolater, even if not actually doing so; thus if someone is in front of an idol and gets a splint in his foot, he should not bend over to remove it, because it looks as though he is bowing down to the idol – if it does not look that way, he is permitted to do so. But there are objects that are assumed to be destined for idolatrous worship, and these under all circumstances are forbidden for Israelite trade. Israelites simply may not sell to Gentiles anything that they are likely to use, or that they explicitly say they are intending to use, for idolatry: that includes, for example, wine. Whatever Gentiles have used for idolatry may not be utilized afterward by Israelites, and that extends to what is left over from an offering, such as meat or wine. Israelites also may not sell to Gentiles anything they are going to use in an immoral way, for example, wild animals for the arena, materials for the construction of places in which Gentile immorality or injustice will occur and ornaments for an idol.

Israelites may, however, derive benefit from, that is, conduct trade in, what has not been directly used for idolatrous purposes. The appurtenances of wine, such as skins or tanks, may be traded, but not used for their own needs by Israelites. In the case of jars that have served for water, Israelites may use the jars and put wine into them; Gentiles are not assumed to offer water to their idols, so too brine or fish-brine. Gentile milk, bread and oil, for instance, may be traded by Israelites. When it comes to milk Israelites have supervised, or honey, Israelites may purchase and eat such commodities. What Gentiles never use for idolatry is acceptable.

When the halakhah comes to treat idols themselves, we find few problems that require subtle analysis. Idols are to be destroyed and disposed of – no surprises there. The Written Torah has provided the bulk of the halakhah, and the Oral Torah contributes only a recapitulation of the main points, with some attention to interstitial problems of merely exegetical interest. When it comes to the asherah, the merkolis, and the nullification of an idol, the halakhah presents no surprises. Here the Oral Torah shows itself derivative of, and dependent upon, the Written, introducing no unfamiliar problems, executing no discernible generative problematics. When it comes to libation wine, the issue is equally unremarkable, although the details show that same concern noticed in connection with trade.

That concern may be defined as: how is the Israelite to live side by side with the Gentile-idolater in the Land? Here the sages find space for the house-holder-farmer to conduct his enterprise, that is, Gentile workers may be employed, and their produce may be utilized. The contrast with the blanket prohibition against participating in trade-fairs proves striking; here the sages find grounds for making possible a kind of joint venture that, when it comes to the trade-fair, they implacably prohibit. Thus they recognize that the Gentiles do not deem as wine suitable for libation the grapes in various stages of preparation. Gentile grapes may be purchased, even those that have been trodden. Gentile workers may participate to a certain point as well. Israelite workers may accept employment with Gentiles in the winepress. The basic point is not particular to wine-making; the halakhah recognizes that faithful Israelites may work with other Israelites, meaning, those who do not keep the halakhah as the sages define it, subject to limitations that where there is clear violation of the law, the Israelite may not participate in that part of the venture. The halakhah generally treats the Gentile as likely to perform his rites whenever he can, but also as responsive to Israelite instructions wherever it is to the Gentile's advantage or Israelite supervision is firm.

The halakhah presupposes not Gentile hegemony but only Gentile power; and it further takes for granted that Israelites may make choices, may specifically refrain from trading in what Gentiles value in the service of their gods, and may hold back from Gentiles what Gentiles require for that service.

Israelites, while subordinate in some ways, control their own conduct and govern their own destiny. They may live in a world governed by Gentiles, but they form intentions and carry them out. They may decide what to sell and what not to sell, whom to hire for what particular act of labor and to whom not to sell their own labor, and, above all, Israelite traders may determine to give up opportunities denied them by the circumstance of Gentile idolatry. The halakhah therefore makes a formidable statement of Israel's freedom to make choices, its opportunity within the context of everyday life to preserve a territory free of idolatrous contamination, just as Israel in entering the Land was to create a territory free of the worship of idols and their presence. In the setting of world order Israel may find itself subject to the will of others, but in the house of Israel, Israelites can and should establish a realm for God's rule and presence, free of idolatry. If they are to establish a domain for God, Israelites must practice self-abnegation, and refrain from actions of considerable weight and consequence; much of the Torah concerns itself with what people are not supposed to do, and God's rule comes to realization in acts of restraint.

When it comes to dealing with the outsider, the halakhah focuses not upon the Gentiles but upon Israel: what, given the world as it is, can Israel do in the dominion subject to Israel's own will and intention? That is the question that, as we now see, the halakhah fully answers. For the halakhah constructs, indeed defines, the interiority of an Israel sustaining God's service in a world of idolatry: life against death in the two concrete and tangible dimensions by which life is sustained – trade and the production of food, the foci of the halakhah. No wonder Israel must refrain from engaging with idolatry on days of the festivals for idols that the great fairs embody – then especially.

Gentiles are idolaters, and Israelites worship the one, true God, who has made himself known in the Torah. In the Oral Torah, that is the difference – the only consequential distinction – between Israel and the Gentiles. But the halakhah takes as its religious problem the concretization of that distinction, the demonstration of where and how the distinction in theory makes a huge difference in the practice, the conduct, of everyday affairs. What is at stake is that Israel stands for life, the Gentiles – like their idols – for death. An asherah tree, like a corpse, conveys uncleanness to those who pass underneath it, as we noted at M. 3:8: 'And he should not pass underneath it, but if he passed underneath it, he is unclean.' Before proceeding, let us consider a clear statement of why idolatry defines the boundary between Israel and everybody else. The reason is that idolatry – rebellious arrogance against God – encompasses the entire Torah. The religious duty to avoid idolatry is primary; if an individual violates the religious duties, he or she breaks the yoke of commandments; and if that single religious duty is violated, so too is the entire Torah. Violating the prohibition against idolatry is equivalent to transgressing all Ten Commandments.

The halakhah treats Gentiles as undifferentiated, but as individuals. The aggadah – the lore of the Torah, its exegesis of Scripture and its theology –

treats Gentiles as 'the nations' and takes no interest in individuals or in transactions between private persons. In the theology of the Oral Torah, the category – Gentiles or the nations – without elaborate differentiation,
encompasses all who are not-Israelites, that is, who do not belong to Israel and
therefore do not know and serve God. That category takes on meaning only as
complement and opposite to its generative counterpart, having no standing –
self-defining characteristics – on its own. That is, since Israel encompasses the
sector of humanity that knows and serves God by reason of God's
self-manifestation in the Torah, the Gentiles comprise everybody else: those
placed by their own intention and active decision beyond the limits of God's
revelation. Guided by the Torah Israel worships God; without its illumination
Gentiles worship idols. At the outset, therefore, the main point registers: by
'Gentiles' the sages understand God's enemies, and by 'Israel' they understand, those who know God as God has made himself known, which is,
through the Torah. In no way do we deal with secular categories, but with
theological ones.

The halakhah then serves as the means for the translation of theological
conviction into social policy. Gentiles are assumed to be ready to murder any
Israelite they can get their hands on, rape any Israelite women, commit bestiality with any Israelite cow. The Oral Torah cites few cases to indicate that that
conviction responds to ordinary, everyday events; the hostility to Gentiles
flows from a theory of idolatry, not the facts of everyday social intercourse,
which, as we have seen, the sages recognize is full of neighborly cordiality.
Then why take for granted that Gentiles routinely commit the mortal sins of
not merely idolatry but bestiality, fornication, and murder? That is because
the halakhah takes as its task the realization of the theological principle that
those who hate Israel hate God, those who hate God hate Israel, and God will
ultimately vanquish Israel's enemies as his own – just as God too was redeemed
from Egypt. So the theory of idolatry, involving alienation from God,
accounts for the wicked conduct imputed to idolaters, without regard to
whether, in fact, that is how idolaters conduct themselves. That matter of logic
is stated in so many words.

1. A '... and let them that hate you flee before you:'

B. And do those who hate [come before] him who spoke and brought
the world into being?

C. The purpose of the verse at hand is to say that whoever hates Israel
is as if he hates him who spoke and by his word brought the world into
being.

(Sifré to Numbers, 84:4)

The same proposition is re-worked. God can have no adversaries, but Gentile enemies of Israel act as though they were his enemies.

> D. Along these same lines: 'In the greatness of your majesty you overthrow your adversaries' (Exod. 15:7).

> E. And are there really adversaries before him who spoke and by his word brought the world into being? But Scripture thus indicates that whoever rose up against Israel is as if he rose up against the Omnipresent.

> F. Along these same lines: 'Do not forget the clamor of your foes, the uproar of your adversaries, which goes up continually' (Ps. 74:23).

> G. 'For lo, your enemies, O Lord' (Ps. 92:10).

> H. 'For those who are far from you shall perish, you put an end to those who are false to you' (Ps. 73:27).

> I. 'For lo, your enemies are in tumult, those who hate you have raised their heads' (Ps. 83:2). On what account? 'They lay crafty plans against your people, they consult together against your protected ones' (Ps. 83:3).

> (Ibid.)

Israel hates God's enemies, and Israel is hated because of its loyalty to God (a matter to which we shall return presently).

> J. 'Do I not hate those who hate you, O Lord? And do I not loathe them that rise up against you? I hate them with perfect hatred, I count them my enemies' (Ps. 139:21–22).

> K. And so too Scripture says, 'For whoever lays hands on you is as if he lays hands on the apple of his eye' (Zech. 2:12).

> L. R. Judah says, 'What is written is not, "the apple of an eye" but "the apple of *his* eye," it is as if Scripture speaks of him above, but Scripture has used an euphemism.'

> (Ibid.)

Now the consequences of these propositions are drawn:

> V. And whoever gives help to Israel is as if he gives help to him who spoke and by his word brought the world into being, as it is said, 'Curse

Meroz, says the angel of the Lord, curse bitterly its inhabitants, because they came not to the help of the Lord, to the help of the Lord against the mighty' (Judg. 5:23).

W. R. Simeon b. Eleazar says, 'You have no more prized part of the body than the eye and Israel has been compared to it. A further comparison: if a man is hit on his head, only his eyes feel it. Accordingly, you have no more prized part of the body than the eye, and Israel has been compared to it.'

X. So Scripture says, 'What, my son, what, son of my womb? What, son of my vows?' (Prov. 31:2).

Y. And it says, 'When I was a son with my father, tender, the only one in the sight of my mother, he taught me and said to me, "Let your heart hold fast my words" ' (Prov. 4:3–4).

(Ibid.)

The proposition announced at the outset is fully articulated – those who hate Israel hate God, those who are enemies of Israel are enemies of God, those who help Israel help God – and then systematically instantiated by facts set forth in Scripture. The systematic proof extends beyond verses of Scripture, with a catalogue of the archetypal enemies assembled: Pharaoh, Sisera, Sennacherib, Nebuchadnezzar, Haman. So the paradigm reinforces the initial allegation and repertoire of texts. The context then of all thought on Israel and the Gentiles finds definition in supernatural issues and context in theology. In the Oral Torah the sages at no point deem as merely secular the category of Gentiles.

Now let us see how the Gentiles are characterized in this-worldly terms, as we have noted how 'being Israel' is assumed to mean a given set of virtues that will mark the Israelite as an individual. When God blesses Gentile nations, they do not acknowledge him but blaspheme, but when he blesses Israel, they glorify him and bless him; these judgments elaborate the basic principle that the Gentiles do not know God, and Israel does. But what emerges here is that even when the Gentiles ought to recognize God's hand in their affairs, even when God blesses them, they still deny him, turning ignorance into wilfulness. What is striking is the exact balance of three Gentiles as against three Israelites, all of the status of world rulers: the common cluster – Pharaoh, Sennacherib, Nebuchadnezzar – vs. the standard cluster – David, Solomon, and Daniel.

A. 'On the eighth day you shall have a solemn assembly. [You shall do no laborious work, but you shall offer a burnt offering, an offering by fire, a pleasing odor to the Lord ...These you shall offer to the Lord at your appointed feasts in addition to your votive offerings and your freewill offerings, for your burnt offerings and for your cereal offerings and for your drink offerings and for your peace offerings]' (Num. 29: 35–39):

B. But you have increased the nation, 'O Lord, you have increased the nation; [you are glorified; you have enlarged all the borders of the land]' (Isa. 17:25).

(Pesiqta deRab Kahana, 28:I.1)

The proposition having been stated, the composer proceeds to amass evidence for the two contrasting propositions, first Gentile rulers.

C. You gave security to the wicked Pharaoh. Did he then call you 'Lord'? Was it not with blasphemies and curses that he said, 'Who is the Lord, that I should listen to his voice?' (Exod. 5:2).

D. You gave security to the wicked Sennacherib. Did he then call you 'Lord'? Was it not with blasphemies and curses that he said, 'Who is there among all the gods of the lands?' (2 Kgs. 18:35).

E. You gave security to the wicked Nebuchadnezzar. Did he then call you 'Lord'? Was it not with blasphemies and curses that he said, 'And who is God to save you from my power?' (Dan. 3:15).

Now, nicely balanced, come Israelite counterparts:

F. '... you have increased the nation; you are glorified.'

G. You gave security to David and so he blessed you: 'David blessed the Lord before all the congregation' (1 Chr. 29:10).

H. You gave security to his son, Solomon, and so he blessed you: 'Blessed is the Lord who has given rest to his people Israel' (1 Kgs. 8:56).

I. You gave security to Daniel and so he blessed you: 'Daniel answered and said, Blessed be the name of God' (Dan. 2:20).

(Ibid.)

Here is another set of opposites – three enemies, three saints: a fair match. In each case, the Israelite responded to God's favor with blessings, and the

205

Gentile with blasphemy. In this way the Gentiles show the price they pay for not knowing God but serving no gods instead. Like philosophers, the sages in the documents of the Oral Torah appeal to a single cause to account for diverse phenomena; the same factor that explains Israel has also to account for the opposite, that is, the Gentiles; what Israel has, Gentiles lack, and that common point has made all the difference. Idolatry is what angers God and turns him against the Gentiles, stated in so many words at b. A.Z. 1:1 I.23/4b: 'That time at which God gets angry comes when the kings put on their crowns on their heads and prostrate themselves to the sun. Forthwith the Holy One, blessed be he, grows angry.' That is why it is absolutely forbidden to conduct any sort of commerce with Gentiles in connection with occasions of idolatrous worship, for example, festivals and the like.

When we come to the halakhah's treatment of the same topic, our first question must be: why do the sages define a principal category of the halakhah in this wise? It is because the sages must devote a considerable account to the challenge to that justice represented by Gentile power and prosperity, Israel's subordination and penury. For if the story of the moral order tells about justice that encompasses all creation, the chapter of Gentile rule vastly disrupts the account. Gentile rule forms the point of tension, the source of conflict, attracting attention and demanding explanation. For the critical problematic inherent in the category, Israel, is that its anti-category, the Gentiles, dominate. So what rationality of a world ordered through justice accounts for the world ruled by Gentiles represents the urgent question to which the system must respond. And that explains why the systemic problematic focuses upon the question: how can justice be thought to order the world if the Gentiles rule? That formulation furthermore forms the public counterpart to the private perplexity: how is it that the wicked prosper and the righteous suffer? The two challenges to the conviction of the rule of moral rationality – Gentile hegemony, matched by the prosperity of wicked persons – match.

Yet here the halakhah turns out to make its own point, one that should not be missed. The halakhah presupposes not Gentile hegemony but only Gentile power; and it further takes for granted that Israelites may make choices, may specifically refrain from trading in what Gentiles value in the service of their gods, and may hold back from Gentiles what Gentiles require for that service. In this regard the halakhah parts company from the aggadah, the picture gained by looking inward not corresponding to the outward-facing perspective. Focused upon interiorities that prove real and tangible, not matters of theological theory at all, the halakhah of Abodah Zarah legislates for a world in which Israelites, though apparently subordinate, govern their own behavior and steer their own course.

What then is the difference between the Gentile and the Israelite, individually and collectively (there being no distinction between the private person and the public, social, and political entity)? A picture in cartographic form of the theological anthropology of the Oral Torah would portray a many colored

Israel at the center of the circle, the perimeter comprising all-white Gentiles; since, in the halakhah, Gentiles, like their idols, are as we have seen, a source of uncleanness of the same virulence as corpse uncleanness, the perimeter would be an undifferentiated white, the color of death. The law of uncleanness bears its theological counterpart in the lore of death and resurrection, a single theology animating both. Gentile-idolaters and Israelite worshippers of the one and only God part company at death. For the moment Israelites die but rise from the grave; Gentiles die and remain there. The roads intersect at the grave, each component of humanity taking its own path beyond. Israelites – meaning, those possessed of right conviction – will rise from the grave, stand in judgment, but then enter upon eternal life, to which no one else will enjoy access. So, in substance, humanity viewed whole is divided between those who get a share in the world to come – Israel – and who will stand when subject to divine judgment and those who will not.

Clearly, the moral ordering of the world encompasses all humanity. But from the perspective of the Torah God does not neglect the Gentiles or fail to exercise dominion over them. For even now, Gentiles are subject to a number of commandments or religious obligations. God cares for Gentiles as for Israel, he wants Gentiles as much as Israel to enter the kingdom of Heaven, and he assigns to Gentiles opportunities to evince their acceptance of his rule. One of these commandments is not to curse God's name, so Mishnah-tractate Sanhedrin 7:5 I.2/56a: 'Any man who curses his God shall bear his sin' (Lev. 24:15)': It would have been clear had the text simply said, 'A man.' Why does it specify, 'Any'? It serves to encompass idolaters, who are admonished not to curse the Name, just as Israelites are so admonished. Not cursing God, even while worshipping idols, seems a minimal expectation.

In fact there are seven such religious obligations that apply to the children of Noah. It is not surprising – indeed, it is predictable – that the definition of the matter should find its place in the halakhah of Abodah Zarah.

> T.8:4 A. Concerning seven religious requirements were the children of Noah admonished:

> B. setting up courts of justice, idolatry, blasphemy [cursing the Name of God], fornication, bloodshed, and thievery.

> (Tosefta-tractate Abodah Zarah, 8:4–6)

We now proceed to show how each of these religious obligations is represented as applying to Gentiles as much as to Israelites.

> C. Concerning setting up courts of justice— how so [how does Scripture or reason validate the claim that Gentiles are to set up courts of justice]?

D. Just as Israelites are commanded to call into session in their towns courts of justice.

E. Concerning idolatry and blasphemy – how so? ...

F. Concerning fornication – how so?

G. 'On account of any form of prohibited sexual relationship on account of which an Israelite court inflicts the death penalty, the children of Noah are subject to warning,' the words of R. Meir.

H. And [the] sages say, 'There are many prohibited relationships, on account of which an Israelite court does not inflict the death penalty and the children of Noah are [not] warned. In regard to these forbidden relationships the nations are judged in accord with the laws governing the nations.'

I. 'And you have only the prohibitions of sexual relations with a betrothed maiden alone.'

(Ibid.)

The systemization of Scripture's evidence for the stated proposition continues:

T.8:5 A. For bloodshed – how so?

B. A Gentile [who kills] a Gentile and a Gentile who kills an Israelite are liable. An Israelite [who kills] a Gentile is exempt.

C. Concerning thievery?

D. [If] one has stolen, or robbed, and so too in the case of finding a beautiful captive [woman], and in similar cases:

E. a Gentile in regard to a Gentile, or a Gentile in regard to an Israelite – it is prohibited. And an Israelite in regard to a Gentile – it is permitted.

T.8:6 A. Concerning a limb cut from a living beast – how so?

B. A dangling limb on a beast, [which] is not [so connected] as to bring about healing,

C. is forbidden for use by the children of Noah, and, it goes without saying, for Israelites.

D. But if there is [in the connecting flesh] sufficient [blood supply] to bring about healing,

E. it is permitted to Israelites, and, it goes without saying, to the children of Noah.

(Ibid.)

As in the case of Israelites, so the death penalty applies to a Noahide, so Mishnah-tractate Sanhedrin 7:5 I.4–5/57a: 'On account of violating three religious duties are children of Noah put to death: on account of adultery, murder, and blasphemy.' R. Huna, R. Judah, and all the disciples of Rab say, 'On account of seven commandments a son of Noah is put to death. The All-Merciful revealed that fact of one of them, and the same rule applies to all of them.' But just as Israelites, educated in the Torah, are assumed to exhibit certain uniform virtues, for example, forbearance, so Gentiles, lacking that same education, are assumed to conform to a different model.

Gentiles, by reason of their condition outside of the Torah, are characterized by certain traits natural to their situation, and these are worldly. Not only so, but the sages' theology of Gentiles shapes the normative law in how to relate to them. According to the Torah, if an Israelite is by nature forbearing and forgiving, the Gentile is by nature ferocious. That explains why in the halakhah as much as in the aggadah Gentiles are always suspect of the cardinal sins, bestiality, fornication, and bloodshed, as well as constant idolatry. That view of matters is embodied in normative law, as we have seen. The law of the Mishnah corresponds to the lore of scriptural exegesis; the theory of the Gentiles governs in both. Beyond the Torah there is not only no salvation from death, there is not even the possibility of a common decency – the Torah makes all the difference. The upshot may be stated very simply: Israel and the Gentiles form the two divisions of humanity. The one will die but rise from the grave to eternal life with God. When the other dies, it perishes; that is the end.

In the Torah Moses said it very well: choose life. The Gentiles sustain comparison and contrast with Israel, the point of ultimate division being death for the one, eternal life for the other. If Israel and the Gentiles are deemed comparable, the Gentiles do not acknowledge or know God, therefore, while they are like Israelites in sharing a common humanity by reason of mythic genealogy – deriving from Noah – the Gentiles do not receive in a meritorious manner the blessings that God bestows upon them. When it comes to the halakhah, as we have seen, the religious problematics focus not upon the Gentiles but upon Israel: what, given the world as it is, can Israel do in the dominion subject to Israel's own will and intention? That is the question that the halakhah fully answers.

4 DEFINING THE COMMUNITY IN ISLAMIC SOURCES:
THE QUR'AN, HADITH, FIQH

The identity of the community is not as clearcut in Islam as it is in Judaism. Whereas in Judaism very little consideration is taken of those outside the holy people, Israel, in Islamic sources a great deal of attention is given to people of other faith communities, many mentioned by name. These are accorded greater differentiation than 'the goyim' are by Judaism. But the principal points of differentiation remain focused upon matters of faith and practice. Attention is given to people who do not believe in God (*kuffar*), to people who pretend to believe but do not really (*munafiqun*), and to those who believe in multiple gods (*mushrikun*). Indeed, in many ways, the Muslim community defines itself *vis-à-vis* the communities of non-Muslim monotheists and non-monotheists. Yet because the Qur'an recognizes that some people among other faith groups are true believers, and that ultimately it is only God who judges, the lines between the identity of the community of Prophet Muhammad and those outside that community are not neatly drawn in scripture.

The Qur'an, in fact, uses a number of terms to designate the faithful. The most general is 'believers' (*al-mu'minun*), those who accept the existence of the one God, *al-ilah* (the [only] God) or Allah. Addressing the Prophet's followers, the Qur'an says:

> Indeed, God has blessed the believers by bringing forth among them a messenger from among themselves, who recites for them his verses and purifies them and teaches them the Book and wisdom; surely, before that they were obviously misguided.
>
> (Qu'ran, 3:165)

The verse continues, contrasting the believers (al-mu'minun) with the hypocrites (al-munafiqun). Referring to the Battle of Uhud between the Muslim community at Medina and their enemies in Mecca soon after the emigration (Hijra, 622 CE), the Qur'an explains that the defeat of the Medinans by the Meccans was a test given by God.

> And what happened to you on the day when the two groups met was by God's command, that he would know the believers and the hypocrites. And it was said to them, 'Come and fight in the way of God and defend.' They said, 'If we knew how to fight, we would follow you.' That day they were closer to disbelief (*kufr*) than to belief, saying with their mouths what is not in their hearts. God knows what they are hiding.
>
> (Ibid., 3:167–168)

The hypocrites are here likened to unbelievers, those who engage in kufr. Kufr means both ingratitude (for God's favors) and failure to recognize God at all, that is, unbelief. Although the meanings of ingratitude and unbelief are far apart in English, within the Qur'anic worldview the two are intimately bound; clear recognition of the only God is assumed inevitably to result in obedience, submission, worship. These, seen as marks of gratitude, demonstrate the Qur'an's equation of true belief with responsive behavior. In the foregoing verse, the only distinction between outright unbelievers and hypocrites is that the hypocrites do not admit their atheism. Nevertheless, it demonstrates itself in their actions, and in any case, God knows and will judge accordingly.

As we saw in the previous chapter, belief in the one God, integrally related to or expressed in righteous behavior, is the focus of the Qur'an's teaching. Thus, nearly ninety verses are addressed directly to 'those who believe'. For example:

> O you who believe, enter in peace completely and do not follow the footsteps of Satan. Indeed, he is the clear enemy of you.
>
> (Ibid., 2:208)

> Indeed, believers are brothers, so make peace between brothers and take protection with God so that he will be merciful to you.

> O you who believe, do not criticize, one people against another who may be better than they, nor women against women who may be better than they, and do not backbite among yourselves nor insult. Insult after belief is evil and those who do not repent are wrongdoers.

> O you who believe, avoid much suspicion, for some suspicion is sinful.
>
> (Ibid., 49:12–13)

The difficulty of naming more specifically the community of God's followers is reflected in the following verses of the same chapter.

> O people, we created you from a male and a female and we made you tribes and clans so that you would know one another. Indeed, the most distinguished among you with God are those who are most pious. Truly, God knows, and is aware.

> The Bedouin say, 'We believe.' Say, 'You do not believe; instead, say, "We submit," for belief has not entered your hearts, but if you obey God and his messenger, he will not take anything away from your deeds. Indeed God is forgiving and compassionate.'

> Truly the believers are those who believe in God and his messenger,

then have not doubted and have expended every effort with their wealth
and their persons in the way of God. They are the truthful ones.

Say, 'Do you acquaint God with your religion, when God knows what
is in the heavens and the earth and God is well aware of everything?'

They count it as a favor to you that they submit. Say, 'Do not count
your submission (*islam*) as a favor; God bestows favor on you that he
has guided you to belief, if you are truthful.'

Indeed, God knows the hidden things of the heavens and earth and
God sees what you do.

(Ibid., 49:14–19)

The Qur'an seems to be distinguishing here between true belief (*iman*) and
submission (*islam*) or obedience, with the implication that even before true
belief develops, it is spiritually advantageous to obey the teachings of Prophet
Muhammad. Nevertheless, it is clear that the Qur'an again emphasizes that
true belief is recognizable in people's actions, rather than in their words or in
how they identify themselves.

Because of the importance of true belief expressed in the Qur'an and many
verses addressed to the believers, it seems clear that 'the believers' was an early
designation of the Muslim community. This is attested to by the fact that the
earliest leaders, after the death of Prophet Muhammad (632 CE), called themselves 'leader(s) of the believers,' *umara* (singular: *amir*) *al-mu'minin*.

It is in this context that the term 'Islam', as it is used today to designate the
religion, appears in the Qur'an, although only eight times. We saw one
instance above, where people were told that their *islam* is not a favor to God
but is rather God's favor to them. Indeed, the Qur'an teaches that this submission results from God's guidance: 'Whoever God wants to guide, he instils
submission (*islam*) in his breast.' (6:126; cf. 39:24) But we are also told that
the only true religion is submission to the will of God, or *islam*.

God and the angels and those with knowledge, upholding justice, bear
witness that there is no god but God; there is no god but he, the great,
the wise. Indeed, the religion of God is submission (*al-islam*). And
those who were given the Book did not differ except after knowledge
came to them, in mutual error. And whoever disbelieves in the signs of
God, truly God will quickly take it into account. Then if they dispute
with you, say, 'I have submitted myself, as have those who follow me.'
Say to those who have been given the Book [Jews and Christians] and
to the unlearned, 'Have you submitted?' Then, if they have submitted,

they have been guided, and if they turn back, then it is for you to
announce [the message], and God sees those who serve.

(Ibid., 3:19–21)

Similarly, 'Whoever seeks other than submission (*islam*) as religion, it will not
be accepted from him and he will be among the losers in the afterlife.' (3:86)
True religion, then, is submission to the will of God, even if those involved call
themselves Jews or Christians. It is not described as Prophet Muhammad's
mission to make them change their group designation but to announce the
truth to them. God will judge them by their actions and intentions.

It is interesting to note the use of the term translated as 'religion' (*din*) in the
Qu'ran. For example:

And Abraham charged his sons with this, and Jacob: 'My sons, indeed
God chose the religion (*din*) for you so do not die until you have submitted.'

(Ibid., 2:133)

And fight [those who fight against you] until there is no oppression and
religion (*din*) is God's. But if they stop, then no hostility except toward
the oppressors.

(Ibid., 2:194)

There is no compulsion in religion (*din*). Right has been clearly distinguished from wrong. So whoever disbelieves in idols and believes in
God has hold of the strongest, unbreakable bond. And God hears and
knows.

(Ibid., 2:257)

Indeed, the religion (*din*) of God is submission (*islam*).

(Ibid., 3:20)

O People of the Book, do not go beyond your religion (din) and do not
say anything about God except the truth. Indeed, the Messiah, Jesus,
son of Mary, was a messenger of God and his word which he sent down
to Mary, and a spirit from him, so believe in God and his messenger
and do not say, 'Three [Trinity].'

(Ibid., 4:172)

And they were commanded only to obey God, making religion (*din*) his
in sincerity, being rightly guided, and to perform prayer and give zakat.
And that is the religion (*din*) of value.

(Ibid., 98:6)

213

The term *al-din* is used in this way at least sixty more times. But the same term is also used to mean 'the final judgment,' at least eighteen times. For example, the Qur'an opens with:

> In the name of God the merciful, the compassionate, praise belongs to God, the Lord of the worlds, the merciful, the compassionate, the master of the day of judgment (*din*).
>
> (Ibid., 1:14)

> [God] said, 'O Iblis [devil], what is the matter with you that you are not among those who bow [before the human being, as God instructed and the rest of the angels did, acknowledging his special role in God's plan]? He said to him, 'I am not going to bow before a person you created from clay and shaped mud.' He said, 'Then leave from here for you are damned. And indeed on you will be a curse until the Day of Judgment (*din*).'
>
> (Ibid., 15:33–36)

> But you disbelieve in the judgment (*din*). And indeed over you are guardians, honored recorders; they know what you are doing. Indeed, the virtuous will be in bliss and the evil will be in hell, burning there on the day of judgment (*din*). And they will not be absent from there. And what makes you realize what the day of judgment is? Again, what makes you realize what the day of judgment is? The day a person has no power over a[nother] person and [all] power that day will be God's [alone].
>
> (Ibid., 82:10–20)

One of the noun forms of the same term (*al-din*) means 'debt' or 'what is due,' and the term is also used in the Qur'an apparently with that sense on occasion. For example: 'On that day God will pay them their due and they will know that God is the clear truth.' (24:25) Based on that usage, some hypothesize that the common bond between 'religion' and 'judgment' is that is that they are both something 'owed'. Correct belief and behavior are owed to God the Creator, explaining why 'disbelief' and 'ingratitude' are the same term in Arabic; and the last judgment is only for God to make, while we for our part will receive what we are owed.

In any case, the term *al-din* is used to refer to the religion of Abraham, as we saw, and it is also the religion of Noah, and of all the prophets: 'He has prescribed for you as religion what he has charged Noah with, and what we revealed to you and Abraham and Moses and Jesus: "Establish religion (*din*) do not separate over it." ' (42:14) But *din* is not the only term used for 'religion'. The term *millah* is also used, for example:

And who turns from the religion (*millah*) of Abraham except the foolish?

(Ibid., 2:131)

And they say, 'Be Jews or Christians to be guided.' Say, 'Rather, the religion (*millah*) of Abraham the rightly inclined (*hanif*); he was not among the idolaters.'

(Ibid., 2:136)

And I followed the religion (*millah*) of my fathers Abraham and Isaac and Jacob. It is not for us to associate anything with God. That is by the grace of God for us and for [other] people, but most people are not grateful.

(Ibid., 12:39)

So the *din* of Abraham and the *millah* of Abraham are one and the same, the true religion, for Abraham is at once rightly inclined (*hanif*), a true believer (*mu'min*) and one who submits (*muslim*):

And when Abraham and Ishmael raised the foundations of the house: 'Our Lord, accept from us for you are all-hearing and seeing. Our Lord, make us submitters (*muslimin*) to you and [make] our offspring a submitting (*muslima*) people to you.'

(Ibid., 2:128–29)

Abraham was neither a Jew nor a Christian but he was rightly inclined (*hanif*), submitting (*muslim*), and was not an idolater.

(Ibid., 3:68)

Say, 'God was truthful, so follow the religion (*millah*) of Abraham, rightly inclined (*hanif*), for he was not idolater.'

(Ibid., 3:96)

So again we see the term that came to be used to designate the religion, *islam,* does not have the kind of exclusivist connotation in the Qur'an that would develop later. It seems instead to indicate all those who believe in the one God, who has intervened in history, sending messengers with truth, and whoever accepts those messages and lives in accordance with them – those who submit (*muslimun*).

In this context, the Qur'an uses yet another term for the community established by the Prophet Muhammad: *ummah,* a 'nation' (coming from the same root as the word for 'mother', just as 'nation' comes from the same root as 'nativity' or birth), 'people', or 'community'. There are numerous mentions of previous communities (*umam,* plural of *ummah*), that have failed to follow God's guidance and so have passed away. For example, referring to the descendants of Abraham, Ishmael, Isaac, and Jacob:

> That is a community (*ummah*) that has passed away; for them is what they deserved, and for you what you have earned, and you will not be questioned about what they were doing.
>
> (Ibid., 2:135)

> Or do you say that Abraham and Ishmael and Isaac and Jacob and the tribes were Jews or Christians? Say, 'Are you more knowledgeable than God?' And who is more oppressive than the one who hides the testimony he has from God? God is not ignorant of what you do.

> That is a community (*ummah*) that has passed away; for them is what they deserved, and for you what you have earned, and you will not be questioned about what they were doing.
>
> (Ibid., 2:141–142)

Abraham himself is described as a community, probably indicating that he was the founder of the community of true believers.

> Indeed, Abraham was a community (*ummah*) obedient to God, rightly inclined (*hanif*), and he was not among the idolaters. Grateful for his favors, he chose him and guides him to the straight path (*sirat mustaqim*). And we gave him goods in this world and indeed in the afterlife he will be among the righteous. So we have revealed to you to follow the religion (*millah*) of Abraham the rightly inclined (*hanif*), and he was not among the idolaters.
>
> (Ibid., 16:121–124)

Accordingly, the followers of Prophet Muhammad are told:

> Thus, we appointed you a median [or moderate] community (*ummat wasat*) so that you may bear witness to the people and the Messenger [Prophet Muhammad] be a witness to you. And we only made the direction of prayer (*qiblah*) you were facing so that we would know one who follows the Messenger from one who turns on his heels.
>
> (Ibid., 2:144)

The Qur'an says that at one time, all people were one community.

> People were one community (*ummah*), then God brought forth prophets as announcers and warners and sent down with them the

216

Book of truth so he could judge among people on things upon which they differed. And none differed on it except those to whom it was given after clear signs came to them, out of jealousy among them.

(Ibid., 2:214; cf. 10:20)

The Qur'an confirms elsewhere that this multiplicity of communities was part of the divine plan.

And if your Lord had willed, he would have made people into one community, but they continue to differ, except those upon whom your Lord has mercy. And for that he created them and the word of your Lord is fulfilled.

(Ibid., 11:119–20; cf. 16:94; 42:9)

Furthermore, God has sent a messenger to each community.

And to every community (*ummah*) a messenger, so when their messenger comes, it is judged among them with justice and they are not oppressed.

(Ibid., 10:48)

And we have brought forth in every community (*ummah*) a messenger. So serve God and turn away from temptation. For among them are those whom God has guided and among them are those truly turned toward error. So travel the land and see what happens to liars.

(Ibid., 16:37)

Every community has also been given rituals to follow.

And for every community (*ummah*) we made a ritual of sacrifice so they could mention the name of God over the animals of the herds he has given them. God is one, so submit to him and preach in humility.

(Ibid., 22:35)

For every community (*ummah*) we have made a ritual sacrifice so do not let them argue with you on the matter and call to your Lord for indeed you follow the correct guidance. And if they argue with you, say, 'God is more knowledgeable about what you do. God judges among you on the Day of Resurrection about the things on which you differ.'

(Ibid., 22:68–70)

hus again the Qur'an, in keeping with its overall emphasis on expressing true belief through good works, guides people away from arguing among themselves about their various creeds and practices. It explains further that every community will be judged together in light of what their respective messengers have taught them.

> And [one] day we will bring forth from all communities (*umam*) a witness. Then those who disbelieve will not be allowed leave nor to intercede.
>
> (Ibid., 16:85)

> And [one] day we will bring forth from all communities (*umam*) a witness for them from among themselves and we will bring you as a witness against them. And we have sent down to you the Book to make everything clear and as a guide and in mercy, and announcing to those who submit.
>
> (Ibid., 16:90; cf. 28:76)

Believers are then encouraged to come together again as a single community.

> O you who believe, take refuge in God as you should, and do not die without having submitted.

> And cling to the bond of God together and do not divide. And remember the favor of God on you when you were enemies and he brought your hearts together so that by his favor you became brothers. You were on the edge of a pit of fire and he saved you from it. So God makes clear his signs to you, guiding you.

> And let there be a community (*ummah*) of you, calling to good and prescribing righteousness and proscribing evil. And it is those who will thrive.
>
> (Ibid., 3:103–105)

The unity of the community of true believers is stressed when the Qur'an tells Muhammad's followers that they belong to the same community as the followers of earlier messengers. After mentioning Moses, Aaron, Abraham, Lot, Isaac, Jacob, Noah, David, Solomon, Job, Ishmael, Idris, Elijah, and Jonah, the Qur'an recounts the story of Zechariah.

> [W]hen he called to his Lord, 'My Lord, do not leave me alone, for you are the best of heirs.'

218

Then we answered him and gave him John, and cured his wife for him. Indeed, they competed with one another in good works, and called on us in hope and fear and they were humble before us.

And the one who remained chaste [Mary], so we breathed into her from our spirit and we made her and her son, a sign for the worlds.

Indeed this, your community (*ummah*), is one community (ummah) and indeed I am your Lord, so worship.

(Ibid., 21:90–93)

The term *ummah* appears to be the designation used earliest by Prophet Muhammad as he organized his followers and their dependants into a sociopolitical entity. This is apparent from the Constitution of Medina, preserved in Muhammad Ibn Ishaq's *Sirat Rasul Allah* (Life of the Messenger of God), based on oral (hadith) reports, collected and placed in narrative form just over a century after the Prophet's death. The document defines the community (*ummah*) as consisting of his followers, referred to as 'Believers' and 'Muslims', both those who emigrated with him from Mecca (*muhajirun*) and those who welcomed them in Medina (*ansar*), including the Jewish tribes who lived in Medina. The other inhabitants of Medina, who were not monotheists, were not included.

In the name of God, the Merciful, the Compassionate!

This document is from Muhammad the Prophet, governing relations among the Believers and the Muslims of Quraysh [Meccan tribe] and Yathrib (Medina) and those who followed them and joined with them and struggled with them.

1. They are one Community to the exclusion of all other men.

[2–10: The various tribes shall handle their own retaliation and prisoner redemptions, according to their customs.]

11. The Believers shall not desert any poor person among them, but shall pay his redemption or blood-money, as is proper.

12. No Believer shall seek to turn the auxiliary of another Believer against him.

13. God-fearing Believers will be against whoever among them is rebellious or whoever seeks to sow injustice or sin or enmity among the

Believers; every man's hand shall be against him, though he were the son of one of them.

14. No Believer shall kill a Believer for the sake of an unbeliever, or aid an unbeliever against a Believer.

15. The protection of God is one: even the least of them may extend it to a stranger. The Believers are friends to each other, to the exclusion of all other men.

16. The Jews who follow us shall have aid and equality, except those who do wrong or aid the enemies of the Muslims.

17. The peace of the Believers is one: no Believer shall make peace separately where there is fighting for God's sake. Conditions [of peace] must be just and equitable to all.

18. In every raid, the riders shall ride close together.

19. And the Believers shall avenge one another's blood, if shed for God's sake, for the God-fearing have the best and strongest guidance.

20. No idolater [of Medina] shall take Qurayshi [Meccan tribes] property or persons under his protection, nor shall he turn anyone against a Believer.

21. Whoever kills a Believer shall also be killed, unless the next of kin of the slain man is otherwise satisfied, and the Believers shall be against him altogether; no one is permitted to act otherwise.

22. No Believer who accepts this document and believes in God and Judgment is permitted to aid a criminal or give him shelter. The curse of God and his wrath on the Day of Judgment shall fall upon whoever aids or shelters him, and no repentance or compensation shall be accepted from him if he does.

23. Whenever you differ about a case, it shall be referred to God and to Muhammad.

24. The Jews shall bear expenses with the Muslims as long as they fight along with them.

25. *The Jews of the Banu 'Awf are one community with the Believers; the Jews have their religion and the Muslims have theirs. This is so for them*

and their clients, except for one who does wrong or treachery; he hurts only himself and his family. [*Italics added.*]

26–35. The same is true for Jews (who are members and confederates) of the other clans of Yathrib: honorable behavior is without treachery.

36. None of them may go out [to war] without Muhammad's permission, but they shall not be prevented from taking vengeance for a wound. Whoever murders a man murders himself and his family, unless he has been wronged. God is [the guarantor].

37. The Jews shall bear their expenses and the Muslims shall bear theirs, and they shall render mutual aid to whoever wars against the people of this document. There shall be mutual advice and consultation, and honorable behavior, without treachery. A man is not guilty of treachery by the act of his confederate, and help shall be due to one who is wronged.

[The document concludes with ten more provisions detailing miscellaneous issues of protection and mutual aid.][70]

It appears, therefore, that at this point *ummah* or 'community' was the most encompassing category of believers (monotheists), capable of including a number of 'religions' and legal codes brought by various messengers. Indeed, this became the model for including other monotheists, such as the Christians, who were likewise allowed to join the community, keeping their own worship and personal law, paying a tax to substitute for the zakat paid by Muslims in order to contribute to community support.

Other hadith literature preserved in the authoritative collections displays, however, an evolving sense of group identity among those who accepted Muhammad as their prophet, as distinct from those who maintained loyalty to their own prophets, in the case of the Jews, and those who accepted Jesus as the redeemer and fulfilment of the covenant, that is, the Christians. The reports in question reflect another trend in certain Qur'anic verses, one in which Jews and Christians are described as generally untrustworthy.

O you who believe, do not take Jews and Christians as friends. They are friends of one another and whoever makes friends among them is one of them. Indeed, God does not guide oppressive people.

(Qu'ran, 5:52)

For you will find the strongest people as enemies of the believers to be the Jews and the idolaters.

(Ibid., 5:83)

And they say, 'No one will enter paradise unless he is a Jew or a Christian.' These are their hopes. Say, 'Give your proof if you are truthful.'

Rather, whoever submits himself to God and does good works, his reward is with his Lord. They have nothing to fear nor shall they grieve.

And the Jews say the Christians stand on nothing, and the Christians say the Jews stand on nothing. And they read the same Book. That is what is said by those who do not know, like what they say. So God will judge between them on the Day of Resurrection on those things on which they disagree.

(Ibid., 2:112–114)

Thus, the Constitution of Medina included Jews within the ummah, and by extension, others were also allowed religious freedom. Yet there remains suspicion about the motives of those who do not leave their religions and become Muslim, reflected in the fact that violation of provisions for their inclusion automatically results in exclusion from the community.

The specific nature of the differences between Muslim communal identity and that of other monotheists does not take concrete form until the development of Islamic legal texts (*fiqh*, human articulations of practical implications of revelation and the normative practice of Prophet Muhammad). It will be recalled (see our companion volume *Comparing Religions through Law: Judaism and Islam*), that these texts developed in the context of an expanding sociopolitical power, the community led by *amir al-mu'minin* (the commander of the believers) or caliph, which allowed religiolegal freedom to Jews and Christians. Jews and Christians were allowed to maintain their own legal systems, while Muslims had to develop their own. As we have seen, there was much in the Jewish and Christian heritage that was sanctioned by the Qur'an and the practice of Prophet Muhammad, but there were differences as well. Thus, the development of the Islamic legal system involved a dual dynamic. Not only was it necessary to distinguish Islamic law from that of the other monotheists, but it was necessary to develop a system that allowed for certain differences of opinion within the Muslim community, but one that at the same time maintained an overall coherence. While the latter effort took precedence over the former, its results influenced the growing sense of Muslim group identity and therefore its substantive separation from other religious groups.

The Islamic legal system developed over a period of some 200 years. The ultimate source of Islamic law was the Qur'an; upon this all agreed. There was agreement as well that the Qur'an is complemented by oral tradition, carried in reports (*ahadith;* singular: *hadith*) relating the words and deeds of Prophet Muhammad, collected and codified by the third century after the death of

Muhammad (632 CE). While many hadith reports disagree with one another, and there remains disagreement among scholars regarding individual reports' reliability and applicability, virtually all Muslims accept the principle that the Sunna of the Prophet, though secondary to the Qur'an, is essential to the understanding of scripture. It acts as authoritative explication of written scripture.

But as Muslim rule spread beyond the Arabian peninsula, issues arose that were not specifically covered in the Qur'an and the Sunna. Efforts were needed, therefore, to determine how to derive needed legislation from the revealed sources. Within the first three centuries of the Islamic era, a number of schools of legal thought developed in this regard. While all agreed on the ultimate sources and methodology for deriving legislation, they differed on the relative importance of sources as well as on specific points of interpretation and customary practice. The earliest school of legal thought (*madhhab*) to develop was that attributed to the work of Abu Hanifa (d. 767 CE), although none of his own works has survived. The oldest surviving comprehensive work of fiqh is that of Malik b. Anas (d. 795/6 C.E.), *Al-Muwatta'* ('the leveled path'). The earliest works of fiqh are attributed to followers of either Abu Hanifa, and are thus said to belong to the Hanafi school of thought, or to Malik, and thus said to belong to the Maliki school. The Hanafi school was also sometimes called the Iraqi school, since that is where Abu Hanifa and his main followers (Abu Yusuf and al-Shaybani) worked. The Maliki school was associated with Medina. In both regions there was an established body of hadith literature which was consulted for subjects not specifically dealt with in the Qur'an, or for amplification of those that were. *Al-Muwatta'*, for example, includes some 1700 hadith reports circulating in the city of Medina, Malik's home. Legists then extrapolated from such precedent as was available, relying on their informed opinion (*ra'y*) to determine the established or agreed-upon practice in each region; the term used to describe such agreed upon interpretation was *ijma'*. Ijma' means consensus, but in the context of early Islamic law it refers to practice that has been agreed upon as appropriate. 'The ijma' of Medina,' for example, was a common phrase, meaning that something or other was the agreed-upon (legal) practice in Medina. Malik generally concludes his arguments in *Al-Muwatta'*, after having cited authoritative hadiths, by claiming that the practice in question is the one his community in Medina usually follows. In these sentences Malik uses the terms *sunnah* and *'amal* (practice) and *al-amr al-mujtama' alayh* ('agreed upon practice') interchangeably.[71]

As Muslim sovereignty continued to expand in range and complexity, so did its legal system. A more formal syllogistic reasoning (*qiyas*) was developed to extract rulings from the sources for novel cases. Whether by means of ra'y or qiyas, the exercise of reasoning to determine application of principles established in the Qur'an and authoritative hadith reports to novel cases was called *ijtihad*. The earliest schools of law, therefore, generally started with the Qur'an, went next to the hadith reports considered authoritative in their regions, then exercised their reason on these two sources, concluding with what was established practice (ijma') among them.

The culmination of efforts to systematize Islamic legal reasoning was the work of the eponym of a third school legal school, al-Shafi'i (d. 820 CE).[72] In his system, ijma' was the third source of Islamic law, after the Qur'an and the Sunna (which he equated with authoritative hadith reports, although the process of determining exactly which hadith reports were authoritative had not yet been completed). But for al-Shafi'i, ijma' did not refer to regional consensus. For him it meant the consensus of the entire Muslim community. The goal of this re-definition of ijma' was no doubt greater uniformity in Islamic law. But given the vast extent of the Muslim world by that time and the virtual impossibility of determining consensus among people spread from Spain to Iran, its effect was greater reliance on precedent (taqlid) in determining legislation. In fact, al-Shafi'i held that the soundest basis for law was precedent and that ijtihad should be used only as a last resort. And then it must be ijtihad narrowly interpreted as qiyas, for which he articulated rules, rather than the more liberal ra'y.

It is al-Shafi'i's view on ijma' that concerns us here. His insistence that it consists of the consensus of the entire community, not just those of a given region, meant that it was, for practical reasons, a thing of the past. All authoritative ijma' had been done since it was no longer possible to achieve such consensus. In his effort to convince others of the validity of his case, al-Shafi'i articulated clear lines of distinction between 'those who hold what the Muslim community holds' and those 'who hold differently.' In his *Risala* he recounts being asked what proof he has for his view on consensus. The questioner says he agrees that it would be unlawful to give an opinion at odds with a clear command of the Qur'an or Sunna of the Prophet. But how do we know that we should accept an established opinion ('consensus of the public') as authoritative (rather than engage in our own reasoning based on the two main sources)? Al-Shafi'i's answer assumes general acceptance of an already prevalent hadith report according to which the Prophet said that his community will never agree on an error.

> That on which the public are agreed and which, as they assert, was related from the apostle, that is so ... . So we must accept the decision of the public because we have to obey their authority, and we know that wherever there are sunnas of the Prophet, the public cannot be ignorant of them, although it is possible that some are, and we know that the public can neither agree on anything contrary to the sunna of the Prophet nor on an error.[73]

Next, al-Shafi'i was asked, 'What is the meaning of the Prophet's order to follow the community?' In reply, al-Shafi'i said that there is only one possible meaning. The questioner then asked, 'How is it possible that there is only one

224

meaning?' In response, al-Shafi'i articulated the difference between Muslims and non-Muslims that would become definitive.

> When the community spread in the lands [of Islam], nobody was able to follow its members who had been dispersed and mixed with other believers and unbelievers, pious and impious. So it was meaningless to follow the community [as a whole], because it was impossible [to do so], except for what the [entire] community regarded as lawful or unlawful [orders] and [the duty] to obey these [orders].

> He who holds what the Muslim community holds shall be regarded as following the community, and he who holds differently shall be regarded as opposing the community he was ordered to follow. So the error comes from separation; but in the community as a whole there is no error concerning the meaning of the Qur'an, the sunna, and analogy [qiyas].[74]

In practical terms, those who agree with what the legal scholars decide shall be considered Muslim, and those who do not follow Islamic legal scholars' rulings are not. Undoubtedly, it took time for al-Shafi'i's articulation of the roots of Islamic law (usul al-fiqh) to be accepted – at least a century. That it did become the basis of 'an organically structured and independent science ... a full-fledged methodology,' is, however, undeniable.[75] That is due primarily to the fact that his opinions were not innovative; his genius lay in the fact that he was able to achieve a synthesis of prevailing opinions. Ongoing arguments about the details of his synthesis need not concern us here. Of interest in this context is the clear definition of 'the Muslim community.' From this time on, if not before, with few exceptions, it was defined as those who accept the articulated sources of legislation and follow their rulings. All others 'shall be regarded as opposing the community.'

5 HOW THE OUTSIDER IS TREATED IN THE LAW OF ISLAM

This is not to say that religious freedom was abandoned in Islam: on the contrary, Jews and Christians – and later Zoroastrians and Hindus – were accepted as members of the Islamic polity, although not of the ummah, defined as the strictly Muslim community. It is simply to stress that the identity of the Muslim community came to rest on Islamic law, rather than on issues of belief or behavior. This, too, reflects Qur'anic teaching.

> And so let the People of the Gospel [Christians] judge according to what God sent down to it, and whoever does not judge by what God has sent down are sinful.

And we have sent to you a Book with truth, confirming and safeguarding the Book that was sent before it. So judge between them by what God has sent down and do not follow their desires, turning from the truth that came to you. We have appointed for each of you a law (*shir'ah*) and a path.

(Qur'an, 5:47–48)

The fact that there are numerous prophets, more than one book of revelation, and more than one legal system is, therefore, not considered problematic. Like the existence of more than one religious community, it is described by the Qur'an as part of the divine plan.

Some of the followers of the earlier texts may even be saved, as the Qur'an affirms.

Surely, those who believe and those Jews, Christians and Sabians who believe in God and the last day and do good deeds, their reward is with their Lord; they have nothing to fear nor shall they grieve.

(Ibid., 2:63; cf. 5:70)

And if the People of the Book had believed and taken refuge with God, we would have forgiven their sins and admitted them to the garden of bliss.

And if they had observed the Torah and the Gospel and what was sent down to them from their Lord, they would have eaten from what was above them and beneath their feet. Among them are a just community *[ummah]* but many of them do evil.

O Messenger, deliver what has been sent down to you from your Lord, for if you do not, you have not delivered his message. And God will protect you from people, and God does not guide disbelieving people.

Say, 'O People of the Book, you stand on nothing until you observe the Torah and the Gospel and has been sent down to you from your Lord.' And, indeed, what has been sent to you will increase in many of them disregard and ingratitude, so do not grieve for an ungrateful people.

Surely those who believe and the Jews and the Sabians and the Christians, whoever believes in God and the Last Day and does good works have nothing to fear nor shall they grieve.

(Ibid., 5:66–70)

[The People of the Book] are not all alike. Among the People of the

Book is an upright community, reciting God's verses during the night and prostrating [in prayer].

They believe in God, the last day, and command good and proscribe evil, hastening in good works; and they are among the righteous.

(Ibid., 3:114–115)

Indeed, God will admit those who believe and do good works into the garden beneath which rivers flow; indeed God does what he wants.

(Ibid., 22:15)

This promise of reward for those who believe and do good works refers to divine judgment, however, and not to group identity. In this sense the People of the Book may even be considered *muslim*, in the Arabic sense of 'one who submits,' as we noted earlier.

Indeed the religion of God is submission (*al-islam*). And those who were given the Book did not differ except after knowledge came to them, in mutual error. And whoever disbelieves in the signs of God, truly God will quickly take it into account. Then if they dispute with you, say, 'I have submitted myself, as have those who follow me.' Say to those who have been given the book [Jews and Christians] and to the unlearned, 'Have you submitted?' Then, if they have submitted, they have been guided, and if they turn back, then it is for you to announce [the message], and God sees those who serve.

(Ibid., 3:19–21; cf. 2:273)

The reference here is clearly again to divine judgment rather than group identity. The Jews, Christians and Muslims have each received correct guidance and revelation and each has a law; that is as God has ordained. Accordingly, they should show their belief through righteous behavior (according to the Qur'an), reciprocate loyalty (according to the Constitution of Medina), and discuss their differences.

And debate with the People of the Book only on what is best, but not with those among them who are wrongdoers. And say, 'We believe in what has been sent down to us and sent to you; our God and your God are one, and we have submitted to him.'

(Ibid., 29:47–48)

Still, as we saw earlier, Jews and Christians should not be taken as friends.

O you who believe, do not take to the inside other than yourselves ... . Hatred has shown itself from their mouths and what their breasts hide is [even] greater. We have made signs clear for you, if you understand.

(Ibid., 3:119)

O you who believe, do not take Jews and Christians as friends. They are friends with one another, and whoever makes friends with them is one of them.

(Ibid., 5:52)

Truly, your friend is God and his messenger and those who believe and those who observe prayer and give zakat and who bow (in prayer).

And whoever takes God and his messenger as friends and those who believe, the party of God [hizb Allah], they shall prevail.

O you who believe, do not choose friends from those who were given the Book before you [and for whom] your religion is a joke and game, and the disbelievers – and take refuge in God if you are believers –

And [those who] when you call to prayer, take it as a joke and a game. That is because they are a people who do not understand.

(Ibid., 5:56–59)[76]

Some People of the Book may even have to be fought if they fail to live up to their own standards, rejecting Muslim rule and thus interfering in establishing a godly society.

Fight those among those who have been given the Book who do not believe in God and the Last Day and do not forbid what God and his Messenger have forbidden, nor follow the true religion, until they hand over the alms tax and are humbled.

(Ibid., 9:29)

This is because they remain under suspicion in that, having been given true revelation in the past, they fail to recognize it now by accepting the religion of Prophet Muhammad.

And when they meet those who believe, they say, 'We believe.' But when they go off with one another, they say, 'Do you tell them what God has revealed to you, so they can argue with you about it before your Lord? Don't you understand?'

228

Don't they know that God knows what they hide and what they announce publicly?

(Ibid., 2:76–77)

And when a Book from God came to them, confirming what was with them, and they had been seeking victory over those who disbelieved, yet when what they knew came to them, they disbelieved in it. So the curse of God be on the unbelievers.

(Ibid., 2:90; cf. 6:93)

And when it is said to them, 'Believe in what God has sent down,' they say, 'We believe in what was sent to us.' And they disbelieve in what is after that, but it is the truth, confirming what is with them. Say, 'Why did you kill the prophets of God before, if you are believers?'

(Ibid., 2:92)

Indeed your Lord knows what your breasts hide and what they reveal.

And there is nothing hidden in heaven and earth that was not made clear in the Book.

(Ibid., 27:75–76)

And when our clear verses are recited to them, those who disbelieve say of the truth when it comes to them, 'This is sheer trickery.'

So they say, 'Did he forge it?' Say, 'If I forged it, you cannot help me at all against God. He knows best what you are engaging in. He serves as a witness between you and me, and he is forgiving and compassionate.

Say, 'I am not an innovator among prophets and I do not know what will be done with me or with you. But I only follow what is revealed to me and I am only a clear warner.'

(Ibid., 46:8–9)

And they say, 'Be Jews or Christians to be guided.' Say, 'No, the religion of Abraham the true believer; he was not among the idolaters.'

Say, 'We believe in God and what was sent down to us and what was sent to Abraham and Ishmael and Isaac and Jacob and the tribes and what given to Moses and Jesus and what was given to the prophets from their Lord. We do not distinguish among any of them, and to him we submit.

And if they believe as you believe, they have been guided, but if they turn away, then they are in schism and God will be sufficient for you against them, for he hears and knows.

(Ibid., 2:136–138)

O People of the Book, our messenger has come to you, making clear – after a gap in the messengers – but you say, 'No announcer has come to us nor a warner.' Indeed, an announcer has come to you and a warner, and God has power over everything.

(Ibid., 5:20)

We took an agreement with the Children of Israel and we sent messengers to them. Whenever a messenger came to them with what they themselves did not want, they lied to some and killed others.

And they reckoned there would be no temptation, so they were blind and deaf. Then God forgave them, then [again] many of them they were blind and deaf and God watches what they do.

For they disbelieve who say that God is the Messiah, son of Mary, when the Messiah said, 'Children of Israel, serve God my Lord and your Lord.' Indeed, whoever associates others with God, God has forbidden him Heaven and his refuge will be fire, and the oppressors have no helpers.

They have disbelieved who said that God is third of three. There is no god but the one God. And if they do not stop what they are saying, a painful punishment will come to those of them who disbelieve.

Won't they turn to God and ask for his forgiveness, since God is forgiving and compassionate?

(Ibid., 5:71–75)

The suspicion with which Jews and Christians are viewed as a result of their failure to become Muslims is heightened by the Qur'an's claims that the coming of the Prophet Muhammad was actually announced in the other monotheists' scriptures, before they concealed such references.

Do you expect that they will believe you when a group of them hear the word of God and then tampered with it after they understood and they know [it]?

(Ibid., 2:75)

Do you say that Abraham and Ishmael and Isaac and Jacob and the

230

tribes were Jews or Christians? Say, 'Are you more knowledgeable than God?'

(Ibid., 2:141)

O People of the Book, why do you disbelieve the signs of God when you have witnessed?

O People of the Book, why do you mix truth with lies and hide the truth knowingly?

(Ibid., 3:71–72)

Those who follow the Messenger, the unlettered prophet, whom they find written about with them in the Torah and the Gospel, who commands them with good and proscribes evil, and allows the good and prohibits the bad and removes their load from them and the bonds that were on them. So those who believe in him and aid and support him, and follow the light that was sent with him, these will prosper.

(Ibid., 7:158)

Nevertheless, despite these suspicions, as noted above, it is not for Muslims to force the People of the Book to change their religion, nor to judge them. They are allowed to retain their own systems and God will judge them when the time comes.

[God said,] 'As for those disbelieve, I will punish them severely in this world and in the afterlife, and they will have no helpers.'

But as for those who believe and do good works, he will reward them fully; and God does not love the wrongdoers.

(Ibid., 3:57)

Indeed, those who believe and those Jews and Sabians and Christians and Zoroastrians and the idolaters, surely God will distinguish among them on the Day of Resurrection. Truly, God is a witness over all things.

(Ibid., 22:18)

Say, 'Travel the land to see how those who came before you ended up; most of them were idolaters.'

So set your face to the established religion before a day comes when there will be no avoiding God; on that day they will separated.

Whoever disbelieves, his disbelief will be against him and whoever does good works, they are providing for themselves,

That he will reward those who believe and do good works out of his bounty; he does not love the unbelievers.

(Ibid., 30:43–46)

Thus, Jews and Christians are separate communities in the Qur'an, to be respected in that they have received true revelation, and allowed complete freedom provided they do not interfere with Islamic sovereignty. Hadith material makes relatively minor mention of other religious communities. The most attention is paid to Jews and Christians, for example, in discussions concerning how to address non-Muslims, it is universally agreed that Muslims are to greet one another with the phrase *al salaam 'ulaykum,* 'Peace be with you.' It is also agreed that Muslims must respond accordingly, generally by adding further blessings: 'And with you, peace, and the mercy of God and his blessing.' There is also discussion about whether this greeting is necessary for all individuals or just for most of the community, whether riders greet walkers first or the other way around, whether those in a small group should offer the greeting to a larger group first or the other way around, and so on. But also included are appropriate greetings for People of the Book, meaning Jews and Christians, who are not to be greeted first. If Jews or Christians greet Muslims, they are to be responded to accordingly; whether they offer 'peace' (*salam*) or 'poison' (*samm),* the appropriate response is 'and to you.' It is also reported that Muslims are not to give way to Jews and Christians on the road: 'Abu Huraira reported Allah's Messenger (may peace be upon him) as saying: "Do not greet the Jews and Christians before they greet you and when you meet any one of them on the roads force him to go to the narrowest part of it." '[77] Other than such minor issues, hadith material generally confirms Qur'anic teachings concerning the People of the Book.

The status of non-believers (*kuffar*) and polytheists (or idolaters, *mushrikun*) is a different case entirely. They are addressed in the Qur'an, as well, but there is no heritage of true belief in which they can take refuge. They must accept true revelation or they will receive the severest punishments in the afterlife:

Haven't you seen that whoever in the heavens and on earth, and the sun and moon and the stars and the mountains and trees and animals, and many human beings submit to God? But many earn punishments, and whoever God declares feeble, none will honor. Indeed, God does what he wants.

(Ibid., 22:19)

God will punish hypocrites – men and women, and idolaters – men

and women, and God forgives the believers – men and women; and
God is forgiving, merciful.

(Ibid., 33:74)

This cosmic judgment is reflected in Islamic law. Those who refuse to accept
Islam or at least to make a treaty with Muslims whereby a tribute is paid and
Muslims and their allies living within their territory are protected, these
non-believers are subject to military expeditions whose purpose is to force subjugation. Al-Mawardi, the tenth-century Shafi'i jurist responsible for articu-
lating the role of the leader of the caliph, in fact described it as an essential
duty to 'wage holy war [*jihad*] against those who, after having been invited to
accept Islam, persist in rejecting it, until they either become Muslims or enter
the Pact [*dhimma*] so that God's truth may prevail over every religion.'[78] (See
Comparing Religions through Law: Judaism and Islam, chapter 7, for a full discussion of jihad.)

6 CONCLUSIONS

It is clear from the foregoing that Jewish and Islamic [Christian] scriptures use different
criteria to determine group identity, inclusion and exclusion, at least at one
level. In Judaism, revelation is addressed to one subject group, identified as
chosen by God to live in accordance with specific regulations. These regulations are designed to re-create an ideal life in relation to God, the Creator.
Observance of the regulations is therefore of primary importance. In other
words, living according to Jewish law defines inclusion in the group. To be
'Israel' means, to accept God's dominion and his unity, and to accept 'the yoke
of the Torah.' That is what brings each affirming individual within the framework of 'Israel,' and it is why 'Israel' in the authoritative sources may refer to
an individual or to the entire community; there is no difference. The story
Judaism tells itself about Israel is that God has devised in the Torah his final
solution to the problem of humanity – free will making them like God but
also leading them to rebel against God's will. The issue is not individual but
the character of humanity as a whole: from creation like God, with free will,
humanity rebels, and the Torah is given to purify the human heart and teach
people to want the same things God wants – 'to do justice, love mercy, and
walk humbly with God,' in a classic formulation. So by 'Israel' Judaism means
not an ethnic group or a particular nation like other ethnic groups of nations.
It means a unique social entity, 'a people' that is *sui generis* by reason of how it
comes into being through all time: those that embody God's kingdom on
earth.

Islamic scripture, by contrast, is addressed to a far more amorphous group:
believers in God (monotheists), those who submit to the one God ('muslims'),
and those who claim to believe or submit but do not really (hypocrites) – and

233

only God can tell which is which – as well as those who believe in more than one god or who associate others with God (polytheists). At this level, 'muslim' includes all those who believe in God and respond accordingly by doing good works as judged by God. On the practical level of daily life, however, 'muslim' (Muslim) means those whose lives are regulated by Islamic law. These two levels are not in contradiction to one another; they simply refer to different levels of concern. The former level, that stressed in the Qur'an, is concerned with salvation or earning eternal reward. Ultimately, only God can judge inclusion in that group, since the criteria include not only true belief but good works which have been properly motivated. The latter level is developed in Islamic legal texts. It contains certain rules laid out for followers of the Prophet of Islam. Even at this level, the followers of other revealed texts are not entirely excluded, since Islam allows for the co-existence of its law with that of other faith groups, although not at equal levels of jurisdiction; the concern of Islamic law as such is with Muslims.

To compare the two conceptions of the community of the faithful is not difficult, because Islam and Judaism concur that to love God means to participate in a community of those that love God, affirm his unity, perpetually give thanks to him, and therefore submit to his rule (Islam) or live and rejoice in his kingdom (Judaism). The contrasts prove subtle; each draws its own consequences for the character of the social order from the commonalities of faith. Judaism invokes the metaphor of 'kingdom,' God's rule being spoken of as 'the kingdom of Heaven.' The Sabbath prayer captures the mode of thought and expression: 'those that keep the faith with the Sabbath and call it a delight will rejoice in your kingdom.' Islam, with its critique of what it perceives to be the exclusivity of Israel as God's people, frames matters by using more theological than political metaphors. Its points of differentiation – the sincere, the hypocrites – yield nuances that God alone can perceive.

Judaism and Islam concur that religion is public, communal, corporate – fully realized only in the social order. But their respective narratives define in very different ways how that social order is realized, by whom, and, above all, in what context. No wonder in contemporary affairs a vast labor of mediation awaits. Points in common require articulation, so points of difference may be identified and understood. In our judgment the former vastly outweigh the latter. No two religions among all the religions of the world, concurring on so much, have better prospects of mutual understanding and conciliation than Islam and Judaism.

NOTES

1 Ibn Ishaq, *The Life of Muhammad*, trans. A. Guillaume. Karachi: Oxford University Press, 1978, 186–187.
2 Ibid., 113.
3 Malik b. Anas al-Asbahi (d. 179/795): *Kitab al-Muwatta'*. Recension of Yahya b. Yahya al-Andalusi (d. 234/848), ed. Hasan Abdallah Sharaf. Cairo: Dar al-Rayan li-l-Turath, 1988, vol. 1, 25–26.
4 Al-Qayrawani, *al-Risala*, Cairo: Muhammad Ali Sabih and Sons, ND, 20–22.
5 Al-Qayrawani is using Qur'anic language throughout this passage. Here, for instance, the end of the Sura of Daybreak (89) reads: 'O serene soul, return to your Lord, both pleased and pleasing! Enter unto my servants; enter my garden!'
6 Al-Qayrawani, 24–25.
7 Ibid., 22–23.
8 Ibid., 27–28.
9 *Weekday Prayer Book*, ed. by the Rabbinical Assembly of America Prayerbook Committee, Rabbi Jules Harlow, secretary. New York: Rabbinical Assembly, 1962.
10 Judah Goldin, trans., *The Grace After Meals*. New York: The Jewish Theological Seminary of America, 1955, 9, 15*ff.*
11 Al-Qayrawani, 51.
12 Ibid., 53.
13 Ibn Ishaq, 112.
14 Malik, vol. 1, 41.
15 Al-Qayrawani, 9–10.
16 Ibid., 11.
17 Ibid., 13–15.
18 Malik, vol. 1, 357–358.
19 Al-Qayrawani, *81.*
20 Al-Qayrawani, 77.
21 Ibid., 77.
22 Al-Qayrawani, 75–76.
23 Al-Qayrawani, 80.
24 Malik, vol. 1, 362.
25 Ibid., vol. 1, 378.
26 Ibid., vol. 1, 382.
27 Al-Qayrawani, 107.
28 Ibid.
29 Ibn Ishaq, 494.
30 Ibid., 495.
31 Ibid., 496–497.
32 Al-Qayrawani, 115–117.
33 Ibid., 121.
34 Malik, vol. 2, 141-142.
35 Abdullah b. Abd al-Hakam, *Al-Muktasar al-Kabir fi-l-fiqh*, ms. fas. 810, fol. 25 a–b.
36 Ibid.

37 Al-Qayrawani, 120.
38 Al-Qayrawani, 79.
39 Al-Qayrawani, 83–84.
40 Ibid., 79.
41 Ibid., 79–80.
42 Malik, vol. 1, 376–377.
43 Al-Qayrawani, 78.
44 Ibid., 80–81.
45 Al-Qayrawani, 85.
46 Allama Sir Abdullah al-Mamun al-Suhrwardi, *The Sayings of Muhammad*. New York: Citadel, 1990, 53.
47 Ibid.
48 Imam Muslim, *Sahih Muslim*, trans. 'Abdul Hamid Siddiqi. NP, 1971, II:466.
49 Ibid., II:467.
50 Joseph Schacht, *An Introduction to Islamic Law*. Oxford: Clarendon Press, 1982, 130.
51 See discussion in Neusner and Sonn, *Comparing Religions through Law: Judaism and Islam*. London: Routledge, 1999, ch. 6.
52 Imam Muslim, *Sahih Muslim*, II:469.
53 Ibid.
54 Ibid.
55 Ibid., II:472–73.
56 Ibid., II: 470–71.
57 Ibid., II:475.
58 Ibid., II:477.
59 From Ibn Hazm's *al-Muhalla* (6:156), cited by Fazlur Rahman in 'Islam and Problem [sic] of Economic Justice,' *Pakistan Economist*, 24 August 1974, 33.
60 Majid Khadduri, *Islamic Jurisprudence: Shafi'i's Risala*. Baltimore: The Johns Hopkins Press, 1961, 164.
61 Ibid., 165.
62 Ibid.
63 Ibid., 166.
64 Imam Muslim, *Sahih Muslim*, II:483.
65 Ibid., II:478–479.
66 Ibid., II:479–480.
67 Ibid., II:481.
68 Ibid., II:484.
69 All translations of Judaic texts in this chapter derive from Roger Brooks, *Support for the Poor in the Mishnaic Law of Agriculture. Tractate Pe'ah*. Chico: Scholars Press, 1983.
70 Imam Muslim, *Sahih Muslim*, II:485.
71 John A. Williams, ed., *Themes of Islamic Civilization*. Berkeley: University of California Press, 1971, 12–15.
72 This usage was pointed out by Fazlur Rahman in *Islamic Methodology in History*. Islamabad: Islamic Research Institute, 1965, 13.
73 See Neusner and Sonn, *Comparing Religions through Law: Judaism and Islam*. London: Routledge, 1999, for a full discussion of the four major schools of Sunni law.
74 Majid Khadduri, *Islamic Jurisprudence: Shafi'i's Risala*. Baltimore: The Johns Hopkins Press, 1961, 285–286.
75 Khadduri, *Islamic Jurisprudence*, 287.
76 See discussion by Wael B. Hallaq, 'Was al-Shafi'i the master architect of Islamic jurisprudence?' *International Journal of Middle East Studies* 25/4, November 1993, 600.
77 This, of course, is even more important with regard to non-believers: 'O you who believe, do not take unbelievers (*kuffar*) as friends instead of believers.' (4:145)

78 Imam Muslim, *Sahih Muslim,* trans. `Abdul Hamid Siddiqi. NP, ND, III:1185.
79 See al-Mawardi's *Al-Ahkam al-Sultaniyya,* trans. Bernard Lewis. In *Islam,* Vol. I: *Politics and War.* New York, Hagerstown, San Francisco, London: Harper Torchbooks, 1974, 171–179.

INDEX

ablutions: before meals 46; Islam 1, 40–5,
57–8; Judaism 1, 45–56, 57–8;
menstruation and 40, 43, 46, 55; sex and
42–3, 55
adultery: divorce and 113; Islam 90–4, 126;
Judaism 74–84, 126
afterlife: Judaism 182, 185, 207
Aisha 5, 88–92, 120
alimony (maintenance after divorce) 124–5
almsgiving 89; Islam 129–46; Judaism
150–67
animals: slaughter of 57–8
annulment of marriage: Islam 122–3
apostasy: Judaism 182, 183–5

beauty: prayer and 27
betrothal 59, 125–6; children 60, 61;
deception 62–3; fathers and 60, 61;
Islam 63–7, 126; Judaism 60–3, 126;
money and 60–1, 64
blessings: Judaism 14, 20–30; meals 14,
20–5
blood: slaughter of animals and 57–8, see
also menstruation
bribery 174

call to prayer 2, 9–10, 57
charity 129–30, 178–9; almsgiving 89,
129–46, 150–67; Islam 129, 130–49,
178; Judaism 129–30, 150–79; required
130–46; voluntary 146–9
children: apostasy and 184; betrothal of 60,
61; fasting and 37; guardians of orphans
100–2; marriage and 86; orphans 67;
parentage of 69–70; uncertain status
103–4, 117, see also inheritance
Christianity: Islamic view of 213, 221–2,
225–32; marriage 85; prayer 1
cleansing see ablutions
commercial transactions with outsiders:
Judaism 192–5, 198, 200–1
communal meals: in Judaism 23–5

communal prayer: Islam 2, 9, 10
community 180–1; Islam 181, 210–25,
233–4; Judaism 180–90, 233, 234
concubinage 66
creed (Shema') 11, 15–17
crime: Judaism 185–90, 208–9; outsiders
208–9

Day of Atonement (Yom Kippur) 36–8
death penalty: Judaism 186–8, 209;
outsiders 209
deception: betrothal and 62–3; charity and
162
dhikr (repetition of the name of God) 2, 10
divorce 59, 126; inheritance and 112; Islam
117–25, 126; Judaism 61, 112–17, 126;
maintenance after 124–5

eclipses: prayers at 10
evil occasions: blessings on 25

family relations 59, 125–8; betrothal 59,
60–7, 125–6; divorce 59, 112–25, 126;
inheritance 59, 94–112, 126–7; marriage
59, 67–94, 126
fasting: at spiritual retreat 32, 34–5; children
and 37; illness and 37–8; Islam 1, 30–6,
57; Judaism 1, 36–40, 57; menstruation
and 33, 35; pregnancy and 33, 34, 37;
Ramadan fast 1, 30–4, 35; sex and 31,
34, 35, 36; travellers and 37–8; vomiting
and 33–4; votive 32, 34–5, 38–40
fathers: betrothal and 60, 61; marriage and
86
festivals: Gentile 192–3, 198
food: charity 156–78; outsiders and 194–5,
see also meals
foreigners see outsiders
forms of prayer: Islam 7–9; Judaism 12–14
fornication: Islam 66; Judaism 193

Gentiles see outsiders

239